BATHHOUSE BABYLON

The Good, The Bad and the Horny

Jameson Farn

ISBN-13: 9798504813936
ISBN-10: 1477123456

Cover design by: Art Painter
Library of Congress Control Number: 2018675309
Printed in the United States of America

Thank you for every emotion.
JMM & RO

Raymond
07871626149.

Bathhouse

You arrive in the middle of the night
From God knows where
You're higher than a kite
But you just don't care

You've taken time for the outside
Yet the inside's a mess
When the clothes come off
Who cares how you dress

Look down on others
When you're shit don't stink
Gonna make a big comeback
But you're really on the brink

You think you're wanted
But it's the shine of the lights
Why is it so lonely
Why is it a fight

You just can't stop
When perfect won't do
A guy will follow
A pill will fool.

What you think isn't noticed
Cannot be seen
You're always in trouble
Why is it about me

CONTENTS

PREFACE

One of the things Coronavirus has unusually given us all is time. As I write this, here in France we appear to be nearing the end of our third lockdown since our virus numbers continue to be so high with hopes of slowly opening up more fully by July 2021.

When France completely locked down the first time during the middle of March 2020, people were naturally confused with many people in a panic. For myself, the only way I thought of surviving this for the long haul for my businesses, is to evolve with it all.

With that, on my part came a renewed surge of energy and ambition, the last of which I have always had but it just became even more intensified with a strong sense of focus.

More than a year later, my businesses have changed over this past period, much of which has been for the better and I'm grateful to still be busy.

When summer 2020 came to an end, which is typically known as my busiest season of the year, since we were still not allowed to properly socialize because of the virus situation, I was looking for some side projects that would change things up from my typical work routine during the winter months.

At around this same time I came across an online article

discussing whether or not bathhouses would survive the pandemic and how would the ones that do make it might have to change the way they do business.

It's been a good number of years since I worked in the bathhouse industry and it feels like a different lifetime now in many ways, especially since my home has been in Europe for years. With talk of these types of venues possibly being finished, at least for a short while, it got me thinking about a few things.

My opinion and predictions are, the longer countries and cities are locked down that have bathhouses, like any other business that provides services to customers, bathhouses are no exception to the Covid19 impacts and will continue to suffer if they haven't closed for good already.

It will also depend on how deep owners' pockets are, type of insurance coverage, and if they are getting any kind of financial help from the government to be able to just hold on to a business while being out of operation for any unknown length of time along with being able to afford to maintain it.

As even if temporarily closed, water, electricity, heat, all the regular elements of the business do still have to be paid even if not at their regular high usage rate and everything within the premises will still need to be closely monitored and maintained on top of the monthly rent. With these establishments usually being quite sizable operations, this can still be a considerable expense when there is no revenue coming in.

As with past decades, bathhouses have come and gone only to be replaced by those individuals or groups with the substantial funds required who can, with at least some know-how, patience, and time, open a bathhouse.

If you love a good bathhouse, have faith, and if the one you go to gets the chance to open again, support them if possible.

Bathhouses have somehow succeeded through many archaic cities and government regulations and bylaws through the decades, along with being raided by the police in the past. Only then to deal with the AIDS epidemic and that downfall, to rise again to then have to evolve with when the internet became available worldwide and online dating sites were introduced, followed by dating apps throughout various forms of social media.

No matter what, simply because humans need to interact and actually touch each other, bathhouses have survived and had always been an integral part of the LGBTQ community, so I believe in whatever shape or form they come in, they will still be around.

Although bathhouses are more of a want rather than a need, like it or not, they are a part of the gay culture and some even say a rite of passage for many men. They also create jobs not only for those that work in the venues but for all the suppliers it takes to stock a bathhouse to help keep it clean and in top working order.

New rules might now come into place because of Covid19, and given the amount of human interaction that happens in bathhouses, besides vaccinations, and for overall health reasons, a bathhouse may be required to take everything a step further. If not by an owner, then definitely by a government regulator who might implement new rules for their customers to prove that they are staying above board such as customers needing to show their vaccination card, QR Code, temperature controls, etc., before entering the premises. At least for the first while until things get moving to a normal pace again.

In reading that online article, it gave me an idea that has always been at the back of my mind as during my time working in bathhouse establishments, I had kept several random diaries, simply because I was fascinated with the variety of men that came to bathhouses that I was able to meet.

No matter their ethnicity, financial and educational backgrounds, the human dynamics in this kind of business were very intriguing, to say the least.

It was always interesting to observe how men that are sexually motivated act in various situations in a bathhouse along with the range of men for whom, this is their place of work. The minute you start working in these venues, you notice immediately that it does take a village to run an operation such as a bathhouse, especially if they are open 24/7, but more importantly, what customers might not even realize is, who makes up that village can say a lot.

I also found that keeping a diary was not only a form of stress relief if things were getting crazy or I had a bad day (or even many good ones), but it also helped me plan out things a lot better whether at work or in life at the moment or for in the future.

For well over a decade, (about 13 years) bathhouses were my job in some manner in North America. And that lifestyle to a very small extent has followed me to where and how I live my life now in Europe, even though I am no longer in that industry and lead a completely different lifestyle.

That former life in many ways set me up perfectly for what I do now in the luxury real estate world. It's taught me many lessons and prepared me to be more open in ways both culturally and otherwise. Also to know when decorum and privacy matter most and how to maintain it, and to strategize and negotiate with ease with those in and around the ultra-high-net-worth (UHNW) world. And many in my extensive business network know of my former background and tend to be completely fascinated with it, which oddly, has helping me to have a better rapport with them and see through the bullshit in others.

Inevitably, because it is a part of my history and comes up in conversation at some point, either privately one on one, with a couple, online, or during a gathering with friends, even business associates who find it extremely captivating. Someone will know or eventually find out what I used to do so then it becomes a topic of conversation.

If it comes up during a social gathering, people will want to hear some of the outrageous sex stories that went with my experience or even how much money can be made in that business.

Right off the top, I'm no expert or guru of any sort when it comes to bathhouses, I can only speak of my experiences. The way bathhouses operate also changes over time, updates in technology have also helped enhance the experiences of an individual, couple, or group. It also depends on what you are looking for, even with the kind of bathhouse you would like to visit.

Each person's experience will be different, no matter how much information you offer up to them. Some men will love a bathhouse, some men will hate it.

Over the years during these private conversations or at parties if people happen to become aware of what my job used to be, and especially if they have only known me for what I do for a living here in France. Without hesitation, the first words tend to be, "You should write a book! You must have a ton of sex stories?!"

Believe me, I've thought about it over the years. Time has always seemed to be an issue, and I certainly don't consider myself to be some kind of literary genius.

Now, thanks in an unusual way to Covid19, with varying levels of isolation, and the fact that I like to keep busy now has been the opportune time so I've dusted off the diaries to see what I could come up with in regards to a book.

I also think it's important that the LGBTQ community have a huge perspective on a range of topics for future generations to refer to. And I didn't want to write something that was all just about sex stories (although there will be plenty), as that route seemed too easy and I think we are all much more than just sex.

I think it's important to show all aspects of a business, both good and bad, that are not traditionally considered to be normal in what society dictates.

This is all from my own experience in the bathhouse industry, and it's going to make some of those people I worked with happy to reminisce and some will be upset but I have no intention to hold back as this work in the past has taught me to navigate how some men in particular, with or without an agenda, operate with their intentions and goals and their potential mindset at any given time. It has prepared me to expect the unexpected which has been extremely helpful in my life and career.

I've discovered with writing all of this that it has been extremely cathartic in many ways, teaching me more lessons and bringing back every feeling and memory from halfway across the world from where it all took place years ago. It has shown me that distance does make a difference in how strong the clarity can be with events from the past. Memories not already noted or that I thought I forgot came flooding back and all for the right reasons.

This way of living while working at the baths became my normal and very second nature instinctually in many ways, so my observations here are just something I wanted to share so that others can see a more in-depth side of how things worked at the time.

CHAPTER ONE

For most of my twenties, I was an administrative assistant for a major architectural and interior design firm that had approximately 60 employees. The company had already been in business for at least 20 years, was highly reputable, and extremely connected within the layers of City Hall while being responsible for many of the major projects and high-rises in and around the city.

At some point every year, usually in the winter months when things tended to be quieter in the city, I would get a part-time job somewhere to make extra money for my vacation to Europe every summer.

I would take on part-time or casual jobs which consisted of more administrative work at various offices helping with everything from building data entry templates to then doing data entry, archive filing, and accounting or more regular admin work on weekends.

The location where I had lived for years was and from what I understand still is quite beautiful with gorgeous natural surroundings while in many regards then was considered in the scheme of things a small city but a unique place to live.

If you were living in the downtown core like I was and where much of the gay community was also located, those of us in this part of the city was frequently considered to be a very cliquey crowd, especially if you just moved to the area.

It was unexplainable as to why this was happening but even if you met someone at a party and then happened to run into

them the next day on the street, rarely would either acknowledge each other. It was, and I understand, still is a unique
phenomenon but at least you got to know who was who and
whether they became your friend or not right away. Yet the
funny thing about all of this is, it was rare to meet someone in
this LGBTQ community who was born and raised right in the
city and if you did, they tended to be more receptive to making
new friends without having any protective guards up about it.

For myself having grown up about an hour's drive from the
city, the next step after high school for many was to move
downtown where the universities were close by and whereas a
gay man you could feel more liberated to be yourself as this is
where the LGBTQ bars, nightclubs, and the overall scene was
situated. In many ways, once you made the move and got settled in the hub of it all, you'd hear people say it still felt very
much like a high school with the typical dramas with most
people being one degree of separation.

People you already knew or did happen to meet would sometimes have big dreams of what living downtown would be like,
it all appeared so cosmopolitan from a distance so if you were
ambitious enough to strive for what you wanted, you could at
least attain a few your goals. That is until you discovered just
how low the ceiling actually was, but with some effort, you
then found other avenues you'd like to explore and expand
upon in due time.

This was also until, like many other North American cities, everything started to become even more gentrified, so if
you were really seeking something different and adventurous,
you'd have to come up with your own ideas and ways to make
things work.

Or you could consider moving elsewhere, hoping that a
destination cure would do the trick, from those I know that
have stayed, some have become complacent and just bitch constantly about it all to anyone that would listen while remind-

ing others of the good old days.

Perhaps it was my age at the time and the trips to Europe reminding me that there are other options in life out there, but I was feeling restless and definitely needed a change of some sort as I was finding myself getting bored with the predictable weekend nightclub scene in the city. And rarely did it seem people were having parties anymore for fear of being evicted because of possible noise complaints coming from their apartments in a tight and overly expensive rental market so I was seeking out some other kind of fun.

Somewhere along the way, I recalled hearing something in casual conversations about these places called bathhouses and wondered what went on at those establishments? Keep in mind, this was just before the internet was fully available so we couldn't just Google anything that one might be curious about.

And this is also a reason why to this day I tell people it's important to know your LGBTQ history, or at least have mentors in your life that you can ask questions to. Having someone that isn't afraid to tell you what the score is would have been more than helpful as some of my first naive thoughts were, do bathhouses have just big open spaces where people could have baths in big tubs? Why do men go to these places? What's the attraction? And why is it only apparently gay men? There was a sex factor to what I was hearing about but how did it all come together? And were the places sleazy and dirty?

Unlike today where many men openly admit going to bathhouses with quite a number certainly not shy about stating the frequency in which they visit these places or what they get up to in them. Back in the 1990s, at least where I lived, it was still only talked about in hushed tones that a few gay friends had told me what they either assumed a bathhouse was, while the other half would only admit to having gone to one, and only if they were drunk enough, and of course only just the one time to see what it was like for themselves. Not having the actual information could have also just been simply because of the people I had been surrounding myself with at the time.

Even then, some of the men that opened up about it to me would claim it wasn't the kind of place for them to frequent regularly but then again, they would add that they never really stayed long enough to know for sure if they really liked it. Or maybe they didn't want to disclose how often they go?

Whatever I was told, the opinions seemed to be neutral about it all and at the same time it seemed like a place that was popular for a gay person to go to often in the 1970s but when the AIDS epidemic hit, now, these places weren't that high on the list of gay establishments to frequent anymore. This from what I was at least able to gather at the time.

Which then made me wonder what the crowd would even be like now? Sadly, I assumed it must be just old, creepy men but yet my younger friends had been to these places so does that balance it all out somehow?

While wondering, well men must still be going to these bathhouses otherwise how do they stay in business? And why were the advertisements in the local papers and in nightclub flyers making it so enticing and like the place to be? I assumed it was a certain kind of person that went to bathhouses, yet couldn't exactly pinpoint who that individual would be.

Since any real information seemed scarce, I took it a touch further and looked them up in the local yellow pages phone directory and noticed there were two bathhouses listed in the downtown area, under the very categories of fitness and spa sections which led me to assume they must look somewhat like a gym inside, just a men's only private gym or something where you could maybe relax in a jacuzzi or get a massage? Then I wondered if it was then like a gay massage parlor, offering full releases?

More confusion, which was just making me lose the edge I was seeking because I was starting to want definite answers when I should have just got an idea and went to see a bathhouse for myself.

One of the bathhouses I noticed had a sleek, modern advertisement in the LGBTQ community newspaper and I recalled seeing their promo flyers at various bars and nightclubs so I thought for part of my upcoming birthday it might make for an interesting and memorable venue to discover.

When the night of my birthday arrived, I met up with friends for dinner and drinks to celebrate. Naturally when any party is underway is when many confessions start to come out so that is when I disclosed what the rest of my plans were for later that evening.

A couple of close buddies at the party asked me if I wanted them to come with me for support as they had been before, but I like to test out new grounds on my own so they finally told me a little more about this newer bathhouse that I was going to be checking out and what to expect. They didn't relay a ton of information about what happens once inside as they (and I) wanted to experience it for myself with that element of surprise. One bit of advice was, just not to show up flat out drunk or the people working the door might not let you in.

It was a bit too late for that as we were all well under the influence by that time, yet I thought I would take the chance and go anyway while trying to be as sober-looking as possible to get inside.

As the night wore on, I said goodbye to my friends and hailed a cab making my way to the part of the downtown that wasn't yet overflowing with new condominium developments at the time. This was still a part of the city known more for the rugged loft warehouses with dive (but fun) bars or nightclubs, all in a darker part of the city with random street lights and very few stores or restaurants. This is the kind of area where people would converge on weekends for any number of last-minute underground rave parties.

I had the taxi driver drop me off about a block away from this bathhouse so that I could possibly watch for who might be coming and going to get a better idea of the clientele as I made my way towards the place. When I got to the building, that was apparently known as the "new and modern" bathhouse, from the outside at least, it just looked like a large nondescript white cinder block building with no windows and only one wide, tinted glass doorway at the front with the building address number in small letters above the door.

The building looked more like it had been transformed from being perhaps a former storage facility or maybe even a car dealership at one point. It didn't appear very welcoming but it was certainly discreet in appearance, something that many entertainment groups in the city have always been good at pro-viding because of the antiquated bylaws and general city rules making it the no-fun city as they say, so they did what they could that would still be considered acceptable to open their particular alternative venue.

Although it was just past midnight on a weekend, this part of the downtown seemed absolutely deserted with not one soul on the street. Hoping I had the right address, I slowly pushed open the door to an immediate waft in the face of a steamy scent in the air that was a bit reminiscent of a gym mixed with the odor of bleach with loud music booming in the background from behind yet another interior entrance door inside the very small lobby area.

I wasn't sure whether to be nervous or relieved when I got inside as there were a couple of other guys in line ahead of me keeping to themselves by not saying a word or even acknow-ledging each other and there also seemed to be one too many front desk clerks working the small window scrutinizing everyone while they took their money to enter the premises.

When it was my turn to pay, I wasn't sure what to ask for, there seemed to be no sign or information so the cashier just asked me if I wanted a room or locker. I thought a room sounded like some sort of hotel room and I wasn't sure what to expect in the first place so I just asked for a locker as it sounded like something I would recognize like in a gym.

I was asked for my identification which they then used to check what I assumed was my name and age against some very basic and not very secure looking computer database where then I was also told I would have to buy one of their member-ships so I bought a three-day membership as I didn't think I would be back soon anyway and in the end was also never told what that membership was about or included. Once that was paid and signed for, I remember feeling relieved that they were even going to let me in as I still felt a bit drunk.

I was then buzzed through the second set of doors to go inside the bathhouse where at the second counter to my left an employee handed me a white folded towel, with my locker key on top with its number tag on a plastic coil to keep around your wrist, along with a slight warning not to lose the key and a small packet of lube, one condom packet, and a safe sex pamphlet while also getting a quick, blunt lecture on safe sex while in their facilities, which the last part seemed preachy and a bit over the top in the way I was spoken too thinking...I'm a grown-ass man.

Stepping into what was now the official bathhouse, it looked big from the onset but even with clothes on it actually felt cold like the air conditioning was on blast and we were in the month of March.

One of the first things I saw was a bunch of men to my right of all ages and sizes naked except for the towels wrapped around their waists and entranced with some random TV show that was playing on the big screen in the open lounge area.

Not sure where to go as there was again no real signage, I started taking a look around for where lockers might be under the dim lights, in the meanwhile all there seemed to be was row upon row of straight, parallel long hallways with a bunch of closed doors that I passed by, I assumed these where what they meant about rental rooms, they seemed all to be built very orderly and without ceilings within the middle of this space.

As I started to make my way deeper into this gay sauna, I saw an employee with a uniform polo shirt on who was cleaning what looked like an already spotless mirror in such a way as to make himself look busy, so I asked him where the lockers were and he begrudgingly pointed in the general direction.

I then made my way to the location he pointed to, and as I approached, I could hear metal locker doors opening and closing so I moved in that direction to find a few rows of lockers. Once I found the number on a locker that matched my key tag, I noticed some of the other customers that were also in line when I arrived were starting to get undressed so I simply followed what they were doing and instinctively got completely stripped down, wrapped the towel I was given around my waist like the others and went on to take a further look.

Wandering around the bathhouse I quickly discovered that basically men cruise each other, trying their best to catch the eye of the ones they are interested in and if they feel there is a match, even just with a look or a light touch and routinely without words they will make contact.

Their connection and what they wanted to do, again with or without words would take place almost anywhere they wanted, going behind closed doors in a rented room didn't seem to be a requirement. They could get each other off by kissing and mutually masturbating, giving blow jobs or having full-on sex or all of the above and more and anywhere. If they were fine with others passing by who wanted to watch or join in, that didn't seem to be a problem either. Physical gestures guided and dictated plenty.

There were no written rules, everything appeared to be almost second nature as to what goes on and how to behave in a bathhouse, at least from what I was discovering in this place.

What could be a bit disappointing and noticeable right away was a large percentage of the men seemed to be just roaming the hallways hoping to run into Mr. Perfect, if they thought they found him, they'd practically chase him down, which if they were even slightly too aggressive in their approach, could scare him off and lose him.

And if they got rejected, instantly there was a slice of sadness showing on their face but then they would bounce right back and they would be at it again, even while holding off on advances from others if they weren't what they considered perfect enough, and as though they were waiting for husband material but were in a sex club.

It seemed like many of these men working the floor of this place might not have looked in their own reflection in a mirror to see what they are about and what they have to offer back, yet were running on a mental list filled with fantasies of what they were after and how things were going to be.

Some men would hit it off immediately, almost by chance, with subtle interactions but otherwise, it was like most of the individuals here were holding out, which is fine, they just appeared to be sullen and more discouraged as time went on and it made me wonder if this was all it was about? Strange yet still the dynamics of it all were fascinating to observe.

The bathhouse itself was very clean to the point it felt very sterile, many of the colors were stark white with black trim and subtle sharp blue tones here and there, the lighting was either dim and sultry or super bright with the highest wattage light bulbs ever and to which no one wanted to be seen under or around so then that area stayed barren.

It didn't feel like there were a lot of sexual ambiances except for when you might run into men getting a blowjob or having some other sexual act out in the open and even then, that atmosphere would only be relegated to that one spot.

Only in the back wet area of the bathhouse did there seem to be the most potential, even with the bright, bad lighting since it also had an open plan room containing a massive, 10 man jacuzzi that men were busy jumping in and out of while on the other end of the space between the showers, sinks, toilets, and urinals was a frosted glass door that led to a large, open steam room.

The steam room is also where it seemed most of the men in the establishment were situated, almost to the point of passing out from the steam while holding out for somebody to please start with some sort of sexual acts with them as they were getting bored with rubbing their own cock.

There seemed to also be a tension in the air, perhaps it was sexual tension but there was a definite attitude to be felt from some of the patrons, which surprised me since we were all just wearing a towel around our waists, yet many of the men in attendance had a holier than thou attitude yet they weren't exactly what one would consider being the model type but maybe this was normal too and the attitude helped them as a form of defense for their low self-esteem? In many ways, it could be like a nightclub, just without the cocktails.

It was also surprising to feel the attitude coming from men in an older demographic that you would assume had it all together and just knew better? But maybe their age was the reason for the attitude, good looking or not, to try and prove that they were and are still worthy for someone? For certain their attitude would quickly disappear if they got rejected by some 20-year-old twink or the attitude would even come on stronger for unknown reasons which meant for certain no one was going to be attracted to them for fear of rejection.

The atmosphere changed completely when small groups of drunk and obviously coked-up boisterous buddies arrived after the nightclubs closed, (so there went that rule about being too intoxicated to come inside). Rather than mingling and doing their own thing, most of them would continue to hang out together, talking rapidly and loudly while periodic-ally dashing in and out of one of the rooms one of them rented for nose touch-ups. On this first visit, it also seemed odd that the rooms weren't being used for anything else.

You could tell a couple of the men from the nightclubs by their roving eyes wanted to get out there on the floor and meet some other men, yet they would stay within their group which then made it harder for them to meet anyone, if at all, but maybe that's what they wanted to do?

Over time though a few of them strayed for some action, one I actually played around within one of the dark, empty, play spaces, he appeared to be frustrated with himself after giving it his all masturbating to try and get hard, but with not being able to get it up, instead, he kept whispering his apologizes between grinding his teeth. Not knowing what to say, I just quietly drifted away from him.

It was interesting to watch how everyone acted around each other in this environment, I've always been drawn to the vari-ous kinds of human interactions and found the whole scene compelling no matter the amount of action taking place.

All I know from that evening is when 4 am hit, and every-thing was slowly wearing off with everyone. Without much discretion, the men started to give up their game, let down their guards and it all transpired when some hot group sex finally started to take place in the steam room which was mind-blowing to be a part of, as anything and everything went down.

Looks didn't seem important in the dimly lit steam room, it was all wet, slithering bodies sliding up against each other, no matter the shape and no matter the way you looked, men were just trying to be as much a part of it all. Some actions were hard in nature, others soft and everyone seemed to be enjoying the group experience.

Once it all came to varying degrees of climatic closures, it was like everyone got what they came for and disassembled quickly without saying a word, with the showers busy and locker doors being slammed closed as men got dressed. People seemingly were soberer (myself included) and gathered everything they had with them and started to leave en masse.

Whatever it was, and even though it wasn't the most eventful time ever, I was hooked. This is the kind of environment that offered a strong sense of freedom, where fun was taken to a different level, where you could be yourself because that truly got you what you wanted and yet be as experimental if you choose with your sexuality without judgment.

This place explained to me why so many men weren't always picking up others at a bar or dance club. A bathhouse is where they could get what they wanted without any necessary commitment before or after the bars, whether that's a good or bad thing.

And not trying to politely kick a stranger out of your apartment in the morning but first having to make him breakfast. Not that I ever brought many to my home in the first place as that was my sanctuary. In a bathhouse you didn't have to give whoever you meet your real name if you didn't feel like it or at all, you didn't even have to talk or participate in anything period if you didn't want to, and all for about $10 for 8 hours.

Over the next couple of weekends, I did go to this bathhouse more frequently, simply because it was different from the nightclubs. I even got to slowly know the employees and they all seemed to be working there for various reasons.

There was the cute but bashful guy just trying to make a living while figuring out life in general, there were the little bitches that thought they were some kind of models and were too good for anyone, and there were those employees that found the hours worked coincided with their lifestyle and others who needed to make money while at university.

During these later visits, you'd see couples going into a rented room and closing the door so I assumed at least someone was fucking around and meeting others while the majority were just figures roaming the hallways. And every time without fail as soon as you walked into the bathhouse, most of the men seemed glued to the big TV in the lounge area. It was like there was a set routine in place.

Inside the steam room, you'd see a guy who would be stroking himself casually while sitting on a bench for then someone to take a chance and quickly get in there on his knees on the wet tiles deep-diving his head into the crotch to give the guy a blowjob before he could even possibly say no.

Of course, that meant others without hesitation gathered around the two, which would then either put an end to the blowjob if the men felt a bit intimidated to the point of making them stop and decide to leave the steam room while everyone else eagerly followed them with the hopes of being a part of it all. Or, half the time the scene in the steam room would become a fuck fest.

For this place, it seemed after midnight was the best time to go, especially once the nightclubs were closed because then the chances got higher that maybe men would show up. A small rush of men would definitely check in but that wasn't a guarantee of any fun either, but you had hope. Overall, on these visits, there always seemed to be more cruising than actual sex which just seemed weird if it was supposed to be a sex club.

The one thing that could be counted on was around the same time in the morning when the men were bored with cruising and just wanted to get off and get the hell home to sleep.

One such morning at about 4:30 am, one of the well-known local drag queens showed up. Still half in her gear, she quickly transformed herself into her rented room and emerged with just a towel on, followed by removing her makeup at one of the sinks with the remnants of the evening smeared across her towel barely draping around her thick waist.

The drag queen's first visit was then to the steam room where she was followed inside by a group of admirers, after she had enough of that room, a small team of men followed her into the big jacuzzi where another show of sorts was to take place. Here, sitting on the edge of the bubbling pool of hot water, wet, naked, enamored men were climbing over each other (which then led to more sex acts) while basically getting as close as possible to ravage the drag queen's huge cock until he busted his load on to them.

Leave it to a drag queen to get the party rolling. The place was finally coming alive with the party even trickling down into what was previously a largely vacant glory hole area most of the evening.

You could see the look of relief on men's faces after their release as they were finally feeling like all this time spent in the place was worth it, even if the sex was not the greatest, at least they got off in some regard and now they could all zip up and head home for the night, as per the routine.

Knowing there had to be more to this bathhouse world than just what this repetitive experience represented, one of the guys I met in the bathhouse had asked me if I ever go to the other gay sauna in town? I told him I hadn't been yet and he told me it wasn't as new as this place and then suggested I see what it's about and that maybe we could meet up there sometime.

That was all I needed to hear, this bathhouse I had been going to was very clean, seemed interesting enough, offering a very big space with a fantastic steam room and jacuzzi area, I was just confused as to why wasn't it busier? I kept thinking, if it's this quiet on a weekend, I can only imagine what the weekdays would be like. And not even necessarily busier as it just takes one really but it just felt like there was something off about this place.

As the next weekend approached, I became more intrigued by what the other bathhouse downtown had to offer while being surprised with myself about how many hours and how much money I spent for so many years going to nightclubs and not knowing all along there were places like bathhouses where men who are looking for sex really get down to it, if that's what you wanted to achieve. I had naively thought the gay way to meet someone was to go to nightclubs or a bar all night hoping to meet someone to go home with. I certainly should have been widening my circle of friends or something to know more.

It made me wonder why bathhouses seemed to be such a big secret, especially in the gay community? There also seemed to be a stigma about it all. A bathhouse seemed like a sexually healthier choice in many ways as condoms and sex information was provided in a safe environment. And it was easier to meet people since everyone is in a towel or naked, so assumptions were lowered, along with being much more secure than bringing a stranger home.

CHAPTER TWO

When Saturday night arrived, being a bit uncertain about this next bathhouse I was going to visit for the first time but looking forward to seeing what it was about, I figured the best time to go would also be just after midnight so I gathered some liquid courage (yet not too much) and called for a taxi to take me to the establishment.

Immediately I could sense this was going to be a different experience because the street this bathhouse was located on was at the edge of what was always regarded as the bad part of town, although still considered the downtown core and more in the business district.

Like the first bathhouse I visited, this location also had very little in terms of street lights which made it feel that much more uneasy but exciting at the same time with the only people around hastily making their way that cold night to find their next fix at the park at the end of the block which was a known at the time as one of the drug dealing hotspots.

As I opened the entrance doors to the lower level of this older, low-rise office-type building, I was immediately hit again in the face with a waft of that steamy sauna scent telling me that this must be where the bathhouse is situated.

When I reached the bottom of the flight of stairs, there was a common area foyer that had a 1970's vibe to it because of the lighting, wall colors, and the style of rug on the floor. There was a cabaret bar directly ahead from the bottom of that stairs with a handmade logo and arrow painted on the wall pointing towards the direction of its entrance door, and when I glimpsed inside, the bar looked empty and also very retro in its décor.

Next to the bar was the bathhouse. Here there was a large plexiglass sign stating the prices of the rooms and lockers at different times during the 24 hours period per day they are open along with the bathhouse specials all next to the small check-in window. The cashier here was dressed far more casually in both style and manner than the staff at the newer bathhouse I had first visited where they had to wear a uniform.

This cashier was wearing the tiniest of daisy duke style shorts, no shoes, and a tank top but he also had a coy, cute little smile on his face as he kept flipping his shoulder-length locks of hair from side to side and seemed very knowledgeable and quick at his job with an aura that also said not to fuck with him. I asked for a locker rental, then I was asked to sign a legal consent form, then sign my initials on a receipt slip, all while paying, to then be buzzed in through the security door straight into the bathhouse itself.

Stepping inside, you could hear dance music just like at the other bathhouse. Directly inside at the window to my left, I was given a towel and the set of keys to my locker by the cashier and was told that the lockers were straight ahead, down the end of the hallway. Condoms I was told were around the corner in a big bowl on the counter and that they could be found in other parts of the club too, I was also given a packet of lube.

This bathhouse was also dimly lit and was obviously older than the other one, yet also clean which was a relief, there was a lounge area with a big-screen TV to the right after entering the bathhouse that looked more like a rumpus room that could have easily been from someone's suburban basement back in the day, just this one had a large glass container on the wall displaying various sex toys and lube you could buy.

From there to my left was a snack bar area that also looked like it was renovated a few times throughout the years with bits and pieces. More lubes available to buy from another glass case on the wall, along with chocolate bars, soda pop, water in a large drink cooler. Freshly brewed coffee was also available. There was also a vending machine near the entrance filled with many of the same particular items including lube and junk food which seemed logical but a weird mix of products although the lubes were more expensive and there was also a range of cock rings.

Compared to the other bathhouse, this place felt warm (literally) and more inviting even though it had some years on it, the place didn't look or feel like a large converted warehouse of some sort, this could also be because of the color choices on the walls and varying levels of ceiling heights. The overall feeling was more inviting to explore.

Straight ahead and halfway down the corridor and to my right there was a massive bulletin board on the wall between two hallways with a maze of rental rooms, the posters on the board indicated the bathhouse's other special events along with local LGBTQ news and information.

At the end of that same corridor, you entered the locker area. In just these few steps, walking into this place I was amazed at how much busier it was than I expected, but that could also be because of the size of the place too (as it seemed slightly smaller) or maybe just because the layout was more conducive to how men interacted; all I knew was I had to navigate my way around plenty of men wrapped in towels.

Right away I knew this bathhouse was obviously more established and had a history, as though it was altered and built up over time. The hallways here were set into more of a maze, not parallel to each other, beckoning you to survey the surroundings. Many of the rental room walls were built with thick pieces of dark stained wood stacked on top of each other, which décor wise kind of gave the place a log cabin design feeling, even if it wasn't the most up-to-date in style.

At the banks of lockers there was another long hallway of rental rooms and a low-budget-looking fitness area and directly behind that appeared to be the back of a row of glory hole booths with what looked like a dark playroom next to it.

Having changed into a towel I was ready to do some more exploring and see what kind of trouble I could find. There was a couple of shower rooms but everyone appeared to be using the main communal showers across from the large steam room and by using it I mean it was like every half of hour of my visit, there was some level of sex taking place that seemed to start in the steam room and would eventually continue on and linger in the big shower area when the heat from the steam appeared to be too much.

These kinds of sexual escapades also continued on in another dark room around the corner that had a TV in the corner on a stand near the ceiling playing gay porn. This room would get so packed with men every so often that you literally could not go past the entrance hallway to get into it but you could hear and see in the shadows from the light of the TV screen that all kinds of hot and heavy action were taking place which just made men practically climb over each other to get involved in whatever was going on. It made me wonder how anyone then got out of the room once they managed to make their way inside but everyone seemed happy with what was taking place with no complaints.

The general feeling my first night here was that men really came here for the purpose of what the business was all about and had no qualms as to what they wanted and were looking for if there was any attitude it (and there was) it was somehow shot down and disappeared quickly and the person with the attitude would seem to be totally ignored until he realized what he was playing at wasn't going to get him any dick.

With this bathhouse being older, I had assumed it would be full of old men, which was totally not the case. Of course, there were older men in the place, but it seemed like more nationalities were represented here along with body shapes and age ranges. If you had a certain kind of man you were attracted to, they were probably already somewhere in the place or about to arrive.

At this bathhouse, the doors to the rental rooms weren't all closed and seemed to be left open more often by the patrons, and even if sex was taking place in a room, the door would half the time still be kept open, giving an indication of an invite for the more the merrier.

There was also less endless roaming of hallways by the same people, which again could be in part because of the maze-like layout, you couldn't help but run into some kind of sexual activity, if not in the rental rooms, then definitely in the corridors and blacked out playrooms.

As aged and in need of a total update in some areas, it was required more for décor, not for anything broken, it still felt clean and safe with the employees being helpful and joking around with customers and with almost everyone that checked in being friendly and approachable. Also, maybe this is just how the customers liked everything, not so shiny, new, and intimidating?

At one point I was wondering if I was in the right city with all this friendly openness and casual banter as it was not something the city was known for so it was both alarming and refreshing.

Over the next couple of weeks, I was coming to this bathhouse, just for the environment alone sometimes, it felt like I stumbled upon a hidden gem of a secret and I was glad to be a part of this kind of society.

It wouldn't always be crazy busy at this bathhouse either but there was something comfortable and soothing about it even in the quiet times. You got a chance to remove yourself from the world outside and were able to reflect and relax while maybe chatting with someone new.

I found myself at times during my normal day job loving the fact that this could be my secret, fun gay sauna to go to once in a while, and I loved knowing that no one at the office, many of who appeared to have a very conservative, boring lifestyles knew anything of what I got up to on the weekends once in a while.

Working in such a high-end professional environment was fine and I quite enjoyed it as I've always had a keen interest in all forms of architecture, design, and history. But as with many corporations, the big boys were the ones making all the money and it was about that time of year I looked for extra employment for my yearly vacation abroad.

CHAPTER THREE

Eager to try for something different than another part-time office job, I thought I would apply at the bathhouses, more curious than anything to see if I would even get a response back from applying because first of all, I had no prior experience in this kind of business. And I wasn't even sure what then state on my application or resume? That I'm gay and can fold towels?

This was also based on my assumption that the job would entail folding towels and general cleaning. Having no idea and nothing to refer to in my work history, I then ended up keeping my resume for what it was as I did work with and had good communication skills with all kinds of people on a daily business basis and I had a ton of administrative experience in every capacity, so those were the angles I highlighted.

During my lunch hour one day, I changed in the staff bathroom at the office into something less business-like and slightly more casual but still a touch dressed up to go to the bathhouses in town to drop off my resume and see if I could at least meet with the manager about a possible part-time job.

Stopping in at the first bathhouse I ever went to, there was a sense of quietness in the space even with music playing in the background. As I was dropping off my resume to the clerk at the window, I asked if it would be possible to speak to the manager about a job opportunity to be told he wasn't there at the moment. I then thanked the clerk and went on my way to the next bathhouse.

Once I entered the building to the next bathhouse, as I approached the cashier window, a clerk that was chatting with a customer in the back snack bar area came bounding to the window and asked if I wanted a room or a locker. I told him I was just dropping off my resume and would it be possible to speak to the manager? The clerk was nice and held the resume almost in awe as he had never seen one before and then told me the manager wasn't in at the moment but he would be sure to give him my resume when he got back. I thanked the clerk and headed back to my job to continued with the day.

A day or two later once home from work, I got a phone call from the second bathhouse I applied to, the more established one that I started to frequent more from time to time.

The manager Kevin and I had a cordial conversation and he wanted to set up a time for an interview. Since it was the middle of the week and he could see from my resume that I was currently working full time at an office downtown, we set up an appointment for the interview on my lunch hour that Friday as the bathhouse was only a few blocks away from the office.

When Friday came, again on my lunch break, I changed into something less strict in business attire and more casual and made my way to the bathhouse for the interview.

Heading there, I wasn't nervous about the meeting, I found it more exciting as to how the interview would go, and what more I could learn about the business even just from the interview process and what the job duties would be like, it probably also helped that I already had a full-time job to fall back on.

Once again from the bottom of the stairs into the foyer of the building, I could see the same cashier from a few days before at the window, I smiled and told him who I was and that I was to meet with the manager Kevin and in a smiling, delightful tone he asked me to come inside and buzzed me through the security doors into the venue and told me that the manager would be right with me.

As I stood there for a couple of minutes on the landing, not sure where I should be waiting, I started thinking about what I was possibly venturing into, which got me a touch nervous but still excited for how it would go.

Kevin's office as it turns out was across the entrance hall from the cashier area, the way he opened his office door quickly made me kind of jump as I assumed behind that door was maybe a storage room.

Either way, he noticed my little jump, apologized for startling me and we had a laugh about it as we shook hands during our introductions and he invited me into his office.

The office was compact while being both long and narrow, but well organized with many file holders on the wall, order sheets, and schedules, plus the normal administrative office supplies, storage cupboards, and a computer on each end of the office on desks.

Kevin offered me the other office desk chair to sit on and we had my interview which seemed to encompass a range of topics to get to know each other and with a segment of questions to gauge how open-minded and comfortable I would be if I worked in this kind of business, with subjects that wouldn't normally be asked in your average run of the mill business but nothing that would be considered legally labor objective or offensive, at least to me.

All of which I thought was a fascinating process and so different from the regular job interview jargon and how protective of my well-being he was to make sure I wouldn't be frightened or freak out about what I might encounter if I got the job.

I was up for anything and any challenge, I felt very happy

and positive throughout the interview and recall even beaming about getting to experience the whole thing.

With that, Kevin asked about my working hours, reminded me that this was a 24/7 business but that if I wanted, he would take me on as a part-time employee and make sure that my work hours on weekends weren't too disruptive to my normal sleeping pattern which I also thought was also very considerate of him.

We agreed on the start date, which happened to be the next day, Saturday, from 4 pm until midnight and I was thrilled!

Afterward, I was feeling a mix of excitement and nervousness about this new part-time job as the hours to the start time on Saturday approached. Kevin had given me a general overview of what my duties would be during a legit tour of the bathhouse after the interview.

And I was to wear what I wanted that felt comfortable while being told I would be on the move quite a lot helping to take care of things around the place so as to make sure the clothing was light and breathable. Also, that he would be making sure the other staff members and himself would be around to train me however necessary.

The next day, upon arrival at the bathhouse, when I went up to the cashier window, a different clerk working must have been told that I would be starting at 4 pm so with a wave to say hello, I was again buzzed into the bathhouse.

This time I walked directly around the corner to the snack bar area where the cashier and housekeeper were on shift and we all introduced ourselves. Kevin shortly came out of his office to greet me and we proceeded into his office to sign some employment papers. Then I was given my own staff locker in another area of the bathhouse where I changed into regular shorts and a t-shirt similar to what the other staff happened to be wearing.

After that was completed, back at the snack bar the staff invited me behind the counter where I was given a run through explanation of what went on in this area mixed with a conversation about who we each were to get to know each other, all the while knowing I was being slightly scrutinized for being the new employee to see if I was up for the task, which I was totally fine with but still a bit nervous as I wanted to do a good job.

Starting off I would be in housekeeping. Which I expected and where I would do rounds of the place frequently to make sure everything was always as clean as possible but also to help watch the customers to ensure everyone was feeling safe and nothing untoward was happening like men doing drugs, drinking, theft, or damaging the space.

The bathhouse was already busy with men so it felt like I was being thrown into the thick of it all but it was exciting being surrounded by practically naked men taking part in their sexual desires.

The main housekeeper on shift would also be the one training me, he was a bit of a smart-ass twink and hilarious, giving me hints along the way on how to multitask the duties while in certain areas of the club.

I was taken aback by the abundance of different professional cleaning products I had to learn about to do the job with many products used depending on what the cleaning situation might be and how there was a list of specific processes to thoroughly clean the steam room and communal showers.

Each product could take care of cleaning and disinfecting something that in everyday life you might not ever have to clean (unless perhaps in a gay household), like what formula works best to remove certain types of oil or water-based lubes smeared on a mirror or on a wall or vinyl mattress and how to detect that, or various stains on a tile floor or rug in the common area, deodorizers, deep cleaning concoctions, etc.

The list went on and was apparently ever-changing in this business as new professional products came on the market.

Keeping ahead of the laundry was also very important so there aren't huge piles of dirty towels and cum filled sheets to both wash and dry.

Everyone of the staff seemed to do their part in this process if they were going by or in the laundry room as one of the worst things that can happen is the place runs low or out of clean towels, pillowcases and sheets as it then starts a domino effect with rooms not getting completely prepared for the next customer so then a waitlist for rooms forms and you also don't want to hear customers bitch that there are no fresh towels. It was also seen as disrespectful if you left a huge pile of dirty laundry for the next shift coming on to have to do.

It may sound strange that so much attention was to be paid to laundry but this wasn't a general process you might find in a household.

In the bathhouse, I noticed right away it wasn't unexpected to find a towel or fitted sheet rolled up because someone had basically wiped their shitty ass with it after a crazy sex session or even to see used sex toys, cock rings, condom wrappers or condoms would be within the sheets and towels so that was one of the reasons things had to be separated before being put in the machine.

Blood on any of the materials could be the norm as well, along with loads of lube and you just knew cum was going to be on everything along with anything else you can imagine. Latex gloves become your temporary best friend as you have to change them up often.

You also had to make sure the industrial laundry machines were not loaded too full as it would take longer to process and the items would also then be not as clean as they should be if the machine was packed too tight. This could also lead to those towels, once in the dryer, heating up the lube residue and providing a very unpleasant stench with the towel then not being suitable for a customer to use.

Since a client could get a new towel anytime they wanted from the snack bar area, some people really took that offer up so on a whim they would ask for a fresh towel while wearing a new towel and then also ask for an extra one to either casually carry under their arm as they cruised or just to have on hand in their room which meant the laundry bins were full all the time.

I was told it would happen and eventually noticed over time that brand new towels, definitely got stolen if a new shipment came in, so they were distributed sparingly and put randomly after washing within the other sets of towels. Same with sheets and pillowcases.

As with laundry, the rental rooms needed to be kept up with demand so they were another top priority.

The rental rooms always had to be cleaned efficiently and as spotless as possible and I was jokingly warned, I was going to open doors to rooms to then see, smell, and have to deal with every kind of situation and mess conceivable.

These rooms ranged in size from single with a basic vinyl covered foam mattress covered with a fitted sheet and a pillowcase over the vinyl covered foam pillow, all on a sturdy, wooden bed framed built within the walls of the room with two open areas under the bed with large plastic containers to hold whatever won't fit in the locker in your room that is located on the other side of the bed with a built-in nightstand set in between.

In this bathhouse, each room also had two walls with large mirrors alongside the bed and a simple light above the head of the bed with a dimmer switch, as it's very important to manage your own lighting and yet watch yourself having sex with someone.

A double room would be the same deal just basically double the size of a regular room with two times the size of everything. A large room would have triple the space and size of everything. A supreme or VIP room would have four times the size of everything and usually included a sling and maybe a fuck bench, plus a TV with a remote to choose your porn.

As I would find over the years, even many of the regular rooms in new clubs would have all this and a lot more for a client as technology advanced and money was infused into a venue.

Cleaning these rooms, you had to be quick but thorough. For the most part, the men that had rented the rooms would be respectable of the place and even leave you a tip on the pillow or side table, those men were routinely the regulars and the staff got to know who was known for tipping well so they would jump at the chance to clean their room after that person left.

Before entering a room, you have to knock on the door to make sure no one is in there as once in a while other customers would sneak in if the door was left open or the last client's lover would think it was ok that they could stay in the room (because the lover said so), they typically knew the rule but would still try. Once inside, turn the lights up and use your flashlight to look at tighter, darker, harder-to-reach areas to make sure no small belongings were left behind or for any garbage like used condoms thrown in a corner along with drug residues or paraphernalia or empty booze bottles.

After making a quick evaluation of what needs to be done you then proceed to remove all the bedding, empty the trash can, check the lockers to make sure nothing was left behind (and on top), and overall that nothing was broken.

If something is broken, make a note of it with the room number, clean the room as much as possible but also alert the cashier to put the room out of order until whatever is wrong gets fixed.

It helps if you are handy enough to fix things yourself so that the room can be rented again right away otherwise it means a loss of revenue until that room is ready to go. I certainly got to know how to fix a broken lock or change out a doorknob in no time. And maintenance could mean anything from changing a lightbulb to getting an electric sander out to grind down the hardened layers of cum around the glory holes in the booths before repainting them.

What could also hold up a room while cleaning is anything from poppers being spilled, lube, feces, urine, blood, drug remnants, booze...you name it, the last two mentioned customers used to sneak it all the time so you had to monitor for that yet also expect it. If there was something in a room that was going to be difficult to clean, you had to use a variety of heavy-duty cleaners which would mean the room takes longer to clean for the next occupant and time was everything as the rooms had to be kept in circulation.

After all that, you then move on to clean the next rooms on your list but in a timely manner and not too many at once as you don't want the front desk cashier waiting for rooms to be ready to give to clients checking in, it seemed to be best to just do 3-4 at a time and as close together to each other if possible, you figured out the best routine that was efficient time-wise.

This was a large bathhouse for its time in the city almost 20 years ago now, with over 4000 square feet of surface area with a ton of rooms and lockers but we had only a handful of staff per shift which seemed to work well as time went fast and you definitely got a workout.

If there are too many employees working on shift, then eventually nothing gets done as everyone will be too busy chatting with each other or with customers while who knows what is happening in the space along with regular duties being left behind, this could also happen with a general cross over of shifts with everyone together. It also gives an impression to customers that the place isn't busy if all the staff is having a big gab session behind the snack counter.

Something else of which I was to discover by accident the first night was when you go in to clean a room, shut the door completely behind you. Or else it can be perceived as an open invitation to some customers who might want to play and when the door is open, even a little bit, that they are welcome to come inside and then it can be tricky to try and remove them while being polite and joking about it at the same time.

The other side of it I was later told was, it's also an opportune moment to get it off quickly with someone that you are interested in at the venue.

Customers just might not know the rules and for some staff and even managers and owners, some play, as tempting as situations can be, and depending on who you were working with, is ok. That supposed set in stone rule could change and you never seemed to know as it was frowned upon or you could be patted on the back for it.

Amongst ourselves, although told it was a no-no, apparently as long as it doesn't totally disrupt your work it's not necessarily a bad thing, it was considered even a natural thing to do, you had to judge for yourself as you could find yourself damned if you do and damned if you don't, plus it depends what reputation you want to put out there.

Sex and games come into play frequently in a bathhouse. There are regular customers who always want to try and be the first to test-drive the new employee in some way and half the time they will want it to be known that they had you first, to not only other customers but the people you are working with so the choice is yours. There were a lot of mixed messages to come to your own conclusion about and the risks you wanted to take.

Loving the work and atmosphere already but also not wanting to jeopardize my job as I had just started, there was plenty of "Sorry, not right now, I've got to work" comebacks, even if interested, even with a walking hard-on, until I got into the habit of closing the doors fully behind me every time as it seemed the rooms were the target areas. Hell, even climbing a short ladder to change a lightbulb in the place seemed like an opportune time for a customer to try and feel you up.

Overall, it was best to never be rude to the customer about the subtle interaction, the worst thing you can do is insult them by making them feel ashamed. It didn't hurt to keep them hoping for you, I was half-jokingly told. You might even get more tips while relationship building and all that kind of rigmarole.

I knew this would be a part of the game going into the job, men hitting on you, asking you every blunt question under the sun, or just flat-out grabbing hold of you while they are naked and hard, it could be a bit abrupt or unnerving when it first happens as I was in work mode, but I ended up taking it as a bit of a compliment and basically laughed it off as part of working in a sex club and would even hit back at them, jokingly slap or grab their ass as I walked away to help make them feel wanted.

You also had to watch leaving a room you just cleaned as a customer might try and either pull you back in there (a big no-no) or try and sweet talk you into some side action. You learned, not all men want what's available and practically nude surrounding them, some love the challenge of having something seen as apparently forbidden as an employee.

During this first shift and the next ones after, you figured out how to handle these "hands-on" situations. I was never shocked or upset about what was happening, I actually found it all captivating. It's like kids in a candy store, they want everything, even if it's not for their own good or too sweet so you learn to manage the situations.

All I knew was after the first shift, I was exhausted from being consistently on the go but loved it. The staff were fun to work with, they were very upfront about everything which saved time and bullshit. It was a world of its own making. I went home tired but smiling, it was far more fun than my regular work life, even if the pay was less. And the men I was meeting were down to earth, very open-minded, and intriguing to be around, no matter their story.

I found this business was like no other. Normal ways of going about things were instantly enhanced by action or words far more than the routine I was used to living. The pay was lower than in the corporate world, but not by that much at the time once you add in the tips made on each shift and anyway, to me, it seemed like I was learning far more about how the real world operates when you cut out the bullshit than up in some office tower looking down on everyone below. If someone wanted to say or do something in the bathhouse, they just did it.

At this new job, I felt like I had expanded upon my secret that only a certain number of people have for themselves. I couldn't wait until the next shift and would jump at the chance to come in and cover for someone if they were sick or couldn't work a shift.

During this new time period, another unexpected thing started to happen, because you are constantly on the go during your shift, running all over the place, cleaning and carrying everything from laundry to cleaning supplies and stocking heavy inventory, you end up losing a few pounds. It was like 8 hours of straight cardio on shift so it was no wonder you'd lose weight, so then you didn't feel guilty about eating what you wanted to cause the more you moved at your next shift, you burned the calories off. It was almost like Crossfit, except I was getting paid to see dicks of all kinds and get in shape.

And oddly, inevitably, as apparently happens to many new employees, including myself, I ended up catching a cold after that first weekend. You are surrounded by so many practically naked men that even with the top disinfectants and cleaners along with the building airflow ventilation, you come into contact with air-borne viruses so you get sick no matter how much you wash your hands. Even if it was just a 24-hour cold, it seemed to help build up your immune system to help ward off other viruses so it seemed rare to get sick after that first cold.

When it happened to me, I was surprised as I rarely get sick but then other employees told me their experiences, it was nothing really invasive and was something you could let other new employees know might happen when they first start.

As the weeks rolled on, it was observed that I was doing my housekeeping job correctly while helping customers behind the snack counter and I apparently worked well with the other staff and clients, I felt like I was part of a team.

Trust is a big thing working in a bathhouse, and it was something that had to be established. Staff members would give their feedback on you privately and to other employees, owners, and managers whether or not they were asked. I felt I got along with everyone as there were certainly a lot of laughs for almost every situation and we had a good rapport. With that, I was asked if I would like to be trained as a cashier in charge of checking the clients in and out and also managing the snack bar during those shifts.

In any other normal environment, this wouldn't be a big deal, in a bathhouse a cashier is a very valued person that you recognize and appreciate on day one. Besides your accounting needs to be on point every time, you were also a bit like a bouncer, a counselor, and of course, you had to be trusted with the money and credit/debit charges.

You are the first and last person a customer sees. Depending on your skills, over time, you can help dictate the show on your shift, set the tone for the place and your discretion skills come into play as to who comes in and under what circumstances as every walk of life individual and their motivations come up to the cashier window. Most men are allowed inside but you have to be able to also read someone at first glance as best you can to prevent possible trouble and for the security of the other customers and employees along with the physical business.

Not only are you in charge of all the rapid cash handling (it is, for the most part, a cash business), you have to watch the rental room and locker rental situation, be able to try and predict what you will need to have accomplished by the employees under your watch before a rush of men arrives to prevent anyone being held up for a room and put on a waiting list.

Of course, as time went on in the industry, you can now just look at a computer screen for updates with online maps of the place and estimated wait times. Back then, everything was by memory and matching your walls of keys for room and locker rentals and on the printed spreadsheet and receipts you kept updated during your shift so that the next cashier can be given an overview of what is going on at the time of shift change.

In this bathhouse, we used walkie-talkies only half the time, and even with all the technology of today, communication is the key whether it be verbally or even with a quick glance as it can save time and effort in ways a device on hand cannot. Being one who loves technology, it seems best if you can use those key elements at hand and also work with your instincts.

At times we'd have a customer who had been slowly escalating in his actions, it could even be because he simply got turned down by someone he was interested in, and/or maybe he snuck in booze or drugs on his person checking into the place. So while in his room, he will try to build up his self-esteem by getting high or drunk before making his way around the club again.

As staff members, we had such a good, natural rapport with each other that we could detect early if something might be about to happen, so this is when a knowing glance from a fellow employee or even passing each other a note can help prepare everyone along with the other customers close by to stay clear and safe as we might have to remove someone. More than half the time a drama would evolve on some level like yelling at anyone who will listen to how unfair life was, along with, "Don't you know who I am?!" And that he should be able to do what he wants in a bathhouse since he paid to come in.

Communication between yourself, the staff, and customers is a top priority, and at the time working the intercom to tell customers with lockers waiting for rooms to come to the front desk with their belongings to exchange their locker key for a room they have been waiting for, sometimes repeatedly making the announcement for clients on a waitlist as they might be already caught up in some action with other customers. Half the time the customer didn't seem to pay attention to the announcements so one of us on the floor would find the customer to let him know to bring his belongings to the front as his room was now ready. If communication didn't work one way, we made it work another way.

You had to know what was happening around you as best as possible at all times and learn to trust your instincts that you continue to develop as something useful, valuable, and many times paid off.

You also have to be very self-assured but modest in many regards. A customer for example may have been barred for any number of reasons, so unless otherwise stated by the manager or owner, it's up to you to decide after some discussion with the patron on his behavior previously whether to let him back in again or not, for how long and under what circumstances. Many times you have to make the decision also to remove and bar an individual from the premises for a myriad of reasons, which could also be dangerous with certain kinds of men if not handled correctly and strategically.

The choice isn't always yours as to who gets allowed in even if your gut is telling you it's not a good idea by the way the customer was being disruptive in the bathhouse in the past. While a person is barred, an owner or manager can override your decision if contacted by the customer and so then the barred individual can pay to come in like any other man the next time he chooses to.

In my experiences, it's been mostly an owner's decision to override someone who is barred which was not always the wisest idea as he may have only heard the customer's side of the story while having his ass kissed in order to get back in. The only good part about that is if the customer fucks up again (and they do), the owner will then be even more livid as his trust and ego got affected so they will make it very clear that the individual doesn't come in again while the rest of us giving a knowing look to each other.

A cashier has to deal with not only that but manage patrons who want to come in after the bars close and the last thing you want on a busy overnight shift on a weekend is someone coming in so drunk or high or both that they can barely walk and potentially break things, start a fight, fall and harm themselves or in general start some bullshit with other customers.

Add to that list is if they pass out (or even worse start to overdose) either somewhere in the bathhouse like a steam room or in their own rented room or someone else's room which can be a big chore to then try and remove them delicately and safely which also eats up time, manpower and energy. Plus hope you don't need to call the police or an ambulance. But worst of all is the stress it puts on an employee as you can be sure when any shit goes down, it's mainly at the busiest time in a bathhouse. And customers don't want to see a messy man practically falling down or passing out. It's just not a good look anytime, anywhere.

The wrong customer who somehow manages to get in under not the best circumstances ends up being the one individual everyone has to keep an eye on all night in case he tries some bullshit while you have well over 100 other half-naked men roaming the place.

It's about balance, a good cashier will have a thick skin and be able to run on instincts. Of course, men are going to arrive and come in under some kind of influence, as long as they are told clearly about the rules, then the fun can be had. It would be nice to say all booze and drugs to any degree are stopped at the door and some will claim they do but realistically you can only try your best as bathhouses would have zero business if everyone had to be 100% sober before coming inside.

Even without drugs or booze, a man with an agenda can get up to any kind of trouble and can at times be the one to start the real problems.

A cashier also cannot leave his post at the end of his shift unless everything is balancing at the end, and that's not just the money part, but anything else that they may need to let the next employees coming on to shift be aware of such as maintenance issues, deliveries or specific customers that might be being monitored for current behavior.

No one is perfect though and mistakes of some sort will always happen so if an error has been made or something needs to be taken care of or even if they forgot to mention something to an assistant manager or manager, as long as they can let them be aware of whatever it is right away through healthy communication, things can be rectified.

When an assistant manager or manager isn't present, the head cashier runs the show, and even if management is around, they will have their own responsibilities to take care of too so a cashier is heavily relied upon in many aspects and looked at respectfully, which can be quite a lot to undertake, especially on weekends when the bathhouse is packed, so then just imagine what Pride week is like as well.

I was up for the challenge of adding a new position to my role and recall being worried about the first couple of shifts as I didn't want to make any mistakes, the cashiers training me were very good at not showing me where I might have made a mistake but how to find it and learn from it myself.

It was great to start meeting customers coming into the place more face to face than only in passing in the hallways while doing housekeeping. I still had the housekeeping position too and so I was able to swap roles when required. I had a lot of respect for the cashiers and valued what I was continuing to learn from them.

CHAPTER FOUR

Every weekend working at the bathhouse I was full of anticipation, I never dreaded going to work, and used to arrive early
just to hang out with the staff and chat with customers.

You never knew what to expect during the shift and that's
what also made it enjoyable as it usually meant lots of nudity
and antics and it would be entertaining on some level.

We all had our work duties to take care of and ways of
doing things on the job but there always seemed to be a team
effort involved, you certainly knew your back was covered by
a fellow employee. Yet each of us had our unique personalities
that would shine through for the customers and towards each
other.

Looking back, the owner and manager at this bathhouse let
us be ourselves as that is what seemed to make the customers
feel comfortable, especially if it was a patron's first few visits as
it helped keep everything real and casual.

For myself, this was in many ways a crucial time in my life
as I could be considered a quiet and reserved individual, which
was true. I was and still can be a very guarded and private person, but working there helped me lose a lot of what I wouldn't
consider a fear but more of how to manage and navigate the
conservative world it felt like I had been living in.

Being in my twenties and partially because of how I was
raised, just speaking to another man would make me hesitant
and cautious so I always felt more comfortable being around

women.

Working at the bathhouse though meant I had no choice but to interact with men and even though many had a sexual agenda, I had to lose that sense of caution as this was a men's only private establishment, where men of every age, body type, and overall background would have questions, concerns or just wanted to have a conversation with an employee.

Being at the baths helped bring me out of my shell more and it seemed to happen naturally and comfortably so that was a bonus as part of this learning curve of life.

The bathhouse had a very welcoming environment, and no one was going to judge the customers for what they got up to. It may be talked about if it was some kind of over-the-top sexual act on show for everyone to see, but whatever fantasy a customer was hoping to fulfill, no one was going to stand in your way about it, in fact, other customers might even hope they could watch.

The manager Kevin was also very good about letting us approach him with ideas for special events in the club, along with listening to perhaps a more efficient way of taking care of a task. You'd have to state your point, he would listen with a smile and then ask you questions about why you thought something should change or take place, and after some consideration, most of the time he moved forward on it with a positive result.

One of the ideas that we got passed was to have dress-up theme shifts, we used to have a toga night where staff would dress up in a toga with sheets wrapped around our bodies every which way, plus cowboy nights, police officers, pool boys, you name it. Customers could get in on the act and dressed up too if they knew we had something planned.

We just figured, why wait until Halloween? Which that

holiday in itself was a very special occasion for us as we used to plan weeks ahead for it and we loved decorating the place, changing the hallway light bulb colors, dressing up in outrageous costumes, turning some rooms into spaces for either tricks or treats and making the venue spooky yet enticingly erotic. We'd also encourage the customers to come and dress up for Halloween in their favorite costume with prizes, everyone seemed to love it and customers got to fulfill their attire fantasies with each other.

One of the most popular events we had was Blackout Night, held on Thursdays from 6 pm until midnight, although we tended to let it go well past midnight just because men enjoyed it so much.

At 6 pm for that night, without fail, every Thursday of the month, we would have lineups of men checking in for either a room or a locker, with regulars tending to be the first to arrive so they could request their favorite room to rent before anyone else got it, the waiting list for rooms always began early for that evening of escapades.

Blackout Night was also a chance for those men that were maybe not comfortable with the way they looked or even still in the closet, to show up and parade around more confidently in a blacked-out environment because when it's hard to see each other, it's harder to judge although working at the club, it seemed like no matter how you looked, at some point you'd connect with someone as the customer base seemed to be very diverse.

As part of the setup for Blackout Night, rubber curtains were hung up over specific corridors to not let in light from main areas of the venue like the front lounge and snack bar. While the lights throughout the rest of the space were dimmed down even more than normal to practically nothing or shut off completely. This is when we jokingly referred to it as being "Helen

Keller" ready, which is also what we referred to the blacked-out playrooms as most of the time.

When men checked in to the bathhouse, they were given a very small handheld flashlight, but we made sure before the event started to give the lightbulb itself a good coat or two of dark red nail polish on the bulb part so that any light that managed to shine through wouldn't be harsh and bright, especially if it was accidentally shined into someone's face.

Some men that were new to the event wouldn't like the flashlight at first and didn't have to use one if they didn't want to, and once they understood that was the point of it, to have to feel your way around, with the men you passed by simply by using your senses, they got right into it. Regular customers used to outright refuse to use a flashlight as they knew their way around practically as good as an employee and found it even more exciting to experience hands-free.

Blackout Nights were always crazy busy, you would think it was Pride weekend it was so filled with men. If that was the shift you had to work housekeeping, you had to really work your magic while stepping over and around men having sex with whole hallways being blocked off by the heaps of men participating in group sex.

If you had a particular kind of fetish you were into whether that being fisting, heavy nipple play, bondage, or what have you, this was your night because men would get so involved in the ambiance of the place and since no one could see what they were really up too, they would be more adventurous and would give in to the deep desires and discover new uncharted territories.

For me, it was getting to the point that if the bathhouse needed shift coverage during a weekday or night, I would happily volunteer to swap a shift with an employee or even work while calling in sick at my other job knowing being at the baths was going to be more fun. And working a day time shift could be very different from what goes on at night, even weekday shifts were different compared to weekends.

On the Saturday and Sunday during a day shift the general feeling you got from the customers coming in was that they had a full and busy week and just wanted someplace to get away from the world outside and do whatever they wanted. Many of those customers would even just show up to sit in the TV lounge and watch an old black and white classic movie, cult film or whatever was on a sports channel.

Whoever was head of the shift that day would take care of all the necessities around the cashier office, snack bar, lounges, admin work, etc. to make sure everything was available and ready on that shift while preparing for what would always be a busy night on the weekend and that included restocking the toy case as we called it with various new sex toy shipments that might have come in, along with lubes and the same would go with the big vending machine.

Mornings in the bathhouse still had a selection of men from the night before who would either just be waking up in their rented rooms to then realizing they've been there all night so then they'd be in a panic to leave or, they would renew their stay for another 8 hours, have some coffee, buy a toothbrush and toothpaste from the vending machine, shower then spend the day relaxing and having sex with whoever they were attracted to in the venue, whether those men were also still there from the night before or with whoever was coming through the bathhouse doors fresh for the day ahead.

The deep cleaning of the bathhouse would be done early in the morning every day of the week and was far more encompassing as it was considered a reset for the 24 hours ahead and everything needed to be completed in a timely manner, well before noon as that is when the first rush of clients would start arriving.

The sexual desires and acts wouldn't necessarily differ in scale depending on whether it was day or night because the establishment had no windows, so it was like being in a casino in Las Vegas, where the setup is such that you just keep doing what you want to do not knowing what is going on outside or what time of the day or night it is, it's also why we would only have one clock on the wall at the snack bar and most bathhouses, like this one, did not have windows. Not knowing if it was night or day kept men around and renewing their stay.

On weekdays this bathhouse got to be known for the "Lucky at Lunch' special, with the tagline, "If the girls at the office only knew."

Lucky at Lunch was a hugely popular special. Since we were located in the downtown core, this was an especially enticing promotion for the business crowd.

This would also attract the kind of men you would have to once in a while keep an eye on as many of them considered themselves to be straight and were either married and half the time they also had kids at home. Which could feel a bit awkward if they were going on about their family in conversation to you when you know they just had sex with someone, and then just stepped out of the shower room massaging their still semi-hard cock in front of you while asking for a fresh towel from behind the snack counter.

For these straight men, the desire to act upon those sexual urges and fantasies could at times be considered stronger depending on how the person handled their emotions as they could be concealed at first and then practically explode if things didn't happen to go as planned for themselves while in the bathhouse. This would once in a while be the case if it was their first time at the baths and had a whole, very preplanned fantasy in their mind of how things will go for them.

This was certainly not an everyday occurrence but if it did happen, it would be quick with a lot of yelling with the patron then rushing out the door. What could have also set them off is simply because a guy tried to touch their chest, ass, or even grab their dick as they walked by.

Straight men were also known to us to sometimes being the loudest having sex, almost like they were bragging or showing off if it was happening somewhere in the club for everyone to see. And in such a manner that they finally got what they were after all this time, even over the music you could hear the biggest moans and groans about it all. Men even used to imitate them passing by the room or one of the cheeky cashiers was also known to get on the intercom and imitate the sounds over the speakers.

We would jokingly refer to this as "Showtime!" As without fail half the time, they would then feel the need to have to tell us, employees, all the dirty details about it while they were asking for a fresh towel or as they checked out of the place, but as long as they were happy and really, no one seemed to mind.

If a straight man wasn't quite considered a regular of the place yet, without stating as such, their level of paranoia could also be raised about running into someone they knew (who would also happen to be a bathhouse so probably a safe secret) or they would even just worry about being seen coming and going to the bathhouse from outside.

The fear of being caught would actually make them stand out more while pacing right outside the building doorway by the way they were acting about everything, such as: lifting up coat collars, wearing big black sunglasses while constantly pulling down the front of their baseball cap. Even celebrities didn't go to that extent.

Either way, they were always a good crowd and some damn sexy men too who normally knew exactly what they were after and routinely got it, they would also be one of the reasons gay men would come to the baths at that particular time so they could play with some straight dick.

It seemed that lunchtime or early in the evening during the other special, was when the bathhouse would have more straight men in attendance, so all the quirks that came with that within what was considered to be a gay business could really stand out with what was said and done. No one seemed to mind though, as it was all part of the fabric of the place.

The Lucky at Lunch special was only on during the weekdays from 11 am until 2 pm, and you had to arrive within that time frame so that you would be able to rent a single room for $8 for 4 hours or a locker for $4 for 4 hours.

A couple of times a week we'd also have half-price coupons for rooms and lockers. If you paid the full rate on those particular nights when you left you would get a half-off coupon for what you initially checked in for (room or locker) and the coupon could be used on your next full-rated visit for the discount.

The number of people that would try and use that coupon to get half off an already discounted rate, even when it was stated that it wasn't allowed on the rate list at the entrance to the club and on the coupon itself was an eye-rolling experience.

They'd literally yell as they should only have to pay $2 for a locker with the coupon during Lucky at Lunch visit. And would remind you how often they come to the bathhouse. Again, it could be wound-up sexual tension or something but they still came in as they didn't come all the way to the bathhouse for nothing and would laugh about it after they got off with someone and might apologize to the cashier.

This lunchtime special was a great way to get people in the bathhouse during the day and because of the way the 4-hour stays were laid out, if you timed it right, you would still get to have fun with the crowd that was coming in after work or university.

Some of the strangest and hottest times could be had during a lunch special as the crowd was filled mostly with those that commute downtown to work, men knew they had a time limit so there was no wasting time, they got right to it and as often as they could manage.

One of the customers who would come to Lucky at Lunch was this utterly handsome, clean-cut businessman, about 34 years old with a dark, finely groomed short hairstyle, smooth rock-hard, muscular body, and zero ego.

He would show up at least two or three times a month, being a mix of coy and shy while always requesting the same rental room number from the time before hoping it was available as it was close to the front of the club near the lounge.

Once inside the bathhouse, he would always head straight to the glass display case in the TV lounge filled with sex toys and lube, look it all over, and then race over to the snack bar to tell a staff member that he wanted to purchase something from the case.

Every time he would choose a 9-inch dildo, preferably mulatto in color. If he didn't see one in the case, he would ask if we had any in stock and then be slightly disappointed to learn they had sold out so then would he buy whatever other dildo was available at the same size. This customer had become so frequent over time, we started ordering extras of the mulatto 9-inch dildos since it seemed to be his favorite and overall, it was always one of the most popular sex toys we sold.

Once paid for, at the outrageous bathhouse sum of $57. He would go to his rented room and rarely leave, only if he felt like taking a shower, and after about 30 minutes he would exit the room and then practically charge out of the venue in a mad rush, cheeks flushed red.

His pace to leave was always so alarming that if you didn't recognize him from before, you would think something was wrong.

After he'd leave, when it was time for the cleaning attendant on duty to clean his room, they'd discover as soon as they opened the door, that all initially would appear to be very untouched. If he didn't shower, the towel would still be folded and set nicely on the bed, all except for the dildo, which was obviously pulled apart with his mouth due to the visible bite marks on what was left and it was chewed on, almost like he was in a rage.

Thankfully he wasn't swallowing the silicone bits, at least not the big pieces, instead, he spits out the pieces he chewed off the dildo into the garbage container and all over the floor and on an area of the sheet on the bed.

Nothing would be left except for the wire that held most of the dildo in place and the base of balls would be full of bite marks but obviously, that part was too strong to pull apart with his teeth. After the first couple of times this happened, we crowned him "The Chew Master."

CHAPTER FIVE

While working at the bathhouse or even now if it comes up in conversation, people will wonder if a gay sauna is open at Christmas and what it is like for that time of year.

At all the baths I worked at, Christmas can be quite normal, decorations and all. Many men have that week off of work as part of their Christmas holidays, so if they are in town already or have arrived to visit family or friends, they might be looking for a place to get away from the festivities or even all the shopping commotion for a couple of hours for their own merry fun.

Attendance both day and night during this time of year can be the same as any other week with a few lag times in between or even busier than expected. A lot of men either don't have families to go home to or they can't get into the whole Christmas spirit with all the expectations around what it's supposed to represent with the dinners and gifts deal, so they head for the bathhouses for a break. I too have never been a big fan of this time of year myself, so would always offer to work shifts so that other employees who do appreciate Christmas more could celebrate it with family and friends.

Since a lot of men have more time if they were on holidays from work, you'd see semi-regulars who were normally night owls at the bathhouse checking in during the afternoon and being pleasantly surprised at what they assumed would be a quieter time of day so then after that, many men would start changing up old visiting habits.

Christmas Eve could be quieter around dinner time, but

then get busy afterward if men found they could break away from whatever social event they were supposed to be attending. Christmas Day could be quiet in the mornings but then slowly pick up as the day progresses to then being a crazy busy night.

What we would also notice is it seemed to depend on an individual's nationality and if they celebrated Christmas or not at all. At times we'd see one nationality strongly represented in the bathhouse one day but then almost completely disappear from the bath scene the next day. It all depended on their Christmas traditions, ethnic backgrounds, and religious beliefs, etc.

This is also the time of year where there are a lot of social gatherings amongst friends and of course co-workers having office parties. During the whole month of December, unexpectedly on a weeknight but and closer to a weekend, there would be droves of men coming in each after their own office parties at some point during the evening, and once in a while, they'd even drag someone in from work with them, which must have made for interesting water cooler talk the next day at the office.

For ourselves, having our own Christmas party would be tricky. We couldn't just shut down for it so arrangements were made for a number of employees to go out to dinner somewhere, potluck at someone's apartment, or what have you, and we'd always pick names of who we'd have to get a present and still have our own little celebrations behind the snack bar.

Even though I'm not one to get excited about the whole Christmas season, I can respect it and found the celebratory atmosphere during this time of year was always quite wonderful to experience. Men were always in great moods, lots of smiles and laughs, and that included us, employees, as well who wanted to represent the season as best as possible for the customers. We'd even get small gifts from our favorite customers which were always unexpected and appreciated.

As for New Year's Eve, now that is one of the best times to go to a bathhouse. Besides Pride week, anytime there is a holiday or well-known special occasion is when a bathhouse really goes all balls in and the unexpected can happen.

Anticipating both holidays, in preparation for Christmas and New Year's, our manager Kevin would spend a lot of time getting in more stock (towels, sheets, lubes, condoms, snack food, etc.) to make sure we had everything we needed not only for customers but also since a number of businesses that supply goods to the bathhouse might be closed for their own holidays so it was best not to run low or out of any of the routine supplies.

As soon as Christmas Eve and Christmas Day were finished, the talk would soon turn to New Years with patrons planning on celebrating midnight at the bathhouse with a bang or even many would tell us they were showing up before or after the clock strikes 12, it all depended on their plans but they were excited to attend.

One particular New Years at the baths was special because it was about to be the year 2000 aka Y2K with the media outlets bombarding everyone with warnings that there was going to be possible computer glitches around the world for when the clocks changed the dates from 1999 to 2000, many were led to believe this could also be the end of the world as computers crashes would lead to other technological interferences and massive worldwide shutdowns.

With this in mind, New Year's Eve was another holiday I offered to work as my first thought was, if a big fuck up in the world was about to happen, I'd want to be surrounded by a bunch of half-naked men.

As December 31st rolled in and the afternoon went on, the place started to get more packed as men during these holiday events tend to arrive earlier so they can secure their favorite room before a waiting list starts (we never took reservations) and/or just to get the party going, of which we were happy to help bring together.

A holiday or event is one of the best times to experience in a bathhouse as all the customers are so excited along with the employees as there is a sense of celebration in the air. Even if we are crazy busy, it doesn't feel like work as we are in a place filled with lots of laughter, music, and the sounds of sex all around.

This evening was turning into one of those amazing, almost legendary prime events where everyone was in a festive mood and just having a great time while all sorts of crazy naughtiness were taking place.

One of the most memorable moments began when this one unassuming couple who lived out way beyond the suburbs of the city checked in, only this time earlier than their twice-monthly visits. They had a penchant for Room 174, a deluxe room filled with floor-to-ceiling mirrors, at the end of a long hallway in a corner location that was close to the main showers, along with a porn blackout room and steam room.

Although Room 174 was located at the end of what we had long christened, "Oldie Hawn" row, as we affectionately called it, were men of a specific demographic age range liked to rent a room because of its proximity to everything. This corner deluxe room also had a large amount of floor space just outside of it where men would at times congregate as it was between another deluxe room, a single room, and a locked storage area.

This couple though was never overly concerned about proximity, it was more about what the room had to offer as these guys had quickly become known for putting on unique sex shows for all to see.

When word got out to everyone else in the club of who had

just arrived and where they were located, suddenly men came charging up to the cashier window and were trying to switch their rooms or upgrade from lockers to be close to the action that was going to transpire at some point.

The unspoken theory being, if you are seen lounging in your rented room with your door open as an invite next to where a big, open sex scene is taking place for all to see, that means more people will be cruising down that particular hallway more often to see what is attracting so much attention. If they get hard and horny by what they are witnessing, and if you can garner a few more glances and chances while being in the same vicinity, you'll have a stronger opportunity to have more sex as you'll be the next best thing available if onlookers weren't allowed to participate in the show.

There's always a method to one's madness.

The two straight looking guys booking into Room 174 always arrived with a few duffle bags of fetish gear and they were not shy about letting anyone watch what they got up to or of letting others join in, as long as you were prepared to you follow rules and be up on your game, brave and open to trying new things without interrupting the flow with a million questions.

If you saw these two men on the street, you wouldn't have any idea of the tricks they could get up to and as disgusting as it could be to some people, they sure made a name for themselves quickly at the baths and gave zero fucks what anyone thought and if anything, along with being down to earth, nice guys, they were entertaining to many while fulfilling their fantasies and desires at the same time

About two weeks prior, this dynamic duo checked in at their typical weekend time with a couple of big bags of goodies which of course, meant anything could happen.

No matter what they got up to, they always got the place

buzzing, and on this previous visit, after about an hour or so in their favorite room, one of them wrote on the communal chalkboard in the wet area that there was going to be a show at 10 pm so to show up at the door of Room 174 if interested in watching.

The communal chalkboard was an old-school method of communication where you could leave your room number and state what kind of action you were looking for in the bathhouse. Then you could cruise by the person's rental room, if you were both mutually attracted to each other and could offer up what the guy wrote on the chalkboard, then it's a go. It was also a possible way to find out if the guy was an exclusive top of bottom sexually.

What was about to happen in Room 174 though was anyone's guess, like clockwork at 10 pm, the show was on, they opened their deluxe room door for all who wanted to see. Partially dressed in highway maintenance uniforms with the fluorescent vests, boots, and little else. They also had two nude guest attendants in their room, like sidekicks waiting to put in the work effort.

And work it was because one of the men was on all fours on the vinyl bed mattress, extremely lubed up while his new helper slowly inserted a greased-up street pylon from behind with the game seemingly being, how many of the white stripes taped around the pylon will he be able to make disappear up his ass.

While this was taking place, his buddy, also with his own helper, tried to guide, brace and hold him as he had placed his own greased pylon on the floor so that he could slowly sit on it.

This all did take time of course, while jaws continued to drop in awe watching the spectacle, and obviously, the whole of each pylon never completely disappeared up each of their asses. It was just surreal to watch and some of the onlookers were even clapping as each of them achieved the level they wanted.

Fisting sessions in a bathhouse are a regular occurrence, so much so if you happen to pass an open room where it is taking place, it's like, whatever, that guy has two whole hands up his ass or a whole hand deep in the ass well past the wrist and sometimes also in a rigorous in and out punching motion.

We'd just keep going about our business passing by and same with the customers but this particular event in Room 174 was indeed a show of force. When they completed their little event, the door to the room stayed open for most of the rest of the night, and as they continued to push the limits not only on themselves but others who wanted to partake in whatever seemed to be suggested.

What seemed to make this New Years' in Room 174 that little bit more memorable was when they wrote out an announcement this time on the communal chalkboard stating for everyone to show up at midnight for the "Birth of a new millennium!"

This had everyone's curiosity peaked, the cashier at the front desk even got in on the act and added to the excitement by making announcements to head to Room 174 at midnight for a special show.

As midnight approached, Oldie Hawn's row was packed with spectators wondering what they were going to see at the stroke of midnight.

It was a sight to see on that end of the club as men either nude or just wrapped in a towel were practically clamoring for a spot over each other to try and get the best vantage point...and giving blowjobs and everything else while they waited.

Then shortly, just before the beginning of the midnight

hour, the door opened to the room and one of the two men was propped up on to a short, makeshift platform type tabletop that was on top of the wooden base of the bed frame with the vinyl mattress having been moved aside.

The one putting on the show was on all fours facing the mirrors but with his ass, about two to three feet from the wall at the foot of the bed while his partner half held him for balance and gave him quiet encouragement.

Nothing seemed to look unusual, even though this was unusual, except that he was nude and somehow balancing himself while gearing up for something.

As everyone started to countdown to midnight, albeit the timing was a bit off, his partner announced that a baby boy was to be born on New Year's Y2K, and with that, the showman's face squeezed hard, mouth slightly open with some apparent breathing exercises, then he clenched teeth, scrunched his face and after a couple of big pushes, the stunned, hushed audience watched as he shot a full-on plastic baby boy toy doll out of his ass and it flew (and I mean flew) towards the wall so hard the doll made a thud sound before dropping to the floor.

Spectators' mouths were agape, followed by again by some applause, cheers, and a lot of, "Oh, my Gods!" and it appeared a baby boy was born to ring in the millennium.

I guess everyone needs a hobby as that shot out of his ass was clean, obviously lubed up, and done with what had to be some prior practice and strength.

This also wasn't just some long, thin, Ken type barbie doll either, this was one of those cheap, dollar store dolls with some girth that you can buy without clothes in a plastic bag and must have been at least a couple of inches in diameter with an even bigger head that was larger in diameter than the main part of the body itself.

To this day I don't know how he managed that but they both seemed very pleased with themselves and it was the talk of the rest of the night.

CHAPTER SIX

When you come into a bathhouse, essentially what you are paying for is your time to use the venue, what you do with that time is up to you. In the bathhouses I have worked at, you are paying at the check-in window for 8 hours inside unless you have arrived during a special discounted rate period, then you would have the choice to pay half the regular rate and stay for up to 4 hours.

The discounted rate at this bathhouse was used to draw people in at what could be considered quieter times, such as on a workday, even though our venue always seemed to do well during those periods due to the special discounted rate being grandfathered in place so long, and large customer base, either way, it brought men inside.

Unless you work in a bathhouse, it can be tricky to have any comprehension of the time once inside due to lack of windows and clocks, a bathhouse can be set up that way to keep men in the place. Since customers tend to be focusing more on dick and ass, men would often go over the 4-hour or 8-hour time limit, if that happened, we would give them a grace period for being late. If they rented a room, it was easy enough to then find them and remind them that it's almost check-out or renewal time.

There were always a few patrons though who would blatantly abuse that time frame, making it difficult to track them down in the club (some literally trying to hide) so then we would charge them another 4 hours or 8 hours. It all depended on the circumstances and rules set in place by management, or if they were a regular customer, a cashier could let them slide that one time with a polite warning.

A standard set time limit in a bathhouse is different depending on your location in the world and which bathhouse you are going to and if they are open 24/7 or not. We always found that men tended to either show up, get laid once or twice, then leave within even 30 minutes sometimes, then some want to stay and fuck around as long as possible and hopefully without paying extra if they think they could charm their way out of that one.

For those due to check out of the club and planned on staying longer, the rule we had was they could renew from their original 8-hour stay once again for another 8-hours, making it a 16-hour stay. Some men would ask if they could extend their stay an extra hour or two longer but that never worked as 1 to 2 hours would magically turn into 4 or 6 hours. Those patrons were also the ones that half the time would tell you (or even try to argue) that they thought a bathhouse should be free because it must cost nothing to operate.

There were also quite a few men who thought renewing for up to 16 hours in total wouldn't be enough time for them. Many men once at the 16-hour limit would try everything to renew up to 24 hours not comprehending what they are doing, which is insane but again, when you are inside the place and if you have the time and are having fun, who would want to leave?

To stay longer than 16 hours would at times involve a management discussion as it's just not healthy. We'd have plenty of men showing up with a suitcase, wanting and expecting to stay inside a bathhouse the whole of Pride weekend, which could get our guard up as they might have ulterior motives like drug dealing or escorting.

There seemed like no legit reason to stay longer than 16 hours but we'd have men tell us that they would rather be in a bathhouse than sitting in an airport waiting for their next flight. Or maybe they had nowhere else to go while they were waiting to get the keys from their new landlord to move into their place. Whatever the story was, every situation was dealt with differently.

If the basis for why they thought they should be allowed to stay for longer than 16 hours wasn't that legit, we would just tell them to check out, even for 1-3 hours, go for a walk, get some proper food to eat and most of all, get some fresh air and then they could come back in.

Many men will use the bathhouse as a cheap version of a hotel, which could be quite common, just without the in and out privileges, well, that depended on their situation too. If they just got off a long flight and didn't want to be bothered with the process of finding a hotel, couldn't afford one, or didn't want to bother a friend for a place to crash, they would normally tell the cashier at the window that they just wanted a room to try and sleep in and would ask to be put in a quieter, darker area of the club.

On the other side of that, we would get customers contacting us by email or phone to let us know they were flying into town for Pride week and asking if they could (or demand) reserve a room for up to 4-5 days, which always got a no for an answer.

Some men would show up with their knapsacks and suitcase, dressed in rainbow attire at the start of Pride weekend, check-in, and think they can just keep renewing and that we wouldn't notice so eventually we'd have to lay it out to them. These men would often make such a mess of themselves with whatever booze and/or drugs they snuck in within the first 8-16 hours while stating it was in the name of Pride as an excuse so then they would be asked to leave.

Staying well past 16 hours is generally frowned upon as going through night and day transitions inside a place, whether a patron notices or not, the employees and other customers will start to see it taking a toll on not only them as their behaviors start to change for the worse but also in how they treat everyone else in the space.

There have been many instances throughout my years of working in bathhouses where I've seen owners or managers let customers stay for up to 72 hours or more, even a week or two, under the guise of the customer being a good buddy while also letting him stay for free. If you wanna see someone simply look and act messy, see what they are like after 24 hours straight in a bathhouse. It ain't pretty.

This situation would always be total bullshit, employees and management would even plead with an owner not to let this happen as it turns into such a disruption and trouble every single time it was allowed as the "friend" who was given the favor immediately starts acting like they own the place, with assumed permission from the owner to do whatever the hell they wanted.

Customers will notice this person right away too and eventually numerous complaints start coming in about the friend, his know-it-all attitude and it escalates from there so then no one is having fun. Fortunately, it would only happen once, maybe three times with the same "friend" until the message came across to said owner or manager.

Regular customers to a bathhouse are what is considered the bread and butter of the business in almost every way.

These are the men of any age, body type, and background who, without fail, will show up at the club on either their favorite day or night of the week, at the same time and for the same length of stay. Many daily.

If they love your nightly evening special, they will be there for it every night of the week it is running. You can bet on the time they will come in and what locker or room number they will want.

A cashier can make easy tips and the same with a housekeeping clerk just by having everything set up to go the minute they arrive and while they are in the place. Plus, it's not unheard of for them to give those same staff members a Christmas and/or birthday present every year, often something remarkable.

You've got to love these guys in many ways. They may act like they don't notice you on the street, especially if they are in the closet, or with family or friends as they will see the world you work at as being a place of refuge for themselves where they can be exactly who they want to be. You learn early never to take offense by any customer if they don't acknowledge you in the outside world, and you always let them speak to you first as that will tell you it is fine to converse with them and that the situation for them outside of the club is all clear.

You also get to learn more about a regular customer by their moods, laugh at their jokes, they may even really annoy you but they are a big part of the customer base that can be relied upon financially for the bathhouse.

These men always tend to mean well in who they are and will be very protective of the bathhouse for not only themselves but also on behalf of the staff and other patrons first.

If a water pipe is leaking, a TV screen has gone blank, someone is openly dealing drugs, or having a medical issue, even if a lightbulb has gone out, you can bet these will be the first people to show up at the front counter or stop an employee in the hallway to let them know what is happening.

Depending on the situation with a regular, you can reward them with some free passes of which they tend to be extremely grateful for and it makes them feel part of the team.

For a percentage of these regulars, this is their only social life, not that this is necessarily a bad thing. They are getting an eyeful of everything every time they visit, they can also probably run circles around an average Joe with their own sex stories they could tell but typically don't, these are the kind of men that have a more active sex life than you would expect on first sight.

It's also not always necessarily about the sex for a good half of these guys either, more a sense of belonging, freedom, and escapism.

Many of these men would spend their time in the club chatting with staff or other customers, some would come just to watch porn, some would just use the gym facilities. I recall one guy would rent the same room, change into his towel, then leave his door open with the light at a certain level while he read a book during his time, very rarely would he get together with anyone as men passed by his room. Another would change into a towel in his room, then sit in a chair in one of the corridors just to watch the men cruising by.

A bathhouse can be a safe space for these men, you could sense the calmness and happiness in them being there as some were from the days of zero LGBTQ equality rights so just to be in the environment as it was without fear of being hauled out by police was enough for them. These would be the men with little to no ego, yet they were confident in who they are and were happy to just meet others in the bathhouse for a conversation.

Of course, there was the other side of all this too.

You and your fellow employees get to know who is considered to be a regular by the schedule they tend to keep, the rapport between everyone, and overall, how routine they become.

For some though, they may become regulars after a month or so and then their true side shows up.

Their routine schedule will stay the same but you start to see elements of stress building up with them by perhaps being slightly condescending to staff or other patrons. Possibly because of something that has started to come up in their outside lives in their home life or work-related that has changed or needs to be managed.

If their schedule for coming to the bathhouse starts to change because of what is happening in their outside lives, they will try to arrive at a whole new time, if that doesn't go as planned for themselves, they will still come to the club but almost start blaming the place for what is going on with them, it could also be part of sex addiction for them or any other reason but they will be vocal as though the bathhouse somehow obligates them to come to the place, even if we privately tell them there is no pressure ever to come to a bathhouse.

If they have started or are struggling with alcohol or drug issues in their outside lives, they may even try sneaking those substances into the bathhouse. If we have become used to their normal habits, their change in actions now will be red flags for us and will be part of our communications with each other, they may even become barred at some point if the escalations are too much and for their own good.

We would also be able to tell right away if something is different because they will pretty much start blaming the baths for the way their lives are going, as though they are being forced to show up every night, and it could be over something as simple as they didn't like the fresh towel they received after their shower.

The regular patron will eventually escalate in the way they treat anyone they come in contact with at the bathhouse. The worst is when they for some reason get very upset while in the bathhouse, change to quickly get out of the place, and on the way out the door proclaim loudly to whoever is listening that they pay the bills for the bathhouse.

That they spend $300 a month here, that they expect things a certain way and start listing off whatever they think the employees, customers, and the establishment is doing wrong. This is definitely a sign that something is going on in their personal lives.

These are the men that for whatever reason will leave in this manner even if they haven't been barred by us at the club for their antics, they will go further to add more drama to everything and then remark on the local internet message boards why they will never ever come to our bathhouse again, how the place is a shithole and they will then exude the virtues of the other bathhouse in town they claim to now be the best.

More than half the time these guys end up coming back, begging to not be barred any longer (if that has happened), or will just quietly decide to start visiting the place again, then either their circle of behavior starts repeating itself or they change their tune completely and become another one of the guys.

Another consequence of being a regular in a bathhouse, depending on the size of your city, is after a while they have had sex with basically everyone in the place that will have them at some point if that's what they choose. A good portion of regulars though will have various fuck buddies who have their own schedules so each time still seems relatively new and a bond forms and they are all happy with how everything is working between each other.

If they only want to have sex with someone once, which many do, like a new notch on the belt, they may not notice right away but their encounters will start to slowly decrease. We would recognize this by the way these men would start to hang out more by the entrance to the bathhouse so that they can gauge who is new to them and who can be put on their to-do list as their potential next lay.

It can be a fine line for these men if they have spent so much time in the club as they will start asking anyone they feel comfortable enough with if they are losing their edge. They will still look and act the same but what they may not have realized is they have become very recognizable and because of their strong desire to try and sleep with most everyone, word has gotten out about them or men can just sense desperation.

These regulars, if not careful, will start to lose their confidence and become slightly confused. When the bathhouse has become their whole social life, and they notice they have started to have less sex, and in of all places a sex club, they will at first be in denial about it and think something must be off. It must be the clients, the weather outside, time of year, economy, you name it and they will start discussing this with staff and other clients trying to figure out what is happening, how come they aren't having sex as they used to?

In a bathhouse, men are very upfront and will even point-blank to tell them that they are in the venue too much, even an employee will tell them the same thing if they know each other well enough as a sign of how much they care.

Fellow customers will say to them that they know too much about what each other is getting up to and maybe they should take a break, so if the regular will take a break for even a week or two but that can be rare as now their lifestyle has formed a habit of coming to the bathhouse.

We all know their days are numbered and feel a little down about it when a good regular has started wondering why they may not be attracting men as much anymore as they start questioning their looks and attitude, their confidence waivers even more, and they start asking other patrons and staff what they may be doing wrong.

Then they slowly but consistently start complaining to the staff and management about anything imaginable that they may feel might need to change in the bathhouse itself to make things better for them. They won't realize, even if told a million times, a break can make a difference.

One way that can make them finally take a break is when they question the amount of money they are spending at the baths. To put off one of the real reasons at least that's the core of the issue. They may realize how much it costs them monthly to come and play every day and if they aren't getting rewarded with sex, this seems to be the excuse they need to stop for a while, which is good. If financially we lose them for a short time, maybe a couple of weeks or a few months, they always end up coming back with a fresh set of eyes and strong sexual drives again.

After you've worked in a bathhouse for some time, you'll start noticing that customers can be segmented into various groups not only in your mind but you'll quickly find out you are in sync with the people you work with who will also refer to a patron by their personality traits if we don't yet know his name.

Since privacy is part of the game in a bathhouse, you never want to bombard someone with personal questions in a sex club, especially as an employee in order to find out what they are all about. One of the reasons they are coming to a bathhouse is to be anonymous and get away from expectations in the real world.

Naturally, you will start to recognize someone by what they are perhaps into sexually most of the time on their visits if they are out in the open about it, habits they might have picked up while in the club whether they are normal or strange, ethnicities they only seem to be only attracted to, an age range that they tend to go for, suspected drug dealing, along with most anything else.

When we would find out the name of a customer if they have just flat out introduced themselves from the start of their first visit or told us in passing conversation, as part of a natural communications system we developed, we tended to stick to the nickname we made up for them for a number of reasons such as; if they were always late for check out, their personal quirks which was usually the case, or if we needed to monitor them more closely if they were on the cusp of being barred, whatever was needed to make things work. It just made it easier to recognize who we were talking about if we gave him a nickname such as "Big Red" over an everyday name such as "Kyle."

One example of this would be, we had this one customer everyone thought of as a total sweetheart, who was also quite the opposite of the image he was projecting. He was into fist fucking sessions, and we were to learn he was more so into getting fisted than doing the actual fisting so we called him, "Five-Finger Charlie."

Five-Finger Charlie used to come into the bathhouse early on Friday evenings or Sunday afternoons. He was about 6'1", was probably in his mid-forties, had been around the block a few times so he could look about 55 years old. Average body, and had a Daddy/Leatherman look, wearing subtle, cheap-looking colorful bracelets, a receding hairline, a long, dark greyish goatee, and had a following of men that seemed to admire him.

At first sight, you would think he'd come off all gruff and tough, even by the way he walked but as soon as he opened his mouth his voice was very light and airy. Like butterflies were fluttering out of his mouth.

He was always polite and got to know us very well so he would stop and have frequent conversations with members of the staff at the snack counter while drinking a cup of coffee and of course like most chats in a bathhouse, the talk always leads back to sex at some point.

Five-Finger Charlie fancied himself as a fisting expert and for some reason would feel the need to either verbally give us a fisting lesson of sorts with his hands or tell us fisting stories, whether we wanted to hear about it or not.

We gave him the nickname "Five-Finger Charlie" as he would always start showing us his version of a fisting lesson with his arm coming towards us in the air the same way, while telling us how you have to slowly open a man up with lube, with lots of love and intention.

Five-Finger Charlie would tell us you have to really feel the man, learn to move with his body, go in with one finger, then slowly graduate up to two fingers as he continues to dilate, throw in some twirling to increase the circumference until you got your whole pointed hand of fingers, including the thumb, tucked in towards the palm, then you've really worked your way in to give the participant the ultimate in orgasmic pleasures.

Both shocking and amusing, somehow the way he told his stories made you want to hear more even while placing your hand over your mouth while wondering...what the fuck.

If you just arrived on shift, you always knew if Five-Finger Charlie was in the house, because eventually, you would hear him shouting demands from his favorite Room 118 to his new lover while getting fisted with some high-pitched screams thrown in for good measure over the music in the club.

CHAPTER SEVEN

As touched upon, straight men make up a fairly decent percentage of the clientele base in a bathhouse.

If a man is checking into a bathhouse, obviously he doesn't have to disclose his sexual preference to do so, and for many men, their sexuality can even become more fluid especially if they are open to learning more about themselves, experimenting, and indulging in a variety of sexual acts.

Straight men coming into a bathhouse is not some sort of new trend either, it is common knowledge to anyone that works or plays in a gay venue such as this that straight men frequent bathhouses and that this has been happening for decades around the globe, because, no matter the social constraints, a man will find a way to get around to what he desires.

Cruising in a bathhouse you will see men that appear to look straight, or not, and since everyone is wrapped in a towel or naked, you never really know until they start talking with you and open up about themselves or even how they may react during a particular sex act as that's when the confessions start coming out.

Although it is still considered a novelty, straight men are not preyed upon (unless they make it known they want to be) or made to feel like an outcast, they get treated just like anyone else in a bathhouse.

Of course, in this type of environment, if a man feels comfortable enough to somehow get the message out that he is straight, there will be men that will gravitate towards him. Some will treat it like it's their prime opportunity to try and turn him gay, some will want to have what is considered taboo and look at him as a challenge, then some will want to teach him or hope to learn some new tricks from him. There are several reasons why gay men will want to sleep with a straight man.

Before an initial visit, at times men of any sexual persuasion call or email the bathhouse. Gay or bisexual men will have regular questions and just want to confirm something they might have heard in the community or want to know a certain time they should arrive, then they thank you for the information and hang up.

You can always tell when you are on the phone with a straight man as during their first call (there is always more than one phone call or email) they tend to start off sounding a bit nervous yet can go a little deeper and want you on the phone for as long as possible, especially if they feel things are ok after the first couple of hesitant questions. Their breathing will get heavier while they are getting off on the other end of the call. If that would happen, depending on who was working, once in a while, the employee that answered the phone would signal for the other employees to gather around to listen and keep getting him off as a little joke or politely thank him for the call and hang up. It depended on how serious the caller was or if the caller was just really looking to jerk off.

Emails would very rarely come from a business account or a personal email account; it was typically from a fake email address and they would tend to start by sending you headless nude body photos either alone or with another woman (or two) during a sexual act. With the text of the email being filled with both their hopes and expectations from their imagination running wild on what a first visit will be like for them and they will just want you to guarantee that somehow these actions will take place when they go to the bathhouse the first time.

Or they will ask if they could bring their wife or girlfriend, or if we supplied (yes, supplied), the particular kind of men they wanted, that being men with big muscles and very hairy or super smooth and feminine, and in their twenties.

They would also ask if an employee can give them a rub and tug massage, or a blowjob, or sex and how much would that cost and, what does the staff look like? These kinds of random questions. Some would even want you to send someone out to their car from the bathhouse if they promised to park close enough by as though we provided a drive-thru service.

When these straight men are making a plan to explore a bathhouse for the first time, we would occasionally get asked if they could get a tour first. That was usually a no or if they showed up at the cashier window, it would depend on how the employee felt about the situation and also if there was any time to do a tour. In my own experiences, most any tour would not always end well as the man getting to view the facilities already has a million fantasies running through his head and would inevitably be getting so aroused just by walking through the club that he'd practically try and force himself on you, then the freak in him would come out.

Another thing that would happen with straight men that wanted to visit a bathhouse for the first time, is they would ask if there is a back door they can use as an entrance and exit to the business. In which case our rule and ongoing response, backed up by every owner and manager I have ever worked with through the years was that everyone enters and leaves by the same front door, there is no special treatment.

One of the theories being if they expect those kinds of special services from the start, then what else will they demand once inside that should differ from the others who have no problem coming and going through the main entrance? And you don't want to set a precedent, because if one wants, then they all figure they should get.

A straight first-timer, especially if they manage to work up the nerve to come inside the bathhouse, may feel some sort of bond with the one they were in contact with initially for information and may even assume if they did come in and have asked for you, that once you meet with them, you can also provide a hand-holding service as well.

Generally, for any visitor that actually checks in for the first time, an employee or even manager may give them a very brief tour (they've paid to come in and use the facilities so a tour in this instance can be different), even then though you have to be careful as often the new customer will, upon seeing men half-naked, literally start to point out who they are interested in having sex with and want you to try and connect the two of them together. Not happening. We want to help every first-time visitor, no matter the sexuality, by giving them a bit of guidance but part of the fun is discovering everything for yourself.

The first-time straight players could be more nervous about the fact that they have even managed to step into a bathhouse and you can sense that immediately. Whereas men in the LGBTQ community have attended various LGBTQ events or have been in bars and nightclubs so they have a better idea of what to expect as in, the unexpected and to just roll with it all.

Another way a straight man can be easily spotted is they have basically cased the joint like a detective from the outside and from a distance away, they may be hanging around the entrance, pacing back and forth, thinking they are incognito, even in disguise, but actually far from it as acting cagey makes them stand out more.

A man of any sexuality may show up on what they assume is a quieter Monday night for their first experience or even very early in the morning when it's quiet and the place is having a more thorough cleaning, so they can get an idea of the layout for their next visit, which is also a good idea.

When they arrive at those times, this is when you get to meet the real person and you might even be able to have a conversation and answer any of their questions. They may feel awkward and tell you that they might have some dumb questions, so it's best to be empathic and honest with them as it's just because they have no real experience in a bathhouse running at a fuller capacity yet. Those were the men who appreciated speaking with you, you could see them relax a little more and figure out what their next steps should be.

Personally, I used to find it was better for a first-time visitor to show up at a quieter time to learn the lay of the land so to speak, and even get to chat with the employees, then they have a better realistic idea of what to expect.

Otherwise, we have seen instances where a first-timer will show up at peak time on a weekend night (the look in their eyes said it all) and they become instantly overwhelmed with the music up high and the place packed with basically nude men doing all sorts, to the point that they turn around after taking ten steps inside and practically run out. On the other hand, we have seen the reactions of a first-time visitor and their excitement when they realize this can be the best thing that has ever happened to them like they've been handed their freedom and have just discovered a piece of heaven.

Once they enter, they might even disclose to the cashier and that it's their first visit (gay and bisexual men do this to a lesser extent too) so that's when you'll see the makings of a great employee as they will be reassuring to them every step of the way, become a bit more discreet in their mannerisms so as to not stand out and even give them a little pep talk and let them know there is zero pressure to do anything.

We've seen men who will also just pay to come inside, get their towel and key, immediately see there is a lounge area, and watch whatever is on TV while slightly observing what is happening around them. After they have had their initial experience, they might not even go to their room or locker and change, but rather just get up and leave, only to expand upon that visit at some future time.

For many men on their first visit, it seemed they either didn't have sex with someone at all or they couldn't get enough once they've had the first encounter. For straight men though, this can take a touch longer, it can depend on how they carry themselves and what vibes they are giving off as men can pick up on anything in a bathhouse and will navigate around a person if something feels off to some degree.

After a first encounter, if all is well with them, straight or gay, you will literally see the brightness in their eyes, spirit, and confidence level rise or be completely disappointed and even disgusted in themselves. It all depends on the person and their expectations. A bathhouse isn't necessarily for everyone.

Every situation is different yet things tend to always go one of two ways. If a man feels they have more knowledge of the bathhouse on their initial visit, if they meet someone and get some action, they will stick around looking for more or they will at times leave directly after that, no matter if the sex was good or bad. For some, it's like they can't get out of the place quick enough and may even be dealing with some guilt or shame about what they may have done with someone.

We'd notice this immediately as they would literally run out of the place (of course fully dressed) but leaving the room or locker key and everything else behind without a proper check-out. Many in their panic mode will even set off the fire door alarms by using one of the emergency exit doors to try and run out the back way of the establishment and into an alley for fear someone may see them leave from the front door access on to the more public street.

Have to say though, whether it's a good or bad experience for a gay first-timer as opposed to straight. Gay men tend to not freak out and will give everything more than one chance whereas oddly enough, a straight man will make more of a production about it.

Often enough, gay or straight, both sides end up coming back as soon as a few days later to even a month or two and we would always recognize the ones that would be giving it another shot.

One thing you also learn working in a bathhouse is that not only do gay men come with all kinds of baggage, requirements, expectations, and personality but so do straight men.

Overall, it can be hard enough for a gay man to come into a bathhouse for the first time or even a tenth time, so imagine how hard it would be for a straight man in the world he created for himself to feel confident enough in a sexually charged environment. Not that it's any kind of excuse, just in many ways it's best to have empathy on every level. A bathhouse is more of an entertainment venue, want over a need, and it tends to be humans who complicate a situation for themselves when taking the first plunge.

There were numerous occasions when a straight man will gather up the courage to contact the bathhouse by phone or email and insist that we should have heterosexual event nights. Often some random man would practically demand that we must let them in, that it's not fair, how come we can have a place but they can't as part of their tangent.

I recall politely telling one guy who was calling frequently with these particular set of questions and demands that he should try and set his own play space up but that he should also consider all the implications (legal or otherwise) of running such an event as there were a whole different set of legal rules for straight people where we lived if done by the book. Most of the time he just didn't get it and with my patience running thin with him, I just told him we were doing well so we had no reason to stop everything with our customer base so that he could have his way and his fantasy realized.

He then went online stating how the gay bathhouses in town weren't letting him have his straight event and at the time the last I heard he tried to set up parties in someone's basement in the suburbs. What can be scary about this particular kind of person is when they get really angry because they can't make that idea stuck in their head a reality for themselves, which states a lot about them as well.

There are also times when straight men can cause trouble in a bathhouse. Call it nervousness or just being an asshole, any incidents with them have been more memorable as they are more peculiar in nature and it comes down again to men trying to live out some kind of fantasy that they can't with the wife or girlfriend at home.

By being in a bathhouse means they may not be under the same conservative constraints as their routine day-to-day lifestyle, so then they will think anything goes as they are in their secret place and no one will ever find out. Kind of like, what goes on in Vegas, stays in Vegas.

A small portion of these straight men cruising the club will come in with a ton of ego, be overly macho and demanding of others, even condescending and sex can only be done in the manner by which the boundaries they have set for themselves and extremely controlling. Meaning they dictate the whole scenario and it can't come off as being too gay but go ahead and maybe try and stick your dick up my ass.

These men will sometimes, and very loudly, tell staff and customers in conversation, whether we all care or not, that they are straight, almost like a form of protection in a sea of gay men.

If that goes over well for them, or if they just fucked someone, then they will at some point start bragging about their antics in the club. How they love knowing they are screwing around on their wife, going on about how many cars they have, their big house and job, even how perfect their kids are, and very much wanting and expecting the best of both worlds now that they think they have things figured out for themselves.

What would be bizarre is to hear them on their phone talking to their spouse or asking their kids how school was today, while they had a towel wrapped around their waist or were completely nude. After the call, they'd go back in for more action.

If the straight customer found things weren't going their way from minute one, maybe they've had a few drinks before coming inside and it still hasn't taken the proper effect, then they will start to be blatantly rude to the other patrons, perhaps pointing out flaws on someone's body or if a person is being too effeminate, and then they will try to lay in on staff and how useless we all are when they are just asking for a fresh towel or something. This was a big no-no and they were quickly taken down a notch.

We could always handle ourselves very well, we were quick with smart ass, cutting remarks if necessary, so it was always a pleasure to have an in-your-face, get real talk with these men. On top of that, we were always extremely protective of the customers so if we even heard of someone pulling this kind of shit in the club, we were right on it and if they didn't like it, they could leave.

More times than not, after one of us spoke to them they would calm down, even apologize. They would even admit to having some other underlying issue taking place within their lives (which we guessed), then they would confess to all sorts, anything to not be barred from what they still considered their fantasy sanctuary. In the bathhouse, this could be common and we just dealt with everything as it happened.

We had this one incident with a man who for some reason felt the need to proclaim to anyone that would listen that he was straight and how and he was using his time in the venue to fuck around on his wife at home. For some reason, this gave him some kind of confidence yet no one else seemed to care and thought he was obnoxious.

About 45 minutes after he arrived and after hearing his on-going proclamations, he went back to his deluxe-sized rental room where not long after, we were alerted by a customer in the room next to him that he could hear some drilling noises and wanted to change rooms as he assumed we must have been doing some kind of maintenance in there.

A staff member and I went to check on what was going on, knocked on his door a couple of times and when he finally did open, things at first looked ok but then we could see wood shavings both on the floor and on top of the bed, to then see holes drilled into the side of the wooden stationery bed with big hook bolts protruding out and he had also managed to screw in a couple of long hooks into the ceiling.

With a smile, he tried to act like damaging property was no big deal, downplayed everything at first for us, then we found out he intended on installing some kind of makeshift sling from the ceiling along with bondage constraints to hold some-one down on the bed if he felt like switching things up.

When I mentioned he was damaging property, to him he wasn't and this was no big deal. He also assumed the hooks in the ceiling for a sling would hold a human. I told him if it did, we would have placed our own sling in the room, that he just can't go drilling holes wherever he felt like it.

Then he tried to be coy and relay a few of his fantasies on us like that would change our minds. I just told him, this is not happening. And how would he like it if I went to his home and started drilling holes in his wife's French Provencal furniture (assuming) or in his ceiling? He laughed and tried to even argue it was his right to do that as he paid to come in for a good time. I told him he had to pack up and leave or I'd be turning his balls into a set of drop earrings for his wife.

We know that men, especially if they arrive late at night intend on spending the evening in the bathhouse which is fine, but it's also why if they are coming in with big duffle bags it can raise some suspicions, in this case, the guy had enough tools to stock a Home Depot, never mind all the bondage gear.

Fetish gear is something else men of any sexuality love to show off and a bathhouse is a perfect place for it. One of the big reasons men come to a bathhouse is it gives them the opportunity to live out their fantasy, or at least get halfway there if they arrange to see someone at the baths beforehand or meet someone in the club that is also into that same scene.

As employees, we've seen every article of leather put together and the accessories that go with it, every uniform imaginable, sports gear, drag regalia, underwear, and even adult baby fetish gear.

That last one, the adult baby fetish, no matter how many years a staff member had worked at the baths, it was always a bit alarming to turn the corner while walking down a hallway and accidentally bump into a man wearing a big ass diaper, bonnet, with an adult size soother hanging from a string around his neck. And they would get right into the act with the baby sounds and everything. Live and let live but if we ever got complaints, this would tend to be the cause for it.

The adult baby fetish look seemed to really put men off and they would be vocal to us about it. Want to put a stop to an orgy going on in one of the blackout play spaces? Just walk into the room wearing a diaper with little toy trucks or pink flowers printed on it. Customers used to ask us to ask the individual to keep it in his room and if he only had a locker, they would expect him to just stay in one section of the club or something.

There was one straight customer, in his late 40's, average build, nice enough guy, that we had nicknamed "Barry Bits" as he seemed to have a bit of an outfit for every occasion on every visit would show up a couple of nights near the end of every month.

On one visit, Barry Bits rented a room and about 25 minutes later came back to the lounge/snack bar area after changing into one of the biggest diapers I had ever seen and carrying what looked like a plastic yellow and blue paddle with a wooden handle that was about 3 feet long in total.

It kind of threw us off while doing our duties as this area of the club had slightly brighter lighting and the way he stepped out of the lower lit area of the venue and right into our main section put an immediate stop to everything. I think he sensed it too and turned around to start cruising the club again in his gear while the few of us working just gave each other a look and rolled our eyes.

Everything seemed normal as the evening progressed, then a couple of hours later we could hear this smacking noise and wailing cries from two corridors of rooms away. When a couple of us went to see what was going on, we could see some patrons passing by Barry Bits room with a look as though they were wondering what the hell was going on behind those closed doors and others were just giggling.

It sounded like Barry Bits found someone to take care of his needs and he was getting smacked with the paddle on the ass with the diapers still on, hence the louder noise, then throw in some baby wailing sounds on top of it. Amusing as it was, customers didn't seem to care that much and we went back to our work. Only a few minutes later though we could hear loud arguing and the sound of glass breaking.

When we got back to Barry Bits room, his door was open, and whoever was with him must have just left as the yelling had stopped and there were Barry Bits, with his diaper half on, sweating profusely and upset because apparently the guy he was messing around with wasn't obeying what Barry Bits wanted to fulfill, and also somehow managed to cum all over his new diaper and decided to leave but Barry Bits didn't get a chance to cum yet.

An argument ensued and either the lover or Barry Bits in the process of the fight smashed the corner of the big mirror on the wall which splintered a big chunk of it into pieces.

It was time for Barry Bits to pack up his diaper and leave for this visit.

All in all, straight men were always welcome and I personally loved having them around, many had a calming effect on others, were interesting with a good heart, and became very open in how they felt about life in general as they felt safe in the bathhouse.

CHAPTER EIGHT

A lot of things can happen at any given time in a bathhouse full of half-naked men.

When you are in an establishment with a floor space of thousands of square feet, filled with rental rooms designed specifically for men to have sex in along with various types of open play spaces, porn playing constantly, music suitable for any nightclub, steam rooms heating up the atmosphere with the lights set seductively low, something's got to give.

With that, I'd like to clear up a few misconceptions on subjects that I still get asked about to this day.

Do you have a lost and found?

At every bathhouse I worked at we always had a Lost & Found box, typically kept within the cashier area for easy access if the person shows up at the check-in window in a panic about something they might have left behind. If it was something worth any value like jewelry or a wallet with money and identification in it, it was put in an envelope with a note at the time, date and other details then placed in the drop safe for the management to hold in their office until the person came back.

The thing is because it's a sex club if you have the individual's information from an identification they left behind or even had a phone number for the person. We just couldn't call them up or even email them to let them know they left something behind because we may not know their private lifestyle situation outside of the bathhouse. A wife, boyfriend, life partner, or other family members could start asking a lot of questions, and the same with calling their place of work.

Sometimes with some light detective work, we could figure out a way to reach out to the person, more so if we knew him well, to let him know we safely have his belongings but most of the time the individual would figure out what might have happened and then call or email to ask if we found his wallet, etc.

Everything shows up in a lost and found box such as a large number of sex toys of every shape and size, books and naughty magazines, fetish gear, all kinds of everyday clothing, cameras, phones, every genre of porn-related materials, lots of women's lingerie, an extraordinary number of false teeth, important office documents and the most forgetful of customers seemed to be by those in the priesthood since it had their name engraved on items. For example: FR Benjamin Holden

Naturally, men used to leave behind alcohol they might have concealed coming into the club and the same goes for drugs.

We would get so used to placing items in the lost and found box that we would forget to go through the box once in a while, so one or two times in the year, we'd have a shuffle through, and then sometimes the staff members would be allowed to keep a thing or two if the item had been in the box forever. Many employees went for the dildos or fetish gear and you hoped they washed the items first. Phones, cameras, jewelry, any big-ticket items along with wallets, money, and identification never left the box if it was in the manager's office as you just never know if the person would come back and ask.

For booze, if it was a bottle of beer left open, it used to get poured down the drain, but anything like vodka, no matter how full the bottle was, after about a week we'd have permission to keep it if someone really wanted it. Drugs were disposed of right away, although tempting for some, but especially if it was in a baggie, as who the hell knew what that might contain so it was just dumped. Not that a large amount would be left behind anyway.

What age do you have to be to come inside a bathhouse?

Well, in order to come into a bathhouse, you have to be of legal adult age where the bathhouse is located. We would ask for identification if someone looked like a boyish twink and if it turns out they were too young, they would definitely not be allowed inside, even if they tried to come in with an adult, which would happen. There were quite a few teenagers on their own who would nervously show up at the check-in window who were 14, 16, 18 years old, just wanting their first gay experience but that wasn't going to take place in our bathhouse.

Can you be kicked out of the bathhouse for having too much sex?
How many men are you allowed to have sex with?

In terms of having sex, you can't be kicked out for fucking too many men.

We provided condoms, lube, sex toys, information, sex educators, and whatever else was necessary for a bathhouse but ultimately it is up to the individual as to what he wants to do and how often. They also had to sign a legal waiver coming inside stating they know where they are, what may come of their visit, and what they do is their choice.

I lost track of the times I had passed by a rented room or open play area, where a man or men were spread eagle waiting and wanting anyone to come in and fuck him. No matter what you looked like or were into and sometimes there would be lineups of men 15 to 30 people deep, waiting for their turn to fuck someone.

We used to talk about this amongst ourselves at work but for myself, their choice may not have always been with what I agreed with, no matter if it was arousing or disgusting, but only they can decide what is best for them.

Can I call or email a bathhouse to find out who is in there or what is going on?

A bathhouse is set up as a private men's club establishment. Your privacy is the first thing that should be protected so we never would disclose who was in the place at any time. At least once a week we would get a call from a boyfriend, former partner, husband, even a wife asking if a specific person was in the bathhouse followed by a description and it was always considered an emergency situation as to why they needed to speak to the person.

Once a man checks in to the bathhouse, whatever is happening in the outside world for them stays in that part of the world. Unless a patron asks if they have been contacted, we never disclose to anyone outside of the place who is in our establishment.

As funny as it sounds, we used to get numerous calls (more so over emails) on every shift of the day and night to the bathhouse wondering what the clientele was like at the moment.

The main question we would always get asked is, "How many bottoms or tops are in the place right now?"

We never asked a customer checking into the baths if he is a top or bottom when they are coming into the place. Nor does someone go walking around with a list to write down who might be into what, although that too had been suggested frequently.

After the top or bottom question, men would take the time to then also ask how many bears, otters, muscular men, twinks, leather men, businessmen...you name it, we're currently at the bathhouse and even what those individuals might be doing at that moment.

If they asked how many of what kind of men were in the venue, we would jokingly answer the question with, "All of them." It was such a diverse range of men coming and going, who could keep track?

Another thing that was quite common was for men to call and ask how many people are in the place so they could gauge when to come to the bathhouse.

Depending on who you get on the phone, they might tell you the truth or what you want to hear, both ways won't really make a difference. Also, if a bathhouse is consistently low on customers, it's probably going to close down for good at some point and word will be out to that effect.

Here's the thing, by the time you make your way to a bathhouse after you have called, unless you are outside the door on the street, the whole atmosphere can change like the wind.

A bathhouse could be absolutely packed one hour, then a bunch of men will get off in some sort of circle jerk or full-on group sex session, and all of a sudden 10 to 20, even 30 guys will decide that's enough fun for the night and check-out of the bathhouse while a whole new crowd is slowly checking in.

By the time you do get to the bathhouse with all the fantasies rolling in your head of what you will be walking into, the whole dynamics and population of the place can change drastically, then they will claim the clerk who answered the phone must have been lying to entice people in. Lying about the numbers does happen too which I always frowned upon, even though admittedly I have done it once or twice depending on the situation. Overall it was better to be truthful because no matter what, the customer counts will always change hourly throughout a 24 hour period.

There are also peak periods that do take place more than a

few times within 24 hours so just hang out for an hour or so and larger amounts of people will show up. It all depends too on how many specials there are on during a day, an event, civic holiday, season, etc. Then again, as one of the top cashiers used to say...it just takes one good one to get laid.

On the other side of all that, there are men that don't like a bathhouse to be too busy as it can be overwhelming to their senses and chaotic, then they end up getting nothing or become extremely particular in who they want and then still get nothing.

I've also seen a bathhouse be so full of men but very little action was going on. Why? Because men would keep seeing more men coming inside the establishment so then they would hold out for Mr. Perfect to walk in and make their dreams come true or there was simply too much choice and no one knew where to start.

Another part of that scale was, we used to have waiting lists all the time for rental rooms and it would be amusing when someone would complain that the place was too full and they couldn't get a room quickly enough.

No two days or even two hours are the same in a bathhouse, that's what makes it interesting and exciting.

Are bathhouses safe places?

Bathhouses are one of the safest places you can find. It is a much better idea to set up a meeting with someone you have chatted with on an app like Grinder or Scruff for a sex date at a bathhouse or if you have met someone in a bar or nightclub than going home with them for many reasons.

If a bathhouse is well managed, employees will be trained to properly monitor the venue and even have some First Aid training. They will be taught how to handle an emergency situation and have guidelines in place.

This will also give you neutral territory so that if you are meeting someone at the club for a sex date, you can better choose how far you want to go along with it or decide not to altogether without fear of what the other individual might do in your home or his home.

There have been incidents though where an individual has come into the bathhouse and has had his wallet or watch for example stolen by someone with who he has had sex in his rental room. It's very rare though as we used to encourage everyone coming in to use the safe lockboxes designated to their particular room or locker rental and to also lock valuables up inside their room with the locks and storage provided, never just leave something valuable sitting around.

Whereas at home, bringing a stranger over, as exciting as it might be, could also leave you robbed if not then, then at a later date when you are not home. Or the individual could also potentially assault you if things don't go his way. Plus, you might have to come up with lame excuses just to kick them out if things did go well or not and you just want him out of your place.

A bathhouse will have condoms, lube, toys, information, whatever you think you need for a good time.

Is it only ugly men who can't get sex who go to bathhouses?

Definitely not. You'd be surprised who goes to a bathhouse.

The men you'd least suspect that you see on the street or even in your work environment are probably having more intriguing sex lives than you and your friends.

Many a so-called "ugly" man goes to a bathhouse and has very active sex lives and are also sometimes the ones that have sex with those model Instagram influencer men you see online, they just don't make a big deal about it and carry on.

On another side, those super-hot and handsome, muscular men who can be too intimidating to approach by the average person on the street in day-to-day life, also need some form of affection so they frequent the baths too, to a very large extent and with other men you'd never suspect they'd even be attracted too.

Bathhouses are very diverse environments, where men of every demographic and nationality go in many ways to learn more about themselves, who they are attracted to, what they want to try out, to have a sense of community and belonging, even just to learn how to communicate better with other men verbally or physically.

Do bathhouses film you on their security cameras inside the establishment?

A good bathhouse will have security cameras set in place in key areas of the establishment as it is a business and is for not only your protection but for those that work at the bathhouse.

A low number of security cameras can be set up at entrances and emergency exits, in cashier and snack bar locations, anywhere money may be handled, including inside any offices.

You cruising inside a bathhouse is of no interest to the employees or the owners to film and for what reason? Otherwise, word would get out that security footage is being released for some unknown reason and that would ultimately be of no benefit to the business. That alone could shut down a venue.

Security cameras are used in case someone tries to rob the business, to also make sure staff are safe and are not stealing or doing something they shouldn't, it's also helpful for management (who will also be on camera) to know what is going on during a possible incident (drunk patron falls coming in or leaving and a lawsuit ensues) or even for human resources purposes along with other legit reasons.

Are all bathhouses dirty?

Yes and no. It depends on where and how long the bathhouse has been in operation, how is it being managed, and most of all if an owner understands that putting money into keeping the facilities clean leads to more customers consistently visiting the place.

Word gets out instantly if a bathhouse is dirty. It's almost a fear of management and one of the worst things you can hear about your place of work.

A bathhouse should have a top-of-the-line ventilation system built into place, a program that employees follow when it comes to monitoring and cleaning, especially the wet areas including a jacuzzi and steam room.

An insane amount of money is spent just on cleaning products every month and these aren't the regular cleaning supplies you would find in a grocery store; they should be industrial-strength products used by professionals who know how much and where certain cleaning agents should be used.

Towels, sheets, and pillowcases should always be fresh and thoroughly washed with the old products discarded. Common area walls need to be cleaned from top to bottom frequently, along with the rental rooms, lockers, anything where people's body parts touch frequently.

Floors should be impeccable and free of garbage including used condoms, wrappers, popper bottles, etc.

Maintenance is also a big thing in a bathhouse to take care of and is always ongoing, heavy use means things wear out and need to be replaced or repaired frequently so time needs to be set aside quite regularly to make sure things are working and looking perfect as can be.

Do straight men work at bathhouses?

Yes. Some are single or have a wife or girlfriend that are also fine with where they work, or perhaps don't know, but definitely, a straight man can work in a bathhouse.

It is a job and as an employee, you aren't forced to have sex with anyone. It is a legal business; your paycheck will have deductions made for tax purposes and you might even be able to make more tips if you decide to play upon your looks or attitude.

A bathhouse is very much a private club, with a fitness area, steam room, lockers, just that men are also having sex, so if you can deal with seeing that as part of your work environment, you're good to go.

I've never seen a straight man treated any differently than any other employee, they've always seemed to be welcomed and considered very much team players.

Are theme nights a busy time to go to a bathhouse?

Always, unless an owner or manager thinks they are such a good money maker that they get greedy and have the exact same event too many times during one week.

But if you see the same theme night taking place once a week, published online or through some other form of advertisement for a bathhouse, that means whatever the theme is they have set up has worked well in getting men to come to the venue in the past.

Various theme nights once or twice a week seem to work well, every night being a theme night doesn't bring in the men or the money and can confuse your customer base.

Theme nights are also not held on weekends as those are traditionally busier times anyway.

We used to hold Blackout Night (lights off in the club and everyone given a small handheld, a low light flashlight to feel their way around, and others) events once a week. Men would be lined up out the door waiting to check-in for the minute it started and it would stay consistently packed for at least 6-8 hours in a row.

How often is the steam room cleaned and jacuzzi water changed?

Cleanliness is the name of the game. There is nothing worse than walking into a wet steam room and its smells rank. Or a jacuzzi bubbling up peculiar things and colors while being tepid to touch.

A steam room may be closed down and cleaned out at least once every 6-8 hours. A jacuzzi should have a chart set up near it so staff can see what the PH levels were at last testing and test again to see what the current state is, they should also be drained and cleaned at least once or twice every 24 hours. Or immediately if a steam room doesn't smell right or PH levels are out of whack. It depends on how busy things are, day of the week, event, etc.

This also depends on the sizes of a steam room and jacuzzi, how busy it has been in an overall 8-hour period, etc. If there is an accident in a steam room, dry sauna, or jacuzzi, meaning shit, things then get shut down immediately and cleaned thoroughly.

How should I say no to a guy I'm not interested in without being insulting?

There is an unspoken way of communicating in a bathhouse, for many, it comes intuitively. If a guy stops while you are both passing each other by and he brushes his hand against your hand or slightly touches your body. If you don't respond and keep focusing forward and moving on, that can be an indication to him that you aren't interested.

If you choose to stop and lightly touch or speak back to him, that means there's a chance, also though if you keep moving forward but you both glance back at each other.

That's one example of what may transpire but you will know almost right away what feels right for you. It's all in the techniques of cruising that you will learn and it comes naturally, then is built upon as part of flirting with men.

If you have rented a room, depending on what country you are in, many men leave the door partway or fully open so that those passing by can see what you are about and if there is an attraction.

If you have rented a room and someone looks like he is about to come in that you are not interested in, even just by putting your hand up to suggest you are not interested or letting him know subtly but firming that you are just resting right now or even flat out saying you're not interested works as an answer too. This at least seems to work in North America; I know in other countries it works in different ways.

No does mean no though. If someone keeps approaching you and won't leave you alone either with his actions or what he is saying or both, go to the area of a bathhouse where most of the employees are located and let them know. They'll watch out for you and have a talk with the customer.

Some men are just very persistent and don't get it, it could be a language barrier situation, culture, age, whatever. Men though typically recognize that no is a full answer.

And if a customer gets seriously too aggressive, he may be asked to leave and even barred from the bathhouse.

Your safety is the most important thing.

When traveling to a city that has multiple bathhouses, what's the best way to determine the right one for me?

The best bathhouse is only determined by what you like to

do sexually or otherwise. A large city with a number of bathhouse options may have larger or smaller venues and they each may tend to cater to a more specific type of crowd. Such as those venues that are only set up and cater to those more into raw bareback action, pissing sessions, and fisting, while others cater to a much wider demographic.

Google can be your best friend in this instance, so research until your heart's content but also go for the thrill of the unknown if you are arriving in a new city and not sure what to expect.

Also, ask friends what they have experienced and maybe suggest. If they know you well enough and the ones that have been to bathhouses before, especially in this day and age, they likely won't be shy about stating they have been to these establishments.

Online reviews of bars, nightclubs, and bathhouses are also available. Personally, I take those comments with a grain of salt. Just from past experience and having some technological background experience, I know how they can sometimes be skewed to the betterment of a bathhouse owner and also to try and work against a competitor. There is a multitude of ways those reviews cannot be as truthful as stated. If a place has nothing but glowing reviews, my personal alarm bells would go off.

Another way to find out which bathhouse works for you is to try them out. Start at one and stay for a while, then move on to another bathhouse, this way you then get to experience them both and make your choice.

And at least it's good to know we still have some choices available.

Are escorts allowed in bathhouses?

It depends on what rule the owner has set into place but in

my experience, yes, escorts are allowed in a bathhouse, just not actual escorting.

It can be hard to tell who is an escort or not in a bathhouse unless you know them in general or they are frequent visitors. Sometimes their client will pay for them both to come in and play or their client may already be inside so the escort will text him to let them know he has arrived, to come to the check-in counter, and perhaps pay for him to come inside. Or an escort just might pay his own way in and a customer will give him the funds back once he arrives. Depends on the deal they set up.

Escorts sometimes just want to come to a bathhouse for their own bit of fun, they are still men after all and it is a great break away from everything.

The only times an escort can be an issue is if a client rents them a locker while he has a room and after a client leaves, the client just gives him his room and even worse if he then starts to try and turn tricks. That can confuse a check-out process but is easily sorted and it could be a misunderstanding by both parties that this is not how it's done or remind them if so required.

What an escort isn't allowed to do, although it happens, is approach customers who can already have sex with almost anyone in a bathhouse but an escort promises them the world if they want to pay to have them. They usually target a more vulnerable, gullible-looking individual. It's second nature for employees to be on the watch for that though or most frequently a customer will let you know if this is happening.

An escort cannot also set up shop by renting a room and letting people know they can only have sex with him by paying first. They cannot (and some do) try to sell drugs or anything else in the bathhouse on top of it all.

No propositioning allowed is basically the rule for everyone.

Men that hire escorts and bring them or arrange to meet them at a bathhouse sometimes do so as that is just what makes them feel that bit more secure and by choice instead of meeting men on their own in a bathhouse for fear of possible rejection. It does seem weird to go to a place where men are looking for sex and getting it for free, but this is just a preference of some men.

I've always found escorts to be very respectful of the venue, then again they also don't want to eliminate a safe place to meet with a client.

CHAPTER NINE

The laws of attraction in a bathhouse are not always as predictable as one would imagine as you'll often notice that opposites seem to attract. Whether it be leather or muscle men getting together with twinks or a daddy getting together with someone truly more senior. It's all that makes for a great bathhouse experience.

What men want and desire can be such a wide spectrum; you learn that from what we have been told, even within our community isn't always the case in real life. You can't always assume by looks what men are after and even if they say they prefer one particular type of man outside of the bathhouse, that can all change up once they get inside and especially if they let their true self shine through.

In a bathhouse, the general rule is once you get to your room or locker rental, you strip down and wrap the towel given around your waist or even roam completely nude if you want while you cruise the maze of corridors throughout the establishment and venture into the jacuzzi or gym area.

Some men like to add a few more touches and put on their favorite fetish gear, such as a leather harness to signal to men further what they are into and expect either for themselves or to those that consider approaching them. It also might attract those men that maybe haven't dived into that world so much but who are willing to learn. At times it can be all about the signage you choose to display on yourself in a bathhouse.

Being nude or wearing a towel around your waist levels the

playing field in many regards and it shows that everyone has a different body type. This way you might not be able to assume their financial status is or education levels. You see the human first, then you make your choice as to what your next step will be.

Even as employees we'd see men enter the bathhouse in their business attire or a specific style of streetwear and assume they must only go for a certain kind of man with big muscles or twinks, just by how they have initially presented themselves.

Once in a while that would be the case but often enough after they've had sex with someone who unexpectedly came into their realm, perhaps by starting to play together in one of the dark, blacked out playrooms, they'll be all excited to tell you about the encounter afterward while they are getting a fresh towel from you.

It'll turn out that they met someone they normally wouldn't have gone for only to have been pleasantly surprised because the guy gave him either the best head of his life or rimmed him so much the eyes were rolling to the back of his head or he turned out to be a most passionate lover and they happened to bond well together.

Most often this means they've assumed what a man will be like sexually by how he looks, only to find there is a whole other dimension to this man he just met. It could have also been as simple as the other man came with more experience and instinctively knew how to please someone more beyond an instant gratification encounter.

That's why it's always good to go into a bathhouse (or life in general) with an open mind, you might meet the most amazing person ever that will change your perspectives and open up a whole new world for yourself. That person you edited from your mind at first sight before, might just be the one meant for you all along.

You'll also see opposites attract if a customer has come in for a specific special or event during the day or evening that might only have a limited number of hours in which to play.

As mentioned previously, men that come for this specially priced time frame typically have an idea of what they are after and they have to get as much as they want quickly, so they tend to cruise less and get right to it either in an open playroom space, or cruise harder and just approach whoever they are interested in because even if they get turned down, that gives them ample room to go for someone else instead of chasing the same one or two individuals the whole time.

If it is a shorter time frame that they paid for and if the bathhouse is maybe not that busy, it can become a case of any-one will do in order to get off, in doing so, they might surprise themselves with who they have aimed for and if they enjoyed it, it may turn into a new body shape or ethnicity they start to open themselves up to more.

We also used to notice when it was prime cleaning time early in the morning when a bathhouse is not known to be at its busiest. There might only be a handful of men in the bath-house, they could be total opposites in every way, and even with all the space for them to roam around in, they seemed to always be within very close proximity of one another and they might have an element of sex, just to have sex and companion-ship.

What can be slightly uneasy to watch, is to see men that you can tell have planned a whole week ahead for this one night at the baths. They might arrive with a fresh tan, new haircut, generally upbeat, thinking very positively but with the sole in-tention that they are going to meet the man of their dreams in the establishment.

Quite often they will have called ahead a few times over the week, trying to gauge the best time to arrive, then once in the bathhouse, we would hear every detail of what they have done to prepare and all the expectations because of it. Although we might want to say something (and some would), we overall didn't want to burst their bubble as we wanted them to enjoy their time. Although we would be almost cringing with how hard they were setting themselves up and even worry about the disappointment that was likely going to happen at some point on their visit.

Love can be found and long-term relationships can form from visiting a bathhouse. For everyone I've ever known it to happen to, it seemed it was simply because they just happened to be at the right place with a good mindset and the right time in their lives. They mutually felt a certain unexplained connection and it could be because of the sex or the conversations with each other or both and it just happened to be in a gay establishment.

Having witnessed this on repeat how men can set themselves up with unrealistic expectations, the downfall will most likely end in disappointment.

Men are coming to a bathhouse for a number of reasons but overall it is to have sex as that is why business has been built in the first place. Whether that be casual sex, fetish sex, gangbang sex, or just some kissing and cuddling. Initial intentions will always override natural emotions, and you know how good we are at hiding the latter. Friendships, cuddling, kisses, comforting gestures, it all happens but nothing can force love to happen in a bathhouse.

In the bathhouse industry, my former fellow colleagues and I have been given the best opportunities to meet the most wonderful men ever, and they include the ones looking only for love but we've also seen some of these same men that come in with such high expectations that they leave either crying and/ or mad, both at themselves and even at the venue.

We would witness these high expectations with everything surrounding Pride too. An individual will set the bar so high because Pride is supposed to be all about rainbows and everything in the gay world but then they end up being sad if things don't go as planned for themselves. Which then turns into anger, at times for the simple fact that the bathhouse even exists, which then gets trickled down towards the patrons and employees as though they are to blame for them not meeting the man of their dreams yet they normally haven't asked themselves what they are bringing to the show and are they ready for it?

The baths could be packed to the rafters so some men will then assume someone must be looking for a long-term, loving commitment. There will be men like that in the bathhouse but they won't have it stamped on their forehead so you have to be open to every experience, talk to people then maybe, big maybe, someone looking for the same things in life may come your way.

You can meet such beautiful, intelligent, talented, and outgoing men in a bathhouse, just remember the whole purpose of such an establishment...sex, then have fun and evolve with your surroundings.

Ethnicity is also a part of what makes for a diverse and more intriguing bathhouse experience. Opposites can and do also attract in this way.

We've seen the most beautiful bonds come together when a man of one ethnicity interacts with another and especially if they go on to be not only good friends but longtime lovers. I've always been interested in learning about different cultures, the way people live, how they go about handling everyday issues, their traditions, and outlooks on life.

One of the biggest takeaways I've been grateful for from having worked in the bathhouse industry is all the different ethnic groups I have been able to meet and those people I have become friends with over those years. It has even carried into my current career because I live in a very internationally known destination in Europe so I'm fortunate to have business partners from all parts of the globe and am constantly learning from them in the corporate world.

The bathhouses I have worked in were located in North America and in a city known for being very multicultural. This initial bathhouse that I first worked in had been in the city for over 20 years, so at the onset, the way things flowed with the customer base were just grandfathered into place.

Although new customers came to the club daily, when it came to ethnicities, the men from every nationality always seemed to be welcomed and the way everyone interacted seemed very normal.

It wasn't uncommon to see Caucasian men of perhaps a German background only seeking out the pleasures of Asian men, and vice versa. This went for any ethnic group, of course as what can happen in any situation in a bathhouse, no matter the color, body shape, or age. If someone approached you wanting to play around if you weren't interested, a gentle no means no, and both parties move on.

I have seen actual tears because someone culturally didn't know how to react to a soft rejection as it still hit hard.

The only rare times I would see something stand out, would be if someone just arrived in the country and only knew how things worked socially in their place of origin.

They might have had sex with someone and because that person didn't want to continue a form of friendship or relationship of some sort afterward, tears would happen. It was more of a learning curve in terms of interacting with men in a bathhouse and we'd even try and console them. But yes, men would cry because they couldn't understand the kind of connection they just had with nothing being more reciprocated after an encounter, even though this individual was standing in a sex club.

There are of course, and I have seen this in other bathhouses on both sides of the pond, where certain ethnic groups tend to congregate together only with themselves. Again, it could be a cultural thing, perhaps they feel more confident speaking the same language, have a sense of belonging and the same mannerisms with each other as they are still learning the common language of the country they are in at the time.

I know this from experience very well from living in France still grasping the language and social aspects. Being in the same ethnic group could include who they approach to maybe have sex with, it may be easier and a safe bet because when it comes to speaking to each other then they won't be embarrassed if they don't know each other's language.

Again, I can understand this as with my last partner, the moment we met he was speaking Italian to me as he assumed I was Italian and he's from Italy and happened to be staying in France for the summer. When he could see I didn't really know the language, we switched to French and then finally English.

Frequently though, men of any nationality, if they preferred a particular ethnicity, we would get those silly calls again asking how many Black people are in the bathhouse right now, how many Asians, how many East Indians, and the list would go on. Again, we never kept track and treated it like the question of how many tops or bottoms were in the club at the time. Who knew?

Opposites attracting was not always 100% foolproof either. At times, we'd have a customer approach us during their visit and complain with statements like, "There are too many Asians here tonight? How come there are so many Asians?"

How and why would someone want to explain that one? And frequently the same question would come from any nationality across the board. It was puzzling as the bathhouse was never completely one ethnic group and if it's not your so-called preference, wait ten minutes to see who else checks into the bathhouse.

We'd certainly see men of a different nationality becoming quick friends with an ethnic group or individuals that were hanging at the bathhouse, especially if they had visited their country and could speak their language. That individual could become very admired and the key person they would have or hope to have sex with if they happen to be in the venue at the same time or prearranged something.

Men will also go to the other end of the spectrum completely in terms of ethnicity and they would always appear to be some of the happiest, most content men around.

A number of us employees would also see some interesting and even funny interactions take place daily. Whenever an absolutely gorgeous man would arrive, everyone's interests seemed to peak, especially if it was his first visit. No matter the nationality, if he acted confident and looked like some kind of supermodel. We would see usually the regulars or groups of men or individuals either all of the same ethnic background or a mix of nationalities start whispering about the superstar man and then they would form out a game plan, which even now seems weird.

With the bathhouse having a number of cruising hallways filled with rooms set up in a maze, they would lay out a plan amongst themselves as to who would go down which hallway first, who would be circling around all for the purpose of almost trying to corner the poor guy into who he would pick to possibly have sex with, as though that is how things would transpire as it never turned out that way.

You could see them starting off with their plan, everything normal, people cruising at a regular pace, then the model man would suspect he was being followed, be slightly confused about it, or would even then try to throw the game back on them by taking a different hallway or even hiding out in his room or someone else's he quickly met if possible. All so that they could corner the guy and at least get a couple of good feels in.

Sometimes the game would be played so hard you'd have up to 10 men literally chasing around the one guy just trying to have his own fun. There were even times they'd scare the individual so much so he'd quickly change and leave, that was something we didn't want happening. After the first couple of times, this took place, if we could see it build up another time, one of us would just approach the group or individual and tell them to slow things down, that it's no way to meet a man and instead of likely scaring him off, be more subtle about it all and see what comes of it.

If people were like that with one hot guy that just arrived in the bathhouse, imagine how it all looked when this was happening when there were numerous sexy men walking around. We didn't want everyone chased out of the place so we would have to reel it all in before things got carried away for the sake of some possible groping.

CHAPTER TEN

Months into working part-time at the bathhouse things started to change at the architectural, interior design company I had been working at for most of my twenties. The firm had designed and constructed most of the business and residential high rises in the city and along with several other large projects when an announcement was made by the government for a new convention hotel and trade center in the city.

Since the architectural firm I worked at had a solid reputation and history in the city, they went, in my opinion, a bit overboard in their confidence level of securing the new project and hired easily 40 more employees in anything to do with architecture to help put together their large proposals in the hopes to that when they got the project, they would be ready to go while continuing to work on their other ongoing projects as part of a support system.

After the designs had been completed, with the proposal ready to go, top government officials were invited to come into the offices for a presentation of the company's proposals only for everyone to find out a short time later that the whole idea was to be scrapped by the government mainly because of costs and popular opinion.

This set things into a tailspin, many of the partners at the firm were on the cusp of retirement age, they all owned numerous homes and boats in the city and now with all this extra staff on board and no project to work on, they wanted to hang on to what funds they still had available so pink slips were quickly issued out and I was one of the employees let go.

As it so happens, the manager Kevin at the bathhouse in previous conversations with me had mentioned if I ever wanted to work for him full-time, he would see what he could do in finding a position for me.

The same day I got my pink slip, I got home and called Kevin to let him know what transpired and that if he had a full-time position available, I was ready to go.

Kevin was surprised as he thought I'd maybe want a few days to get over the news from the architectural firm but instead of wallowing in what had just happened, I told him it was all good, I was ready to move forward so about a day or so later I was scheduled to start working full time at the bathhouse and could not be happier for it.

I must confess though, a couple of days into the new full-time position at the baths I did have some mild concerns. Doing housekeeping and cashier shifts were fine, the job was fun but being the ambitious type I am, my thinking was already into the future, and I wondered how long I would or should be doing this kind of work as I wanted to maintain much of my administrative and business skills.

I was also working with a couple of other employees at the bathhouse who although we were good friends and seemed happy enough, were at least 10 to 12 years older than me and I did not want to be in the same position they were in working paycheck to paycheck as I knew it wouldn't make me content with my level of drive. For me, it wasn't even about the money, more so of what I wanted to accomplish in life.

Around this same time, I had started to adjust my thinking. An element to all of this seemed to be more of a worry about perceptions from what those in so-called society might think about me working full time in a bathhouse. There had already been questions and assumptions from acquaintances that since I worked at a gay sex club, there was that I was probably escorting there too. They were soon schooled on that one.

The other side of me thought this was a great job, I'm happy and it beats pushing paper for a big corporation where I am treated more like a number. At least at the bathhouse, I could be whoever I wanted and it was more liberating. At this job, I got to experience another side of life that not many get too and I have never been the kind that is content with doing anything limiting in a predictable, restricted lifestyle anyway so I ultimately decided to just stick with it for a while and see what comes of it all.

I didn't have to wait long.

It could have been only a week or so later, but after seeing a few of the other employees and assistant manager who had been there longer than I go into Kevin's office for meetings, it seemed like something was up.

Sure enough, the next afternoon at work, I was folding some towels fresh from the dryer behind the snack counter when Kevin asked me to come into his office. Not sure what to think and assuming I did something wrong. Kevin asked me how I thought things were going, I mentioned I thought everything was fine. Then in conversation, he proceeded to tell me that the owner Brian who also had other bathhouses on the other side of the country wants to slowly retire and that he wanted Kevin to move back and manage the operations there and a new manager would then need to be found for our location.

Kevin then asked me if I would be interested in being the new manager of the bathhouse. I was kind of thrown back in shock and surprise, yet remember smiling and then immediately asking how the other employees would feel about that as a few of them had been at the venue longer than me and I thought for sure the assistant manager would want to be promoted but Kevin said the decision was his, and he had also talked about it with head office. The assistant manager wanted to focus on his DJ career and because I came from a corporate, business administrative background Kevin thought I was the right candidate.

Looking back, I also think I was considered because I was perceived as a "good boy", perhaps even too naïve to want to get into trouble in this kind of business.

Excited but slightly confused and nervous, I asked Kevin if I could have some time to think about it. Kevin thought that was fine and we went back to work as usual. When my shift came to an end for the day, before I left, I met with Kevin again in his office and told him I would like to be the manager of the bathhouse.

Kevin seemed pleased, as was I and so the next day we got the wheels into motion.

Things started to proceed fast. Although Kevin wasn't going to move across the country for at least a month there were a lot of responsibilities to take on right away and I wanted to do a great job of it and still maintain a good working relationship with the other employees, as that was very important to me.

There were also a lot of tests put into place, whether I knew it or not, and I could tell everything was monitored and judged on some level and by numerous people just to see how I would handle things and how I worked with a new task or situation at hand.

As part of the training, I was to fly across the country and stay at a top-end hotel while I got to work at the head office, tour the owner's other bathhouses plus also work in those establishments to learn more of how their operations ran and through all of this get to know more about the people at head office, the owner and his partner a lot better, for which I was appreciative.

I had previously met the owner Brian and his main partner

Callum (the owner had several boyfriends but this was the one that apparently counted) at various times before when they were visiting the city and the bathhouse and was even fore-warned by not only my fellow employees but also Kevin what their personalities could be like and what to expect and would be expected of me upon meeting them, much of it was true as they were quite the characters.

When I got off the plane after arriving from across the country for training, I was picked up by Callum, who was this tall, striking man in his forties. He had a sense of refined elegance to him but also didn't mince words.

On the way from the airport into the city downtown core, one of the first things Callum told me was when I do start the new management position on my own, not to trust anyone and not to fuck with anything because if things go sideways someone could easily fly to where I lived within hours and take over.

Having no intentions of fucking things up, in fact, I planned on giving it my all, I was a bit confused by the bold statement and my first thought was...charming.

Once settled in my hotel, since it was the late afternoon, Callum told me to rest then they would pick me up later to go out for dinner.

Dinner was in a high-end steakhouse restaurant where the maître d' and waiters all seemed to know Brian for more than just being part of their clientele base yet Callum barely got a nod and certainly, nothing came my way in that regard nor expected.

This dinner was a chance for us to get to know each other better and I was glad it was away from the bathhouse environment as they seemed to be more themselves in the restaurant. I was a touch worried though as they both looked exhausted and even mentioned many times that the work is never-ending.

During the dinner, it seemed as the wine and hard liquor flowed so did the honesty in what they wanted to let me know and expect from me. Callum would throw a few digs my way, looking for a response and I guess testing me while warning me multiple times of the responsibilities I was about to take on, the processes would be extensive and the dramas brought on from both employees and customers will never end.

While Brian, although tired, still seemed more enthusiastic about it all and became very animated regaling us with his stories about the 1970s and what fighting for gay equality was like back then, the struggles they went through, and how he loved owning numerous gay businesses, even with all the bullshit. In many ways he was very modest, yet proud and excited to tell me about his establishments and accomplishments and that he couldn't wait to give me a tour of them the next day.

At the end of the dinner, it felt like I had gained more knowledge about not only them but the businesses. As partners, they both seemed like opposites but it somehow worked. In the future, with other bathhouse owners, I was to discover they all had partners that were opposite of their own characters.

The next day was a busy one. I was first taken to one of the smaller bathhouses that Brian owned in a more historic part of the city. The place looked like at one time it might have been a very large brick family-style house, but now converted and I wouldn't even consider it to be like a true bathhouse, it seemed more like a big sex place space with lounges and a very small number of rental rooms and lockers but it also had rooms designed and more defined for all levels of kink and was known to attract more of the leather, rubber, fetish crowd.

Then it was off to the larger bathhouse, in the main gayborhood. It encompassed a whole floor of what seemed like a city block long of a mixed-use commercial building and although grand in scale, to me it needed work badly as it was outdated in many ways. They also had a license to sell liquor at this bathhouse, which was apparently cheap and appeared to be the main focus for the crowd that was there.

The manager's office was filled more with the liquor stock than anything else, working there for quite some time, there was a lot that needed to be taken care of but it also appeared like the list was so long employees and managers just didn't know where to start so they took care of the customers first while management tried their best to keep up with all the paperwork that looked like it never ended.

After that, I was taken to the head office out of the downtown core in a very large warehouse building. Head office staff consisted mostly of those who could do a mix of administrative procedures plus dealing with supplies and final accounting of invoices, payroll, and revenue, they were a good gathering of people.

I would be here for a few days, learning more about how the paperwork is processed and especially about the auditing of the revenue that was quite extensive every day from all the bathhouses.

Beyond the head office was an expansive warehouse area that took up the rest of the building where every product of sex toy, fetish gear, condoms, and lubes imaginable could be found.

There were so many products that it could be quite overwhelming, yet intriguing, and never without its surprises. In this area, I learned not only about each of the products and how they worked or what they had to offer, but also how to keep them clean and long-lasting with suggestions to pass on to customers such as to soak a silicone dildo in warm water first as it makes it more flexible and comforting before usage.

There was also a lot to know in terms of the coding and

pricing as not only did the warehouse supply whatever each of the bathhouses wanted to carry, but it was also (and still is) one of the biggest wholesale suppliers of such goods in North America.

Over this training time, I got to experience more of how each area of the businesses functioned and was managed, along with numerous more dinners where both Callum and Brian who seemed to keep with the same tones as the first night out but enjoyable with even more to take in during the learning process.

On one of the last dinner nights, Brian wanted my honest feedback on his businesses while Callum intently listened. I didn't hold back; I admired all his efforts over the years but Brian also told me he wanted to know from a fresh perspective what was needed so off the top of my head I just told him of some areas I think need to be improved, updated or adjusted and it also led me to have more questions for him. Some of the items I mentioned Callum would be slightly defensive about, then I thought I should keep my mouth shut but Brian leaned forward the whole time while deep in our discussions.

When I first started working at the baths part-time, the industry appeared to be one that functioned better by not bullshitting and getting to the point. As hard as it might be to hear, it saved time and things moved forward. I think because of Brian's level of wealth and a strong segment of the kind of individuals he was surrounding himself with, it made it harder for him to know what his next moves should be, so I felt comfortable enough to be very blunt about some ideas and concerns I had (even being as new as I was) and in turn, he was pleasantly surprised at the feedback, even excited about it because he could then plan out his next steps to what suited.

We seemed to connect better simply but not bullshitting each other and I wanted to hear the full-out, no bullshit thoughts he had on myself as well. From that evening forward, we didn't hold back from each other, many in our circle would even be shocked by the way we would talk to each other and even if a reason for something required more of an explanation, it was a great way to work and kept us both on our toes.

I was then told that my last assignment would be, since I was new to the city, to visit all the other bathhouses and sex clubs in town and observe as much as possible and to then write up a report of it all to him, in which I did and there was really nothing too revealing and nothing ever came of it. The other establishments seemed fine, as were their customers, some places were bigger or smaller or geared towards a specific clientele and it looked like they all operated along the same systems as Brian's businesses. Nothing better, nothing really worse.

Once back in my hometown and at the bathhouse, work was as busy and intense as ever. Kevin had a lot to do in order to move across the country so daily the operations of the club were being left in my hands to manage and it was a lot.

Since this wasn't what is considered in the world a normal business to run, the tests of skill continued and so was the lack of sleep which was something I had to start to get used to and manage for myself. I could also tell right away that any element of lifestyle for myself was going to slowly disappear but I think that also had more with proving myself and accomplishing as much as possible.

The gay dramas I was warned about started to slowly roll in from a smaller scale from the employees (who were testing me) to also the customers since I was becoming the "go-to" person.

It's funny how when I was one of the other employees, we used to handle many of the customers' common concerns or questions on our own before putting them on Kevin's plate. But now that I was becoming the manager I had to learn to deal with every request and concern that everyone had, much of it would be easily taken care of and I knew employees could take care of it too with much of it is petty, but I also noticed the levels of height the smallest things could be taken to, especially if someone wasn't getting their way.

But Kevin was a brilliant mentor in teaching me how to deal with those kinds of situations and again, it was part of testing my character.

If it was anything coming from an employee, they would sometimes demand results immediately, yet half-jokingly, especially if I gave them an arched eyebrow look like...are you serious? Thankfully though we knew each other well enough to know that both parties didn't need any extra shit. We seemed to take care of any issues quickly and/or compromised. I could also tell that I was being monitored by employees being the newbie with reports fed back to Kevin or even head office on how or what I was doing, assumed or otherwise, it was kind of hurtful at first but then I knew what I signed up for and it all appeared to dissipate over time.

Many of the regular customers at our bathhouse were also very protective of the place because as odd as it sounds, this was like a second home to them so I was really on their radar once they slowly found out I was going to be the new manager.

If they were a regular in terms of being at the bathhouse every day, especially at a certain time, they wanted to know that with me now in charge, their schedule with the bathhouse wasn't going to change drastically and I had no intention of messing with that program. Although they like a variety of men coming into a bathhouse to play, they also like knowing their routine wasn't going to be uprooted as they had figured out a routine that worked for them.

Something else I was warned would happen was since I was in a more public role, was to expect to be asked anything under the sun in terms of questions about myself. Being a more private individual by nature, it felt invasive at first as most didn't hold back with any personal questions, I knew some were curious, some were also protective of the bathhouse but there were also a lot more who were just digging for some kind of gossip.

Kevin was and still is respected by many people so it was some big shoes to try and fill at the time and customers just wanted to know that things were going to stay as they were with no big, drastic changes. Or they would also offer up suggestions, which some of it could be outlandish or not very cost-effective but I was happy that they were comfortable enough that we could form some kind of rapport or friendship along the way. There was a good portion of those that came to the bathhouse from those days forward as managers who was definitely kissing my ass and wanting something.

Just like in high school, working in a bathhouse can be a popularity contest and not only amongst the patrons but also for the employees.

Staff members can do very well making tips on every shift so it helps if first of all, they are genuinely friendly with the clients and other staff. Looks of course don't hurt either but you have to be careful.

I've always been a bit guarded around people that run their lives based on their looks, as for me a great personality and intelligence override a person's appearance every time. When it came to hiring staff, my main goal was that they had some form of customer experience in the hospitality industry and were good communicators with people because everyone deserves to be treated well in a bathhouse.

Looks of course came into play to an extent but overall, for myself and the other employees and customers. I wanted to know they could do the actual work involved as otherwise they turned into a hassle and would have to be let go shortly after being hired as I was soon to discover there were a lot of players out there seeking all kinds of side hustles and most I could see coming and got a flat out no from me. I wanted to protect not only the business but everyone involved in a bathhouse too.

There were times working in the bathhouse industry throughout the years where other managers and owners (and their partners) would even say if they happened to see a potential employee applying, that he might not be the sharpest crayon in the box but he looked gorgeous so then they would practically insist that individual be hired even on his looks alone as it would add more eye candy to the place.

They'd even say if he only lasts a month, who cares? The customers will love him. I could see that rational, so at times I'd cave and sure enough, he would work for a predictably short amount of time until customers and employees got used to him being around, and then the employees would complain about his lack of work efforts on top of hearing direct from various patrons how he was being an entitled asshole. Pretty turns ugly quickly. And really, who needs to deal with the added paperwork and bullshit of an employee you know isn't going to be around that long?

Living in a city that was considered a cultural melting pot at the time meant that most of our staff members were from every nationality, country, and background imaginable. It was awesome to see how everyone interacted with each other and although disagreements came up, for the most part, they all seemed to work well as a team.

Very rarely would you see one employee pissed off that another employee was making better tips than they were. If anything, especially if they just started working at the bathhouse, because we all worked in a very upfront, no bullshit environment, a staff member that did well with tips would usually be gracious enough in giving hints on how to achieve that for themselves.

Customers too had their own fan clubs, if they have been coming to the bathhouse for some time, no matter if they were one of those bold, leather men, a muscle God that loved to be worshipped, or an Asian guy with spectacular skin and a witty personality. Customers and employees could easily garner a league of admirers.

Back when I was training for the management position, I was told by the owner and other managers that I was going to have my ass kissed a lot, that someone always wanted something. How I handled it could make life easier or harder so I should figure out a way of how to deal with it as it was part of running the show and it certainly didn't take long to happen, especially once Kevin moved across the country.

I was grateful for the team already in place as we knew each other well enough that kissing my ass wasn't going to work. If, for example, they wanted a particular shift off from the set schedule for some reason. They had to try and swap that shift with someone else but not put them into overtime either or have it mess with their sleep pattern too much since we were a 24/7 business.

Eventually, knowledge of my training and then becoming the new manager got out not only in the bathhouse but the LGBTQ community in general with a seemingly positive response and invites to have small gatherings with nightclub and bar owners, along with media groups, etc. so they could also put the name to the face and see how we could support each other and size each other up.

CHAPTER ELEVEN

The first bathhouse I ever went to ended up being my competitor less than a year later.

When I started working at the bathhouse as a housekeeping clerk and cashier, gossip about anything in general or what was happening in the city or community was a part of the ambiance by both the staff and customers, some of it would be in conversation joking around with each other, some of it would be full of the routine drama.

Being the type of business we were, it wasn't uncommon for us as a group or for an employee working his shift to hear something that was supposed to be about our main bathhouse competitor in town. This kind of chatter could come from a customer looking for a reaction to seeing what he could add to what we had also heard, or even just to a response of some sort to the competition.

Overall, many of us would just joke right back with the customer without handing over whatever information we might have had, not that we went around gathering information, it just seemed very childish and we weren't sure what the customer had to gain for this kind of thing or ourselves.

No matter what we actually knew or were told, it didn't make sense to add any bullshit to some story (although some did) unless we could confirm it was a fact but even then, because we were in the same business, the core of us just kept our mouths shut and maybe went on about it to each other away from the customers for some light entertainment. Work in a sex club could be crazy enough and for the majority of us, we didn't need any more theatrics.

Customers and occasionally employees would be very serious about the latest gossip they heard, but I would just take it as being what it was, a bunch of talk, as even now I prefer to hear things directly from the source.

At some point, if the talk got heavy, I would try to figure out why the other bathhouse seemed to be despised so much by others and especially if they were apparently talking bullshit about us as time went on. Yes, we were technically competitors but shouldn't we be setting a good example to the community? Especially since we are bathhouses?

To me, the other bathhouse in town was just fine, very clean, looked well maintained but I also didn't have a whole lot to compare it to besides the one I was now managing and the others I had been to that our owner had on the other side of the country.

My only personal feeling about the competition's bathhouse was that it lacked ambiance and because of that, no one seemed to be having fun, but maybe they thought things were great with their business, so all the power to them.

When I got the position as manager, once management training began, so were the subtle warnings about the main competitor in town again from seemingly anyone that had spent any length of time in the business or even from those outside of it all as customers.

The story always seemed to be the same when it came to the competition. The word being that there are two bathhouses that were owned by two men in their mid-fifties. One who was a silent owner (who stayed very silent) and his business partner Gary who was the more outgoing (and loud) one that enjoyed being in the "prestigious" position and spotlight of owning bathhouses. I was repeatedly told he was a bit of an old school queen with highly coiffed hair, an infamous, high-pitched voice who liked to dish out ridiculous demands or comments to his employees on a whim and even customers.

Over a short amount of time, this Gary person had grown neurotic from a severe coke habit, this just added to marking his personality and made him even more devious in every way imaginable and that he would try almost anything to take a competitor down because he stated he wanted to "run the gay scene in the city".

Gary and his silent partner also had a very small bathhouse way the hell out in the suburbs that no one ever went to given the location, but this surprised them as they thought it would be a solid investment, so they needed to bring in the funds, mainly because of all the money they also spent setting up their bathhouse downtown close to our location a few years earlier, and they needed to recoup their investments.

I took this with a grain of salt, but did hear the same story from not only other employees (two of which had previously worked for the competitor) but also from random customers and the various ranks of our management.

Taking note of it all, yet still not that seriously also probably because I hadn't yet experienced anything first hand and as naïve as I was about it, this seemed peculiar to me. Competition I understand but to be vile about it? At the time, from everything I basically raised myself to believe in the LGBTQ community, it seemed more beneficial for a city to have as many gay businesses as possible to help designate it as a destination for gay travelers, plus, we all like to have choices in what we want to see and do entertainment-wise.

For another gay-owned business to try and get rid of their competition, especially from a man in that age group who you would think would understand the struggles of the community and bring something positive into it all was just weird to me. Apparently for him though, money and drugs did all the talking.

The first few weeks managing the bathhouse on my own were certainly busy enough and just got busier. There was always a lot to juggle with making sure everything was done, planned ahead, and that everyone was as happy as possible with everything. There was definitely a lot of pressure all the time and on very little sleep being a 24/7 business but it seemed to be something that I thrived upon.

Subtly things began to change, I knew they would and I was told at the beginning it would happen and how it would likely come about. I tend to keep my private life private, but knowing I was in this new position also meant I had to be the face of the business in a sense which meant being more public, outgoing, and available. This also meant that I was the one people came to for answers, there was really no hiding from anything and there were always going to be people wanting something whether it's to kiss ass or complain from who they envisioned to be the top man on the job.

Just under a month of managing the bathhouse on my own, and what felt like it happened all in one week and proceeded from there, some customers both regular and new would have started asking employees if they could speak to me or would just start chatting with me in the club and asking all kinds of questions in the venue to try and figure out more about me. I loved getting feedback and speaking to any of the customers at any time as I wanted to get to know them better too and build a rapport with them all.

Understandably many were just interested in who was the new guy running the show, as a lot of customers loved the place and were perhaps just interested in how things would continue to run and if I had any changes in mind. Normal stuff.

The other side of it was, some would either compare me, to my face, to Kevin, the other manager who trained me in every step of the way but mostly to the other bathhouse owner in town, who had at least 25 years' worth of life experience ahead of me and obviously more experience in operating a bathhouse as I was still very new. Leading me to wonder what could be gained by these comparisons?

Some of these customers from what I could tell would try to tell me this out of care for my own well-being or even to warn me and that I should watch my back. Once I became manager, it felt like some of these men were coming out of the wood-work to try and build a situation that wasn't there from what I knew.

What was also weird about all of this was none of them worked in a bathhouse, was this idle talk and what was it going to accomplish? Most of them I found though, again over time, we're wanting to get to know more about me, and were doing so in a more protective manner as it was their way of letting me know that the other bathhouse owner Gary and his employees were to be watched out for as they are vicious and known for spreading rumors.

With all this added talk, I used to run it by Kevin (who had experienced this to various levels) or friends, but never took any of it as the gospel truth, only the element of it being, if you hear the same thing three times there must be some truth to it. Oddly and almost weekly I would hear something about this Gary from customers, it was strange and just talk but it did have me in a small part more intrigued about who this person was and anything I'd hear would be about him over his employees.

Upon asking a few people that apparently knew of this Gary if the chatter came up, he was briefly a real estate agent, who then bought a little boutique shop downtown and turned it into a place where gay men could go and buy outrageously priced designer underwear. Then he sold that business and got into the bathhouse industry and how he did that was when a previous bathhouse burned (or closed, depending on rumor) down in the suburbs where he lived at the time. He quickly found a space with his silent partner and that is where they built their initial bathhouse before starting up another gay sauna in the downtown core.

This man had, I'm told, spent so many of his prime years tanning that he was often referred to as "Leatherface" behind his back which I found kind of sad. That more times than most he often had to pay for sex, so to save funds he would invite men from bars to his makeshift home on the roof of the warehouse building that contained his bathhouse and was at one time a small set of offices for the property.

Gary's business was directly below, he would also occasionally invite a select group of customers from the bathhouse (usually those that didn't know his history) to come to play in his private domain. He would at times add to the mix of men he picked up at the bars with customer invites from his bathhouse for private parties and play soirees. If true, that was his deal and it made me think, if that is how he lives, he's not going to find much dirt on me to go on, so I felt safe in what I was doing for work and how I was living.

Over the years and to this day, I actually value much of what I learned about working in bathhouses and especially when it comes to competition. It's why I would rather look at a competitor as a part of the LGBTQ community and we should see how we could work together to show support for one another and be an example for the strength of all our equal rights we were and still are, trying to achieve.

Since I was still new at the management position, to try and stop anything before it maybe began, I recall running the idea past a few key people in management and even the owner Brian about getting to know the competition better, introduce myself and meet with this Gary.

This plan was basically laughed at or dismissed as being a waste of time, except for Kevin, who told me it can't hurt to reach out, as he had tried when he first was managing our club too but nothing came of it. I did then make the effort a few times to see if I could meet with Gary or even a manager who was working for him to no response. The only thing that ever came of it was when one of his employees told me over the phone that I was now barred from their business. When I asked why I was told being the competition, I might try to spy on how they operate their business. Which was laughable and something I was also told would likely happen.

At this same time when I started my new work position, the internet had really started to take the world by storm on a much higher scale and was really becoming a part of everyone's daily life. Although still relatively new, it was great as a source of getting information, advertising your business, and connecting with others. Online you'd see what would be considered now, very basic business websites appearing and we already had an email system set up so it was a far quicker way of communicating.

I recalled on my first visits to the competitor's bathhouse as a customer that they had a computer database system in place for check-ins and outs with membership details of which many questioned back then because of data security concerns, so it was no surprise to see how they really took hold of the world wide web and it looked like they spent a large amount of money on a slick and enticing looking website. Claiming (of course) they were the biggest and best bathhouse in the city and consistently voted #1. Not sure by who they were voted number one by as there were no contests about it anywhere just yet, but they liked to post that as often as possible.

The competition also had to move out of their bathhouse downtown, as a new condominium development was going in so they found a space still in the downtown area, on the top of a two-story building that contained a Subway restaurant and a random dollar store on the main level. They were brand new once again, size-wise still only by a couple of hundred square feet bigger than our bathhouse of which they made the absolute biggest deal about for some reason.

Some said setting up this new bathhouse rapidly meant money got tighter so once open the place didn't have all the bells and whistles at first, which customers complained about (not understanding how expensive these businesses are to construct) so they raised their rental rates and charged slightly more on the membership side which gave men even more of an excuse to complain as there was always a concern about who got to view this database of names and addresses of clients going to a sex club.

At least this was the thinking back then as men didn't think it was a secure method and given how weak of a template I saw just as a first-time customer to their establishment, I would have been concerned too.

They did though over a period of time start to do better being a new gay bathhouse in which to cruise and play and they were in a prime gay location surrounded by bars and nightclubs. When customers used to talk to us about it, a lot of the men were saying they were still hesitant to go there because the only door to get inside and up the flight of steps was far too public and people might see them going inside the baths next to the gay bars and such. This again was the mentality at the time because it was still not the trendiest thing to admit you were going to a bathhouse, even at times among friends. The competition must have gotten the same memo though as shortly afterward they opened a back-alley stairwell into their place which helped bring in the privacy concerned individuals.

A few months after the competitors opened their bathhouse, when the honeymoon period was basically over, because we still had our large core customer base that could easily be relied upon and lower prices with no hassles for a good time, we were doing quite well financially.

We were even starting to break our own monthly records with sales that could reach 100k per month, which was no easy task given the population of the city and done with very little sleep at all, and of course, zero days off for myself which is just how I tend to roll, even now. Everyone on the team worked tremendously hard to get those kinds of sales records, and although the pressure wasn't as heavy to hit those numbers after we got past a certain point every month, it was still rewarding to know it could be done in a business well over 20 years old.

With these kinds of sales, head office and the owner Brian, who after giving you a quick thank you, slowly started to expect that kind of sales to be maintained or continually record-breaking, forgetting about how one season can be busier than another, economy changes, the fact that the new bathhouse in town was still developing and increasing their customer base, etc.

With us bringing in the money and the customers, and with the competition trying to pay bills on their shiny new place that was magically supposed to bring everyone to their bathhouse, especially since it was in the heart of the gay community, you could feel a trickle of animosity taking place through rumblings on the street.

We were so busy with this 24/7 operation that any high school bullshit seemed juvenile and not worth our time. One of the things we did notice was happening more often as a team in our venue was a specific selection of new customers that were coming in. Just not for any kind of fun or the intentions they sexually desired.

These were the ones who would keep their street clothes on their whole visit (which really makes a man stand out in a bathhouse) while holding their folded towel and never going to their rental room or locker. Not because it's their first time in the place and were maybe a bit shy but more so they were checking for and focusing on elements of the place that normal clients wouldn't be intrigued by such as where music speakers were, the shower system, the placement of things, lots of looking at the lighting and such, while not paying attention or cruising the men they were walking by or even getting into the sexual aspects of the place.

More so they were checking on the design and how things worked like they were looking for secrets. They would quickly do a couple of loops of the place and sometimes if we noticed this peculiar behavior, we would nonchalantly ask if they needed help finding something in which they would become startled for being noticed or they would ask an employee rapid, invasive questions before handing over the keys to leave which would make the staff member suspect.

This was also when the internet first started having business reviews or discussion forums set up across the board. One of the big LGBTQ media outlets in the country had a very comprehensive, continuously updated website full of information, events, newsworthy articles, and of course LGBTQ business listings and forums where people could meet, post, and discuss most anything imaginable. It was a great way to support each other and welcome those that maybe had just come out of the closet.

Among the businesses listed such as bars, restaurants, and nightclubs, were all the bathhouses in the country on that particular website with the discussion boards on the forums constantly mentioning which bathhouse would seem to be the busiest place to be.

Looking back on it now, those forums were very basic formats in which people could learn quickly how to manipulate and because so many were new to the internet there seemed to be no bounds in what was said, which was both good and bad.

Having done a lot of the previous computer work setting up systems with the architectural firm I used to work at, I could see this was a very simplistic design, with no real monitoring system or manpower set up behind it. To get started on the forums, you could set up 1 or 20 various display names for yourself if you wanted as there were no email confirmations or any other verifications set into place and no moderators so soon the forums became extremely nasty and a free-for-all.

Once people figured they couldn't really get caught at anything they wanted to post and that nothing would come of anything back to what they personally had to say, that is when the online games began.

This initially came to my attention when a customer I knew had just come into the bathhouse for the evening, and being a regular, he mentioned, "Have you seen the latest about your place online yet?" He told me which website to go to and where on the website to look, so sitting in my office, once I got to the forum, I noticed there was a discussion thread started and some random person had posted how he was at our bathhouse the night before and that it was dirty.

It doesn't sound like much and others had commented either agreeing with him but most of the comments were already calling the person out and positively stating that we were not a dirty bathhouse. My heart just sank reading all of that, I was both mad and hurt because I knew how much work we were doing daily to have the place in its best form at all times. I'd also seen the camp film Mommie Dearest a million times and it was a favorite throwback movie by many of us that worked at the bathhouse and because of that, we were obsessed with everything being clean and orderly, as weird as it sounds.

Yes, the bathhouse was over 20 years old but a huge amount of money was spent monthly on professional cleaning products and ironically, we were slowly repainting the whole bathhouse from top to bottom, so maybe seeing some rooms were closed off for maintenance, is what told whoever started the discussion thread with the comment about us being dirty was actually just maintenance and he didn't understand or ask about the situation? Or the person had an agenda?

I remember speaking to Kevin about it all since he loved to repair and rebuild computers at the time and that's when I got an updated lesson about online forums and how people are utilizing them, what to watch out for, how to keep check of it and even to an extent how with some detective work you can get a better idea who posted what and whereas they were also experiencing the same particular online discussions where he lived and ran the bathhouses.

People's opinions are just that, good and bad, this new outlet gave many a way to vent without necessarily having to show their face. One thing for sure, it could eat up your time if you let it.

To read some of the feedback about our place was actually good, if the person didn't want to send a personal email, they would try to get our attention this way and it would work. Criticisms on how we operated, what could change or be better was always a good thing, even if it was tough to hear at times.

And after a while, this was just one more thing to try and be aware of for the sake of the business. You came to recognize the same individual that kept posting, even if they used a different handle. You could even somehow match them up once in a while if they came to our place shortly afterward or had just left, simply by how they were acting while in the bathhouse.

Once in a while the customer would even tell you who they were online so that you were aware and even then they would tell you what they liked or didn't like, that was all great to hear as you want to evolve a business to make things better for as many customers as possible.

It's when the blatant lies started being posted, especially if the individual would complain about your establishment and in the next line talk about how glorious the competitor's bathhouse was, many times you could read the bullshit between the lines and from the direction, it was coming but the words were out there.

One example of this was, a known contributor to the forums of that online LGBTQ website who didn't shy away from who he was, being in his late forties and who also liked to state regularly that he was a journalist (yet you could never find his articles to read), was also known to be a good friend of Gary, the bathhouse competitor.

This silver-haired guy just so happened to check in to our bathhouse for a locker rental one Sunday afternoon. It was rare that he came to our bathhouse and being good with faces, I recognized him as when he did show up, he liked to put on an act like he was something special and he was boisterous about it in his mannerisms, so that's one of the reasons he was memorable to myself and the employees on shift. This time though he was acting like he was on a mission and not at the venue for a lick of fun.

Generally, in our city when the weather was miserable, which was often, that would mean we would be busier than normal, especially on a lazy Sunday afternoon. That day at around 2 pm, we were packed with men having a good time and we also had waiting lists for rental rooms to go with it. A waiting list for rooms alone is an indication that a bathhouse is busy. All of us were on the run that shift trying to keep ahead of the laundry, the cleaning of the rooms, and the overall presence in the club as best as possible, literally sweating from being on the go so much.

Then this guy struts in with tons of attitude. Walks to the locker area and decides to not even bother changing, hangs on to his towel, makes a couple of rounds along the maze of hallways with a devilish smirk on his face, then drops the towel in the laundry bin by the exit, drops his keys on the counter and with a dirty, knowing look at myself and the cashier on duty, he leaves. You just knew what was going to happen next.

Sure enough, about 40 minutes later, I read on the forum from this so-called journalist how he was just at our bathhouse and that it was really dead inside so he decided to leave. Blatant lie.

We made very good revenues that day but it still pissed me off because it makes it seem like everyone's efforts for the benefits of others are useless. The thing is, the city we lived in, it's beautiful but can be very boring. And men don't want to spend their money or waste their time if they think a bathhouse will be dead quiet inside so reading a line like that on a gay online forum can affect a business, whether it is a bathhouse or not.

I was dying to comment back but from reading other discussions on that forum, it just turns into useless arguments that don't solve anything and trolling. So I bit my tongue.

This though seemed to start a trend for a while. And we started to notice, he or they (whoever they were) would start to hit us online when they thought we were at our peak periods at the bathhouse. In some cases, it would work in decreasing the number of men to our bathhouse but many times a regular client would just read something online and call us up and since they trusted the staff, they would point-blank ask them how the night is and the employees would be truthful in their response. It was all just one more thing to tackle.

That wannabe journalist did come back in a few weeks later, so what I did when I saw him show up was, I pulled the previous check-in sheets from that last afternoon he was inside and on a spy mission. I graciously asked him what he meant about our club being dead in the afternoon he was last here. Showing him the pages of check-ins of men who signed in, he really didn't know what to say, you could tell he was burning mad inside though for being caught as his face turned deep red.

I told him, "Now that's not ethical journalism, is it?" And asked, "Why are you trying to cause division within the gay community?" He stumbled with his words then abruptly left. We were all tired of his antics well before all of this anyway.

He never really posted on that forum again, unless he was what appeared to be in a drunken online rant about everything in life. Turns out he had decided to leave the country for some reason shortly afterward, heard he ended up in Costa Rica trying to make a new life for himself but then had to come back to our homeland a few years later, broke and couch surfing in a completely different city.

The online forum posts and comments would continue, you got used to it as a new element of the business, and people weren't always too kind about the competitor as well. It seemed to be like online games for some people.

Our numbers were consistently good or better than average so overall it was fine, just frustrating and more bullshit. I always found it strange how serious some people would try and make an issue of things, which then made me suspect the competitor was maybe paying these people...or not. The level of concern in how many, who, or what was happening in a bathhouse, a business they do not even own was interesting, to say the least.

With forums being so new to me back then, it was a learning curve on how to handle it all and I had to accept that there are going to be those that are either jealous, upset, or even happy, whatever the emotion maybe but it ultimately comes down to how they want to use their personal time and it also says a lot about who they are as a person.

CHAPTER TWELVE

City Hall, no matter where you live, runs the show.

Going through some old files in the bathhouse one day, I came across a large amount of paperwork and photos dating back to when the venue was just trying to open and the tremendous amount of red tape they had to jump through in to get started.

This particular bathhouse was built in the late1970's, in place of what was once a large bowling alley. Reading through the content and seeing the photos, you could determine just how much they were being monitored and inspected along the way during the construction of this new business. How the space was extremely raw at first with every little bit of progress to try and get it to its full potential being under constant scrutiny by the city hall inspectors. Even getting a water fountain installed in the club required an approval first and permit with the subsequent payment being $72, which for the time would have been a lot of money.

There were practically zero equality rights back then when it came to the LGBTQ community, so to get any kind of city hall approvals along with the amount of time it must have taken to get anything accomplished to build a gay business must have been quite a daunting experience but they persevered.

It looked as though just having the funds available to even build this kind of establishment required a large contingency fund set aside because of the delays they knew they were going to incur due to trying to pass the city inspections. Because really, where is the rule book with a city hall on how such a gay bathhouse could be developed and regulated past the health and safety requirements?

In the notes throughout the process, it appeared one inspector would state one thing and another inspector would override or deny most anything they would try to move forward on, as though, and probably so back then, rules were just made up along the way.

How the business even got its initial permit just to open the doors by the notes seemed to be a miracle given the number of times the construction was held up or denied by the inspectors as they attempted to make any progress.

Back then this particular city hall required two types of permits to obtain their full business license and it was still the case when I left the industry just with more ease of restrictions. One permit they had to have was that of a private members club and the second permit was to be as a fitness center. They would have had to prove both through a consistent and slow inspection process in how they would operate and you could also read how they would physically build something within the property and call it one thing for the city hall officials to pass approvals when it was going to be used for a whole other plan altogether once opened.

An example of this was when they were installing a large jacuzzi, the ground floor space around it had to be quite expansive, normal health and safety signage had to be displayed like in many places today but to help get approval, they had large overhead lighting installed on beams so that it looked almost as bright as being outside with a big sign in the corner calling it the "Sun Room."

Once apparently past that part of the inspection stage and when the business was finally good to go, everything stayed in place but the lights were turned down except for cleaning purposes with the only glow being from the lighting within the jacuzzi to give it all a more sensual effect.

This was also one of the most popular areas of the original bathhouse with the occasional drag show taking place for those in and around the jacuzzi.

Getting the gym equipment would be easy enough and was placed in its own dedicated area in the club not far from the jacuzzi by the main locker section. In later years, when the bathhouse was well underway, they had so many problems with the jacuzzi constantly leaking and being maintained because of its grand size, so whoever owned the place at the time ultimately decided to have it filled in and built a floor over it. Then the gym equipment was then placed on top of the former jacuzzi and they then converted the empty fitness area into more rental rooms.

When we had the business, newer and more gym equipment was introduced before I started working there, there was also a large blackout play space set up next to a long row of glory hole booths as part of the gym. It was rare that people used the fitness area when I was there, men were more interested in the gang bangs that would occur in the blackout room when the action from the glory hole booths would spill out into that backroom area.

On one of the visits from the owner Brian, I remember going through these files with him as I found the history intriguing and since he was the one that took over the place from the original owners, he filled me in on more of the details. He loved telling these stories from the past and you felt you were getting a lesson in LGBTQ history from everything he had to say.

Apparently getting the rental rooms set up in the bathhouse was the biggest issue with city hall. Since this was to be a "private men's club", the owners stated in a number of ways that these rooms needed to be built so that the patrons could "relax" after working out in the fitness room or after sitting in the jacuzzi or steam room.

Inspectors must have known that these rooms weren't going to be used just for relaxing and sleep but somehow they managed to get their semblance of rooms for the opening date.

The rental rooms were framed out in rows next to each other that the owner designed and wanted at the time. Each room had what you would normally see in a bathhouse. A built-in bed frame set to the size (single, double, deluxe, VIP) the owner wanted, with a side table also built into the room and a metal locker for personal belongings next to that, these first set of rooms though had only the framing in place for walls, as the inspectors wouldn't allow for full-height walls to make a real room with privacy.

Initially, the rental rooms had walls that were only about a foot higher than the bed level past the height of the top of the vinyl mattress. Which meant you had a door with a lock to your rental room, but basically no walls for privacy. In the eyes of city hall inspectors, these rooms were for private members to rest in and they thought by having things set up this way, nothing untoward could then take place.

Somehow those pseudo rooms worked when they first opened and they must have made for some interesting en-counters since just cruising the hallways you could see every-thing that either was or wasn't going on in these fake rooms with framing in place.

From what I was told, over time, with a clean business record, the owners were able to implement more upgrades which says a lot about the patience they must have had and persistence to improve their business, along with having very open-minded and understanding customers but I guess when this is all you know at the time, you do the best you can and it's accepted as being better than nothing.

And it was all achieved with practically zero legislation for equal rights in the LGBTQ community so it could all be raided, taken away, and closed down without notice at any time.

The old photos I had come across showed the happy faces of the staff and customers who were willing to be in front of the camera and the bathhouse back then looked as though it was a great place to be.

From my experience in dealing with city hall, getting our permits renewed every year was never an issue because the business had already been in operation for over 20 years so luck was on our side.

The only tough time we had was when city hall decided all businesses in the city were not allowed to have people smoking inside a building and it didn't matter if you were a restaurant, office, boutique, or bathhouse. All of which I was personally fine with but many customers got in an uproar about it as it was the main topic of news on TV and it didn't help that the new bylaw was very vague in its rules at first, yet if you didn't comply immediately, you could lose your business permit.

This was not a fun time for any establishment in the city because of the harsh feedback and even loss of business by customers stating it was their right to smoke. The slight cut in profit had to also then be explained to the owner and head office across the country, which they couldn't understand until their local city officials also adopted the same bylaws there.

On top of that, we gathered that the main competitor was contacting city hall as a "concerned individual" about smoking going on in our bathhouse (which was previously allowed in their bathhouse too) only for inspectors to show up randomly and find any and all ashtrays were removed and more than enough non-smoking signage was up everywhere. We also found out it was the competition that contacted city hall because, on one visit with an inspector, the cashier saw the name of the person that made the complaint on the official's clipboard and I had an official on another visit full out tell me, with a knowing smile, who filed the complaint as he was tired of having to inspect our business as he knew we weren't breaking the new bylaw.

Fortunately, after a couple of weeks and as the city bylaw became more clear, defined, and stricter, clients slowly got used to the new rules and realized it was going to affect every business in town, not just ours in particular. I had a lot of discussions with the owner as we thought about building a smoking room but when city hall again discovered people might have found a loophole, they made the requirements for such a room inside a business very detailed, specific, and expensive, it wasn't going to be worth the time and effort.

The main point we had to get across to customers trying to sneak a cigarette in their rental room (we became very sensitive to the smell of smoke) or in the hallways was that the bathhouse might get closed down for good because of it.

Slowly people complied and we allowed them to go outside for a quick smoke if they wanted to. What was funny too was men would then try and sneak smoking a joint in the bathhouse and when we would catch them doing that, then they would try to argue that it's not a cigarette and we would have to explain that smoke is smoke, that one has to light it up and it produces smoke, so please, no smoking of any kind.

Anything else to do with being in the bathhouse industry after all of this seemed like a piece of cake since the LGBTQ community had been given far more rights in terms of equality. It was very rare if ever, there was an issue with city hall.

Now when it comes to government officials and taxes, that's a whole other deal.

When I was a previous customer of the baths, I assumed, like many, that it must be an easy moneymaker, not taking into consideration the amount of work it takes to run the operation at its best 24 hours a day. Those supplies needed to be purchased, maintenance costs add up and payroll needed to be taken care of first and foremost, among a million other things. I also assumed a lot of these places were possibly used for laundering dirty money.

Week one of being trained for management, I learned early the importance of accounting and that it was at the top of the list of priorities when it came to running a bathhouse and that auditing was going to be a time-consuming and extensive daily task.

The training was ongoing as changes were implemented in the accounting procedures over time and intense on how to manage all the money going in and out. And at the end of every month, no matter how much auditing you did daily, you had to take those numbers and audit them again to make sure everything balanced literally to the last dime. If you lost track, you had to start over.

Being the type of business we were, I was told the government was fine with it all but that also meant that they could be suspect and observed us far more closely than a regular business. And since we were making a lot of money, they wanted what was coming to them and without hesitation. We always had an in-depth auditing process in place and I was told the government was using three times the normal manpower to make sure they got every dollar coming to them and we had deadlines to constantly meet to ensure they got their piece of the pie.

That's one of the reasons why auditing and verifying absolutely everything, was so important all the time.

Being open 24/7 meant three 8-hour cashier shifts in a 24-hour period and at the end of those shifts, you had to audit the money coming in by cash, credit card, or debit and compare them to each check-in of a client along with any extras plus whatever the snack bar and sex toy sales brought in during that shift. Before you are given the amounts, the cashiers at the end of their shifts had to do all their own auditing and inventory to make sure things matched up equally on their end first.

I liked to get this kind of work out of the way first, so the next day, once I arrived I would set up the bank deposits, then if there had been an error done by a cashier over one of the past three shifts, they will hopefully be able to recall and explain what might have happened to clear anything up if their numbers were slightly off but overall, they were very good.

Then once everything is matched and added up, you take it all to the bank and deposit it, once back at the office you update everything on the excel spreadsheets and send it off to the accountants at head office who will also audit it again. Looking back, it seems easy enough, even if it sounds like a lot of different steps, and thankfully things are more straightforward now because of more developed computer programs to help a business, then it was just the system that was set into place and doing things the long way helped you to understand the business better.

There were other things to watch for and audit at the time as well, that's why doing the accounting once at work was a good idea because that gave you the chance to go over all the check-in cards to see if anything looked irregular or if there was even a fake check-in. As no matter how much you liked and trusted a cashier it just needed to be done as otherwise, it will catch up with you later by perhaps another accountant which means more auditing of the accounting work and questions that might need to be asked of a cashier about a particular day and time.

The head accountants were tough but appreciated. I recall being out on a monthly audit by .75 cents one time and was made to go through the whole months' worth of paperwork again until I found it. Kind of like they were teaching me a lesson so you developed a way of taking care of things right the first time so there was less stress and effort after.

It was also good to have the accountants on your side because if you wanted to purchase a big-ticket item for the club to entice and perhaps entertain the customers if the owner Brian wasn't sure about the item but the accountants knew about it, they might be able to convince the owner on your behalf how it could be a wise investment choice.

These daily procedures with accounting were only one part of your day out of what felt like a million usual and more often unexpected tasks. Your workday could easily be extended when you are already doing 12-hour shifts, just in making sure everything is accurate.

CHAPTER THIRTEEN

A bathhouse is a fully functioning establishment that offers everything from fitness rooms, lounge areas, communal shower rooms, jacuzzi's, steam rooms, dry saunas, snack and drink stands, laundry rooms, maintenance and supply rooms, play areas, check-in, check-out locations, staff rooms, DJ booth, offices and of course...the breadwinning private rooms of every size for every taste and requirement of an individual.

Add in a large, diverse demographic of men coming and going with their private agendas in a highly charged sexual environment means most anything and everything is going to happen.

Bathhouses to this day, no matter where I am in the world, if I'm outside on some random street, at times I can tell if the building in front of me without even needing to see any signage is a bathhouse simply by the smell wafting out onto the street through the vents on the street impressing friends I might happen to be with at the time.

As offbeat as it sounds your sense of smell can develop and become very handy if you let yourself be in touch with your senses while working in a bathhouse. It will happen quickly and depending on the situation be beneficial to not only you but your employees and customers.

I always found that those employees that care will usually be very protective of their work environment and they will also pick up the trait of utilizing their senses when one needs to help figure out a situation or a concern behind a locked private rental room door or in areas of the club where men might gather for group sex.

There is always going to be someone that breaks rules, whether that be sneaking in drugs or booze into the place, so some things you let go of and some things you observe as best as possible. When the trouble can start is when a customer gets a little carried away either on his own or with a group of others who have gathered for either some makeshift drinks they snuck in or drugs while maybe being part of a party and play session.

Parties are going to happen but if it becomes disruptive to the ambiance and most of all fellow customers are complaining, that is when things have to be reeled in as one issue can quickly lead to another in a bathhouse full of half-naked men.

Depending on the level of tolerance an owner may have of such activities (as they lead with the rules), that's when you take your cue on what to do next as there have been many instances where an individual gets away with something once, then starts to escalate on every next visit.

Doing drugs and dealing drugs always seem to be the big items to watch out for and we could half the time tell if a dealer is checking in since over time you start to be able to surmise an individual's agenda for the most part. They also were half the time straight men who most of the time kept their street clothes on, and would either have a big bravado attitude or try to be as unsuspecting as possible.

They would be in and out quickly after doing a drug run for a specific customer(s) to their rooms in which then we would make a mental note if we noticed this or were told this about the customer(s) and communicate it to each other in case he starts dealing or God forbid starts overdosing. The dealers with the real goals for big sales in mind would rent a room, mainly only on a weekend, and deal out of there, we'd at some point catch them quickly though, and shut that down if possible. Again, it depended on the owners' rules and thinking that could change on a dime as some of them might even use the same dealer or want to get to know this one. Not all, but some.

Of course, we never sold drugs, although there is an assumption out there that many bathhouses do sell drugs to some extent and I do know of managers and staff in which this was a side deal for themselves, but they would tend to let things slip along the way and end up getting caught and fired.

The biggest thing we used to sell in that regard was poppers, which weren't illegal where we lived and we got those from a retired police officer who knew all the tips and tricks on keeping them fresh and how to make them last the longest.

We would get complaints if something smelled bad in an area of the bathhouse. It was like a pet peeve for not only ourselves but for most patrons and we would always try to keep on top of any weird smells as much as we could manage, that's why it was part of the routine just to do a walk around in the space to make sure everything was in order.

On top of checking the ventilation systems frequently and the auto deodorizer dispensers if they needed to be changed, an odd smell could just be a particular customer's hygiene who just arrived and needed to take a shower, or if someone got sick in the wet area or if someone decided to smoke crack in the club which is one of the worst smells ever offering a potent combination of burning plastic mixed with black licorice and horrendously stinking feet, we'd be out in force to try and rectify that situation.

One weekday afternoon, when the bathhouse was busy with mostly men from the business community who made their routine trek from their offices for our Lucky at Lunch Special, nearing the end of the special, while working, a horrendous smell started to drift in from under the metal door to my office. Within seconds you could tell it was the smell of shit as when I opened the door, everyone in my area was squinting their eyes and looking at each other while covering our mouths and noses wondering, what the fuck is going on?!

Alarmed and disgusted, as we could hear customers both complaining and quickly getting changed to leave due to the awful smell, an employee and I made our way through the maze of hallways and wet room areas to try and figure out exactly where and who it was coming from while increasing the air ventilation system and spraying deodorizer in the air.

Shortly we found the hideous smell was coming from Room 136. When we knocked, we could hear the customer making some strange noises from doing who knows what in his room and refusing to answer the door. Having the master key also didn't work at first as he had barricaded the room from the inside somehow.

After some demands to open the door, stating to make sure he was ok, the patron finally opened the door to a grotesque smell of shit. He was nude and obviously high as fuck and rough looking, wearing a pile of cheap jewelry not only around his neck but also with large droopy earrings and bracelets while giving us a smile like nothing was wrong.

Once we got past the looks of him, we immediately saw that he had been in the process of smearing his wet diarrhea shit, loads of it, by hand, back and forth, and as high up along all four walls of his rental room including the mirrors, locker, and bed.

His eyes were wide and glazed. He was told sternly that he needed to leave now. Of course, he took his sweet time about it while we patiently waited as he very slowly put on his clothes. What was also weird about all of this was that he barely had any shit on his body but this was also fortunate for us as then he didn't have to use the excuse to use our facilities in the wet area to clean himself up, not that we would have let him with those antics.

This individual was totally rank and after we barred him and got him out, no matter how much air deodorizer we sprayed (industrial strength) it wasn't enough while it took a small crew of us literally a couple of hours to power clean the room.

One special present we noticed inside the room when we first started cleaning it was that he left the sign of the cross smeared in shit, upside down on the back of his room door. Even after he was long gone, we had to keep going back to intensify the cleaning of this room for another day (which meant we could and wouldn't be able to rent it out) while it all aired out. It was the talk from the regular customers that week who always felt bad we had to deal with people like this once in a while.

When I think back on some of the various characters that used to come to the bathhouse, I always remember the certain kind of individuals that we used to tenderly refer to as, "The Lonely Hearts Club Men."

These tended to be quieter men from a completely different and much older generation, unassuming gentlemen, very well-mannered, and many of which would tell us they had a wife, grown children, and even grandchildren.

Most of these men looked like an everyday gentle soul that minded their own business, someone you might recognize as being your retired neighbor down the street, or the kind you might spot in a grocery store.

These men that came to the bathhouse would seem to be of three types, the ones that arrived very early in the morning as the main cleaning was taking place or finishing up. Or they would arrive in the middle of the afternoon to try and blend in more with the everyday crowd or those that still had a yearning to party and make up for a lost time by arriving around close to midnight to be a part of the more boisterous scene.

This demographic of men seemed to be a part of every bathhouse I worked in the industry.

They could of course do what they wanted upon checking in, many seemed to be observant or would chat with someone they previously met with most just happy to be in the same setting as everyone else, whether they met someone to have sex with or not, some could be very grabby with the hands but men used to take that in stride.

The ones that tended to arrive first thing in the morning normally got a room and were the men that you could tell were taking a break from their regular lives (and wives). They were most of the time in the closet and would go after other men they thought could be easily charmed with their character or just plain horny. They weren't predatory, just they seemed to know the other men that were still there from earlier in the evening might be up for some action with them as a morning release as that seemed to be an accomplishment enough if someone would let them.

The men that arrived for some afternoon fun seemed to be taking a break from their daily errands and blended in well with everyone. They also appeared to get a lot of action as so many that came to the bathhouse during the day either arrived for the special lower price with its limited four-hour stay and/ or had to be home for dinner with the family or back to work, so time was of the essence.

Then there are those that would arrive during the busiest parts of the weekend, meaning late evening into the overnight. They would quietly check in to rent a room, and at times they would want the room in the most popular spots of the club or far away from all the noise. They were in the bathhouse though to definitely get the party on for themselves if they could.

These men would be more open-minded, weren't shy to wear their favorite fetish gear, would somehow be in the middle of every groping and gangbang situation in a blacked-out playroom, and were always interested to hopefully make some new friends. There were very few boundaries to this kind of older man and it made us wonder where they got all their vitality but I think the place was just energizing for them to be around.

One thing all three of these men of a certain age would have in common is a term we used to each other called the, "Pulling a Princess" effect.

Meaning, things were too hot to handle.

No matter what day or time of night, at some point one of these types of men would be soaking up the heat from either the dry sauna or steam room for a bit too long. Maybe if men were having sex in there, they didn't want to leave and miss out on what they were seeing or feeling but they would be in there for so long that they would pass out.

We would be alerted to this by doing one of our random walk through checks on the bathhouse or, as was usually the case, there would be enough men in either of those hot rooms that would all of a sudden see an older gentleman pass out either next to them or close by so then we would be made immediately aware.

Right away we'd turn the lights up, have the heat or steam shut down, barricade the room and outer area to let in fresh air while we checked on them, we would give them some juice to try and drink while attempting to revive them, very rarely we'd have to call for an ambulance who would take care of them on the spot and then be on their way.

One of the first things that would come to mind though too is, you hoped to hell that they didn't die of a heart attack or heat exhaustion in a sex club which thankfully never happened while I worked the baths.

For some of the men that did this, if we recognized them to be a repeat offender of this kind of antic, that's when we would tell each other that someone was "pulling a princess" as we knew it had begun as part of a game for them to play. As they were immediately granted attention, were fawned over, were even physically removed like a damsel in distress by men that were pretty much naked or ambulance attendants. And you knew they were up to no good when they would also try to grab your crotch while being taken out of the hot room, this also let us know that they were going to be ok.

This wasn't something that happened daily or even weekly but a couple of times we did wonder if this was becoming some weird trend or fetish for some. The ones it was happening to for real, were more rigid and heavy with their body and mannerisms and definitely didn't know where they were at first once their body temperature got sorted out and they were more awake again. The ones faking it would sometimes make you think it was Quentin Crisp trying to pull a fast one.

No one was ever barred for doing this but the repeat offenders would be told repeatedly at every check in to the bathhouse, please don't go in the steam room or dry sauna, we want you to be embarrassed if you pass out and we have to pull you out of there. They'd just smile and say in a usually accented old country tone, "Ok, ok."

CHAPTER FOURTEEN

One thing I never considered until I was working in the bathhouse was what about play spaces like this for women?

Situated next to our bathhouse was a small nightclub that we shared a common entry space with inside the building. This was a business that was kind of past its due date and was at the time struggling to stay open.

It was catering more to live bands that were just starting out and when they managed to get some semblance of a crowd into their place, once the nightclub closed for the night, frequently we would get the drunken patrons staggering over, both gay and straight men and women, along with heterosexual couples coming up to our check-in window to either ask if they could come into the bathhouse (without paying) or even demand they be allowed inside.

Not realizing our club was packed with men who were cruising naked and fucking in every room, corner, and hallway, not that would have deterred a few of those inquiring at the window. Some would even try to force their way in if a customer happened to be leaving or sneak in behind a customer who was checking in.

They'd loudly state how it wasn't fair, why aren't women (or straight couples) allowed inside? With one or two stating that they were going to start a business like it for themselves. We'd tease and joke with whoever came to the window acting like that to lighten the mood with the interaction between us all which seemed to work and calm them down a little. We'd also tend to agree with whoever was saying they were going to start their own bathhouse, all the power to them. Why not try and open up their establishment or set up a one-off play party somewhere?

The owner Brian and I used to discuss all sorts of topics about the business and life in general so on one phone call with him I brought up the subject about women being in the bathhouse, more specifically lesbian and bisexual women as that seemed to be the ones who would ask the most about coming inside.

Bathhouses, where I lived, were designated with the city as a "fitness center" first, hence the gym area in the establishment. After the permit was approved then the place needed to also be designated as a private club, for members of our choosing. In this case, a private club for men.

The rules at City Hall could be very archaic, one example being at the time in the city, a bylaw set up in the early 1900s that there could be no more than seven women living together in a home at one time as it could be considered a brothel so you can see how anything a man wanted was swayed in favor of the male gender. And I'm still not sure if that bullshit bylaw was ever implemented past the day it was laid out.

Brian had taken over this particular bathhouse from someone else many years back so he had his version of why women couldn't come into his bathhouse along with stories from the previous owner. It was hard to substantiate what was legit information from the owner before him so he told me his experiences.

The previous owners attempted to have women-only parties so he thought he would give it a shot too. He had been approached by a small group of lesbians a couple of years into owning the bathhouse who asked if he would have a women-only event for one night to test it all out.

Brian tended to be good-hearted and very open-minded, he could even be considered one of the pioneers of the gay rights movement in the country. In meeting with them he listened to their ideas, they all asked and answered questions and he was convinced to give it a try for one night. Brian also agreed that they could staff the place for themselves and ended up doing some quick training sessions for those involved.

Brian said the women in the group were very proactive in getting all the planning done, eager and positive about the outcome with hopes that it could possibly be a once or twice monthly event. This was also of course long before any social media so everything was by word of mouth and by the flyers they made up. Even then I wished he had a flyer somewhere to see as the group advertised the event as a "Pussy Palace Night."

I recall Brian telling me he was nervous about it as he could see this was going to be bigger than he anticipated the closer the event date came up as he hoped their staff would take to running the event well if it got super busy. It was also more than a little controversial in the community, so he found it hard to find a balance with how he wanted to give the group a chance but also not put off his current customer base, especially since he had only taken over the business not long before.

It was just for one night but regulars to the club were pissed off and there was some concern also that this might turn out to be a very frequent and ongoing event. Knowing this same sentiment from my own experience with the regulars that came to this bathhouse who were very protective of their piece of paradise and many of them would question sometimes the slightest changes. Ultimately it was up to Brian though and it did go ahead.

Brian told me their evening event would be run from 6 pm until 2 am. Customers that normally came to the club were notified well before the event on the bulletin boards about the upcoming date and by word of mouth so they wouldn't show up that night but it sounded like that was already taken care of knowing how the word was definitely out in the community already.

The employees of the bathhouse had the evening off except for those that initially helped the women's group set up for themselves and get better acquainted with the venue.

Brian told me, along with a few other long-time customers in the bathhouse in passing conversations when the subject came up what they all witnessed outside before it all began. There was apparently a line-up of women highly anticipating the event down the street on the sidewalk and into the lobby of the building itself to be checked in to the bathhouse which at the time had a capacity for around 150 people.

What the owner told me next was both intriguing and shocking. Brian was told by the group that organized this that they were happy with how excited everyone was and even though the line to get into the place was more than they expected, they were confident they could manage it well but that once they got started, it all quickly got out of hand. Knowing myself how busy a normal weekend could be or Pride Week, I could imagine what this group was attempting to manage on their first go.

Brian said from what he was told, there were so many women trying to get in that there was no real monitoring of what was then happening once they were inside the bathhouse. The only chance they had to take more notice was when incidents started to happen and by then it was too late. Brian also thinks that once they ran out of lockers and rooms, they didn't handle the waiting lists well or pay attention to the capacity so they were allowing women to continue to pay to come in and wait or cruise around.

In those days smoking was still allowed inside businesses, so of course with cigarettes being lit up, the joints started lighting up too. Then the booze started to flow that the patrons snuck into the place which led to parties in rooms and the corridors with a myriad of other activities and incidents.

When the event was starting out, he was told it was busy right from the start but that they then lost control little by little once the party was really underway, and as it continued to get busier, mayhem started to break out in sections of the establishment.

Brian was told by the group afterward (those still involved at that point) how they didn't account for people bringing in alcohol or pot (or so much of it). The bathhouse was absolutely buzzing and how a small portion of the women was shocked to see an ex-girlfriend at the same event (yet they were there too) but especially if they happened to witness an ex caught in a sexual act somewhere in the bathhouse.

Once the arguments and the yelling started, physical fights started to occur, and when those were happening, damages to the business started to take place. A lot of mirrors were broken, rental room doors (light, hollow-core ones) had holes punched into them or were even kicked in breaking the frame. Metal towel racks were taken off the walls near the main steam room, ungodly items were stuffed down the toilets which led to flooding, holes knocked into walls, you name it. For some reason what Brian kept mentioning most were how many doors were busted, even broken in half for some reason. His business was trashed.

Money was made but I'm told it went back to repairing all the damages afterward and to take care of the maintenance needed which ended up disrupting the regular routine in the bathhouse too. It sounded like the group that set it up was alarmed and exhausted by what took place for their event.

An insurance claim couldn't be made because the owner wasn't technically even supposed to have one of those types of events because of how his business permits and the license was established. From the way Brian talked about it all, it sounded like the group, as upset and disappointed they were, were also hoping for perhaps a second chance in the future (it didn't happen) and overall understood why most of the money had to go back to pay for the damages.

Brian also kept mentioning how he did have to close off sections of the bathhouse after the event as they rushed to get things fixed. Which never makes customers happy as they come in expecting to have use of the whole space.

In my time in the bathhouse employees who had been at the club forever or even customers would relay details of finding out a woman who managed to sneak into the place either coming in male drag or even somehow hiding in a group of male friends, simply for the experience.

I have seen women try and sneak it but it never got past the immediate entrance, there were times where if it wasn't that busy and I knew the woman as a close friend, I would give her the three-minute tour of the place while she wore a baseball cap and hoodie and telling her beforehand, don't make a sound, look but don't stare, expect to see the unexpected. It was very rare visits like that happened and it was just for fun, customers would even get a kick to see a woman getting a tour. They'd almost want to put a show on of some kind to try and make her laugh or gasp in disbelief.

The bathhouse always had door alarms on the emergency exits, so once in a while, we would have a customer(s) checked into the place who would think they could push the emergency doors quickly to the back alley to try and let male or female friends in. We'd always catch them; as we were just so in tune with the bathhouse that even if the alarms went off for a second, we were at our stations taking care of it but people were going to try bullshit and it was harmless.

Why I would ask Brian about this too was because at least once a month, I'd have a group of women or individuals who would come to the front door of the bathhouse or call and email to ask if they could organize a women's play event.

I was always on the fence about that as I think times change and things should evolve but ultimately head office or Brian would always say no with the main reason being, we were not legally set up for it, insurance concerns, and it would disrupt the customers and employees routines too much. I could see that point too, as it would have been such an upheaval of sorts and just add to the undertaking of work we already had on hand daily.

These same requests would come in quite strongly from heterosexual couples or swingers' groups too. It was always directed from men that were trying to live out some kind of fantasy, they would really push their agenda but then almost insist it all be done for free. After telling them no a number of times, with reasoning (even though we didn't have to) they would slowly escalate with every communication to the point of being demanding and ultimately threatening in some cases so then it definitely wasn't going to happen.

I'd tell these guys to try and set one up for themselves, in their home, or even rent a large hotel room and see how it goes from there. They always wanted a ready-made space though and were running the ideas off of their imagination. Bath-houses take a lot of time, energy and money to get established, and as the saying goes, if it was easy everyone would do it.

As the years went on at the bathhouses I worked at, thinking did change to the point where we would let various groups from the community come in for self-esteem workshops, mental health seminars, gender awareness, organization meetings, all in a designated area every so often for anyone to attend. It was great to see this kind of progress come about and it worked out well for everyone.

Also, over time, smaller spaces where I lived would also be set up for initially the gay community to hold naked events or even naked yoga classes and a group could rent the space for their own particular event, no matter if they were gay, straight, bisexual or whatever they wanted for their own private parties.

Knowing the owners of those spaces, they would acknowledge the amount of work it would take to set up and the spaces would be considered "raw" meaning not much in the way of furniture and certainly no rental rooms. Just locker rentals, bathrooms, a cocktail bar, dance floor, glory hole booths, and anything else could be brought in so that everyone could experience a play space to call their own.

In reference to a bathhouse getting destroyed by customers, as peculiar as it sounds, unless you work in a bathhouse you maybe wouldn't realize that there are people out there that either for fun, out of anger, depression, addictions, any number of issues or even paid by a competitor that will perhaps go into venues simply to do damage to an establishment.

It seems to happen in many bathhouses besides the ones I've worked at from speaking with other owners and managers over the years and when you somehow catch the individual in the act, their motives can widely range and even surprise you as to why.

At our bathhouse, it wasn't talked about that often as it was just part of our monitoring of the place but small incidents would start occurring frequently every 3-6 months and within a time frame of a week, which once we discovered what was happening, we tended to always catch the person doing it.

It always also seemed to be the same thing that an individual would focus on, which was just weird. What would occur is a customer would find an employee and tell them he thinks something is wrong with their rental room door. The customer might have just come out of the shower, went back to their room, put the key in the doorknob but either couldn't get the key all the way in the lock or they could but the doorknob won't turn.

That would be a telltale sign right away that someone is currently in the space or recently checked out of the club and has been walking around the bathhouse discreetly slipping small pin nails used for delicate woodworking into the key slot of doorknobs, and if it's happened to one doorknob, you better believe other doors will be affected in the place as well.

And when you have a lot of patrons that have rented rooms, expect to have your time eaten up removing doorknobs, fixing the lock or if you are lucky easily pull out the nail with tweezers, all the while the customer might need to be moved to another room or might be hoping to just get inside and change to leave after his stay. God forbid it occurs during a time when you already have a waiting list for rooms.

It's irritating and bothersome but we always seemed to catch the individual, maybe not on that visit but the next and usually by instinct.

Most employees and management in a bathhouse educate themselves through others on the job to be a jack of all trades. Doorknobs and locks you tend to learn all aspects about and how they function inside and out from the first week on the job.

In one of the storage units inside the bathhouse, we used to have hardware areas with every tool imaginable to take care of whatever maintenance issue might have occurred. In cases like these, when your master key and the customer's key won't work, you can just tell by how far the key has gone in the slot or not that something has been put into the keyhole.

We would always be able to handle the situation effectively and while that was all being taken care of because the employees will have been alerted, we would be discreetly on the lookout for who might be currently causing this type of minor damage while also looking to see who recently checked out. You wanted to solve the situation as soon as possible otherwise the person will keep doing this on subsequent visits to the various doorknobs since they felt they got away with it the first time.

The thing is when you work at a bathhouse, the lights are always dimmed very low, but you get to know the place so well you don't even need a flashlight to see your way around. You also get more intuitive to the surroundings and can just tell when something isn't right.

The first time this doorknob situation occurred with me, someone was fucking with the doorknobs as the locks to a storage room containing a lot of our lubes weren't working and when I checked the doors in the vicinity, this person had stuck pin nails in those doorknobs too. At that moment we were all hands-on deck as the sequence in which it was happening told us that the individual was still inside the space.

Pretending to be working on one of the doorknobs like it wasn't a fuss, discreetly I and the other employees on shift acted very nonchalant about everything and casual as we looked around the place.

When I noticed a long-standing regular at the club who was watching me work from a distance on the doorknob and who was also snickering to himself about it.

He was always a bit of a joker, so I walked by him and pretended to go work in one of the other rental rooms I knew was unoccupied but kept the door slightly open just enough that I could keep an eye on him.

It didn't take long as I noticed his fingers on one of his hands were pinched together in such a way that he appeared to be holding something. As I watched, within a couple of minutes, when he thought the coast was clear, he walked by a room and quickly pushed something into one of the door-knobs. I let him walk ahead a bit more, gave it a minute or two, then left the room I was in, checked the door he went to and sure enough he had put a pin nail into that doorknob.

I let a staff member who was close by know to go alert the cashier at the front of the bathhouse. Since I knew who the person was from his very frequent visits to the venue, I just went up and confronted him. He laughed, thought it was a bit of a joke but I wasn't laughing and told him he had to get dressed and leave.

Knowing who this guy was, I was a bit surprised yet wasn't, as he was always a person who had a history of keeping to himself, being quiet, and more observant.

He actually lived only a couple of blocks from me at a beautiful high-rise, in a two-story penthouse suite. He wasn't exactly a toyboy since he was already in his late 30's and just didn't have those handsome looks and body you'd expect, but he was educated and had an older boyfriend that supported him financially since he never seemed to have a job.

I also knew from his conversations with me the past few weeks that things weren't going so well on the home front and he was probably going to have to move at some point but didn't know where or when.

When this happened, I wasn't even that mad, just disappointed and assumed he was taking out his worries and frustrations on a place that he was also familiar with, trying to cause perhaps drama and distractions for himself.

Whatever it was, it was to be the last time in our club. While it may seem minor, locks of every kind are a big part of a bathhouse, and messing with a lock can end up being very interruptive to everyone and these situations can escalate if the desired effect doesn't last for them. He did quietly leave the club and when he did try to come back less than a week later, he was told at the check-in counter that he was barred.

Turns out, we found out through the grapevine that he had developed a crack habit and was even barred from the other bathhouse in town.

Beyond normal cleaning of the bathhouse, at any bathhouse I have worked at, it was always a good idea to walk around and look into areas for anything that others might not suspect beyond those that might be trying to damage your venue.

If something electrical isn't working, you usually know right away if you are able to follow the wire back to see if it has been spliced anywhere. At times men, just even out of boredom or laziness will also leave various leftover food items in some odd nook and cranny which if left can start to smell very bad and put off customers from even renting a room in that area or at all.

Some people liked to stuff whatever they could down a toilet, I've seen plastic mickey bottles of vodka, butt plugs, and dildos, etc. Or they will fuck with the shower nozzles and handles and drainage holes, carve large holes into walls, bang-up lockers and slice up vinyl mattress covers. Even start small fires or damage lighting. We've even caught men throwing shattered glass on the floor of a dimly lit, wet steam room.

It wasn't always pleasant but unfortunately was part of the job, to the point you become less surprised or shocked when someone has done some level of damage in the establishment.

CHAPTER FIFTEEN

Working in a bathhouse and trying to have a dating life can make for a tricky situation.

Most of the people I worked with that were in the bathhouse industry were single, for some, the bathhouse was like one big playpen, for others, many would say they wished they had a boyfriend but one of the issues getting in the way was finding someone that trusted or was even fine with the fact that they worked in a bathhouse.

And if you did meet someone and they do trust you, what do they then tell friends or family when the question inevitably comes up as to what you do for a living and you wanted to be honest about it?

Many assumptions are made the moment when you say you work in a bathhouse. One of those assumptions a number of us used to encounter a lot, was that all we must do all day is fuck and fold towels. Even men that frequented the bathhouses would assume that's all you do so they would flat out ask you if you wanted to have sex.

Publicly bathhouse owners and management will try to put out the notice that employees are not allowed to have sex at work or even after work. Which were more of a front for the most part and total bullshit.

If for an employee, the bathhouse was a part-time job, those seemed to be the ones that if they had another job or income coming in, they would take the risk of getting caught having sex while on shift and losing their job. Not all, but quite a few.

Yet as I've mentioned in another chapter, it was also assumed by those you worked with that at some point on one of your shifts you would have sex on occasion and it could even be encouraged by owners or other managers, even if day one they tell you no sex on the job, again, the rules could change on a whim, there was always a catch-22.

I've even had owners and managers try and set me up with a fellow employee or introduce me to someone they knew that frequented the bathhouse and would strongly encourage me to have sex with that person. He wouldn't even be the type of guy I'm attracted to in the first place that way and never did the deed. This was just how they would at times, as a buddy communicates with you and others. Typical bathhouse guy talk.

One of the rules I had or was told to follow, was to tell employees, at least at the start of someone working at a bathhouse was, no sex while on the job. But I contradicted that rule too as it's just going to happen at some point.

A high level of the employees and managers I worked with fucked around while they were supposed to be working, it was the nature of the place, and I made sure no one felt obligated to do so.

If everything was under control in the bathhouse at that moment, then you knew a staff member would probably do it quickly on the side while at work at some point and not always on every shift. After their shift is fine if they want to hook up with someone or they would give a knowing look to a fellow co-worker and say they are "going for a break", and I used to use that last excuse myself too.

It also seemed most of the time what was allowed by your boss could depend on their mood or time of day. Ultimately playing around was supposed to be only allowed on your days or time off and I've never fired anyone for having sex on the job and had only heard rumblings of those who employees who had been fired because of sex on the job at other bathhouses.

Especially if the employee got so cocky about it that he would basically take over a rental room and have sex most of his shift. The unspoken rule was, as long as it wasn't disruptive to your job, or duties left behind didn't add work for your co-workers, one could turn a blind eye to it all.

My worry used to be if an employee stayed a number of excessive hours after their shift to play around. At first, as a benefit of sorts, I would allow them to stay after work and play without them even having to ask, but if it was then starting to become a habit on every shift, I'd have to discreetly tell them they need to cool down a little as spending more time in the club after you have already worked 8 hours does catch up with them, and their drive to get the tasks done during their shifts starts to decline simply because they are in the bathhouse too much.

It can appear like fun and games from the onset but when you are already working a 40-hour week and then spend another 20-30 hours in this environment, it's just not a healthy habit to sustain. You want employees to have a life outside of the baths.

With dating though, I did know of employees and those in management that were in long term relationships, but the ones I knew who were with someone, depending on how long they had been together, it then became an open relationship (which is more common now) and they had sex with everyone or they had zero interest in sex being surrounded by it at work all the time.

There were many employees that I knew who had crushes on certain men that came to the baths, including myself. You could sense that these men were looking for something a little bit more in and out of visiting a bathhouse. In most cases though, once you got to know the customer better, if the feelings were reciprocated, you both may test the waters in and outside of the place but it would tend to fizzle out quickly and again because of where you worked or just your work hours didn't match up but at least you had hope.

Where I lived at the time, the city was known for, even today from what I hear from friends, to be a place where men just don't even know how to date. There was and apparently still is a lot of apprehension for being possibly rejected just by what could be considered the slightest wrong move, comment, or article of clothing worn. Which could happen anywhere but seemed taken to a whole other level in this town.

It is also a very transient city so it could be hard to hold on to anything good if the individual has no plans to stick around long. And over time, longer-term residents could become more jaded and insular from having their heartbroken too often. Yet they could also be big dreamers in terms of what dating and a relationship are supposed to be by what they have seen on TV in other places or in their minds, so then it gets to the point that people stop dating or if they do go on a date and it does go well, the men won't fully commit just in case Mr. Perfect walks around the corner. It's a tough town where it feels like people make things harder for themselves than necessary.

My friends that still live there will tell me they don't even date now, just meet someone off an app and have some form of sex, they have kind of given up on having a real relationship and it sounds like they wouldn't even know what to do at this point if it was to happen.

There are those small percentages of men though I have worked with that if the trust is there to a high enough level, a relationship can take place with someone they have met either in or out of the bathhouse environment. I do also know of a lot of relationships that started between co-workers who innately understood their surrounding circumstances and for whom it's worked out. The men that I worked with that had strong emotional feelings for their boyfriend, never strayed on them.

For myself, the hours were so long with really no days off and you were also always on call, this I didn't seem to mind as I loved the job but thinking back, I really should have taken more time for myself.

The only times I was in a relationship was when I was in between working at a bathhouse or in the process of setting one up, both partners then knew of what I did for a living and were totally cool with it. I'm also not the kind to be longing for a relationship or even a date as I enjoy my alone time so if it happens, it happens, but otherwise I have found the men who are meant to be in my life appear when I least expect it and stand out from the others.

With being at work so much, with how things rolled, I started to, not technically date but got to know certain men over time better.

Men overall appear to have their guards down more in a bathhouse and the city I was living in was known for being a place that was very hard for making friends, never mind getting to the point of dating someone.

With guards being down in this atmosphere, usually, because everyone isn't judged by the clothes they are wearing as everyone has a towel wrapped around their waist or are nude, you could observe men having wonderful, in-depth discussions with each other, in the gym area, lounges or even in their private rental rooms.

It seemed to be a way for men to get to know each other besides sex or around their sexual relationship.

I definitely wouldn't make a regular point of doing this as my mind would always be about the work in the bathhouse but if interest would spark between myself and a customer. It would start overtime and a number of visits; we'd catch each other's eye then start chatting about life in general in one of the corridors or lounge areas and things would move from there and we'd eventually end up in his rental room.

I knew of colleagues who all they would do is work only to look busy enough but aim for the next fuck in the place. That just wasn't how I worked or was as a person, as much dismay it was to some other managers. I just noticed the ones that played around like that didn't last long in the field as they became known for it and not their work results and/or just ended up with the worst reputation and were never then taken seriously and honestly, ended up looking haggard and finished.

To me, it was enough to work in the industry, without also having the reputation of fucking everything that moves. Although I did sleep around, just not to the large extent as some of the others I worked with in the industry, and I kept it quiet. I felt it wasn't good public relations to be known as the manager that fucks everyone that walks into the place, especially given the size of the city I worked in where everyone was one degree of separation. I would also hear the vile gossip about others that played around excessively and I wanted to be known as a dedicated and hard worker.

How it turned out then at the time was the men I "dated", because of my long hours, I most often met in the bathhouse first, and if we hit it off sexually, then they would be the one every time they came or we set up a time for, so then as the others would say, I too would be on a break.

If we really hit it off then we'd meet outside of my work environment and take things from there, anything that brought a stop to it though would generally and sadly be my fault as I was always worried about work and on-call when I wasn't there and found it hard to break away to get a life. Even if the owners and other management encouraged me to do that as well.

To this day I have a fond regard for these men I dated as they were genuine and different from the rest, at least I'm glad we could be a part of each other's lives.

Many of the employees would also have admirers, men that came to the bathhouse a few times a month but many who would be regulars. Some were seriously crushing hard for a particular employee(s). If the feelings were mutual, the employee would mention later how they went to a movie or out to dinner with a specific customer we might know from the bathhouse. Either they would be excited about how things might transpire or they would feel a bit dismayed if the sparks just weren't there but they were always professional and cordial to the customer afterward.

The 20-something staff members tended to be the ones that would quickly and easily have love in their eyes for a customer they might see in the bathhouse. If they ended up going out with them, because they were used to the no holds barred attitude in the club, once in a while their game I was told, would come off too strong for the other person, and then the fact that they worked in a bathhouse wouldn't help for an actual relationship to work.

The employees who were in their 30's, 40's and 50's totally knew the score, if something happened, great, but the overall experience helped them manage their feelings to be more succinct with their lifestyle. You knew they had so much love to give and you'd wish them all the best in the world, the assumptions would just be so hard from those on the outside though and these employees were grown men that didn't feel they should have to lie about what they do for a living, especially if they were brilliant at their jobs and proud of their work, so it was sad if they got rejected at some point simply because of their job.

Things did improve though with time for the whole dating game, as the internet took over the world, social media, influencers, and most of all those in the gay community showcasing how proud they are of being themselves. Near the middle of my time in the bathhouse industry, it seemed easier to be in a relationship and even a lot more acceptable in society, also intriguing to many for having such a unique job.

I was very fortunate in many ways with this first bathhouse I worked at as Kevin, the previous manager, had done an excellent job at having everything set up and turnkey ready to go. It was just a matter of continuing the flow of how the work was done and once I was more established, I was able to and encouraged to make my own mark on the place, expand upon areas of improvement for both the employees and customers and introduce new systems in how things operated, to even the maintenance and decor of the place over time along with testing new events and specials out.

The one major thing that made it easier to step onboard was the employees that Kevin had hired before I started. Many of which were already considered long term staff who knew the methods of how to handle everything in this kind of business environment, yet were totally of their own character which added that extra dash of personality in the venue and performed their duties very well.

There were of course, like in any business, newer employees that could be trouble week one. You probably know the kind from your own work history. They might have lied on their resume, put on a happy face, looking all eager and ready to go but the moment they get in and feel they have a grasp on the operation, that's when they try to sway things to how they expect everything to be.

Sometimes their true self would show within a few shifts, and sometimes it came out in full force the day their probation period was over or more subtly over time.

It's going to happen, so you just dealt with it, you'd either see them not doing their duties as they should, catch them in lies or a big sign would be when a few of the other employees and customers would have the same complaints about the individual.

It was taxing enough managing a business that's open 24 hours, every day of the week so you wanted to give people a few chances, but when it gets to the point of having to give verbal and written reprimands, it's time for them to go.

Being new to this kind of management, I wanted to be nice and fair as much as possible, but if they would take that as a joke or not serious at all, that's when I learned to be a hard ass fairly quickly.

The job wasn't rocket science, as a group, we were always keen to help each other out and if there was a task an employee was still grasping to learn, other staff and myself would be patient and do our best to help whoever out.

We would have the odd employee that was just not into the job anymore and was looking for something else, which is normal, at least they were honest about it and you have to do what makes you happy.

You could see though if they weren't ambitious enough to apply for other work or tired from trying to find another job that they liked, that their enthusiasm at the bathhouse would start to wane, they would start showing up late, calling in sick last minute or want to leave early, swapping shifts with others more frequently or would do a half-assed job at cleaning a room or whatever other duty was necessary.

Some would even try to mask what was happening in their lives by drinking or doing drugs either after work or before. If it was before, his co-workers and I would be able to detect that right away so then he'd have to go home, which meant calling someone at the last minute.

We had one employee who still stands out who came in as a full-time worker. At first, he was all smiles, an impressive resume in large, fast-paced businesses, in his late 20's, and who seemed responsible.

Slowly he started to bullshit around, we would hear from regular customers either what he was doing that was detrimental to the business in one form or another, but when asked about it, everything would be fine. But as his probationary period was coming to an end, you could see his true self coming to light. Honestly, I should've fired him well before then.

The thing is from the beginning with employees when you go to hire someone, where we lived, it was illegal for a previous company, no matter the circumstances, to give a bad reference, so even if you called a previous employer, the most they can say is, "No comment."

All the telltale signs were there, he disclosed how he emancipated from his parents in his teens, we discovered through payroll that he went by numerous names that weren't legally changed, he started to be full out rude to his co-workers and customers either on a whim or if he didn't get his way and he always wanted to have meetings with me about any complaint imaginable that really wasn't anything serious, he was just making things out to be bigger and always full of drama.

He attempted a mutiny of sorts with a couple of his co-workers, which didn't work and they let me know this (the complaints from staff were piling up about him). He was given verbal and written warnings which he either laughed at or got extremely upset. Legally those warnings had to be given any-time during his work periods in case he was fired so that we wouldn't have to pay out some insane severance package.

He had obviously played this kind of stunt before at another job and this is what it turns out he was after, as when I did fire him (to the relief of basically everyone), he was given his legal two weeks' pay notice, plus all his holiday pay, etc.

Sure enough, we ended up getting a notice from the govern-ment employment standards board claiming he was unjustly let go. The dude was trying to fuck with us as he felt he was fucked with and lost his job.

At least he didn't have a long work record with us, but still details of all the incidents with him had to be put together in his file to present at the employment standards branch.

The day we were all to meet with the mediator, I arrived on my own with his files. You could see him turn bright red with anger as soon as I entered the room. We all sat down in this boardroom, and before the mediator could even talk, he started to blow up spewing all kinds of nonsense. I was stunned by his actions, but stayed calm and listened to how things would proceed by the guidance of the mediator.

He was given a chance to speak first, in which he was all over the map and showing every emotion possible. I stayed calm when it was my turn to speak and just laid out the facts.

What he didn't know was I had found out through some re-search that he had a history of being very disruptive with past jobs. As his previous job was in a small business that was part of a corporation which meant all employees were unionized. Normally that's great, but he made such a shit show of himself that he also tried to take them to the labor board after he was fired and it basically didn't turn out so well for him, even with the union backing him up.

His goal and history stated that he works for a business for a while, does everything to get himself fired, then goes to the employment standards board seeking a big payout so he can avoid having to work, especially if summer is approaching.

He was reprimanded for this by the mediator, which he scoffed at, to keep him from getting even more upset than he was at this meeting and to prevent any possible violence from him, He was awarded from us another two weeks work severance, which was good with me as long as he was gone.

When it came to paying him, he stopped by the bathhouse to pick up his paycheck and when I handed it to him, he swiped it from my hands and exclaimed he should have sued us at a proper court of law. I didn't respond at all, buzzed him out the security door of the club and the cashier who was working at the time, after he left, we both just looked at each other, rolled our eyes, and shrugged.

I was to encounter a few more challenging men like this further into my bathhouse career, but they became easier to deal with and the antics were even expected as time went on.

CHAPTER SIXTEEN

One thing you learn day one of working in a bathhouse is the rank you are in. It's not something spoken about, no issues surrounding it, it is just something that is part of the nature of any business. And like any business, it's important to pay attention to what those at the top are saying and doing. What can be difficult is trying to keep up with what is expected and the ever-changing rules with those at the top as time goes on.

A strong core of what keeps a bathhouse running smoothly is the employees on the floor, those being the housekeeping clerks and cashiers as they are the ones experiencing everything as it happens and they are usually the first and last person a customer sees at a bathhouse.

If things aren't functioning well with that main crew, it will all then slowly make its way up to those at the top level.

Then there are those in the assistant manager position, they can be a manager's right-hand man or their worst enemy. If you work as a tight team, almost anything can be conquered easily and quickly while continuing to build up the business.

Or, they can put on a false front like they are by your side but in reality, are ready to stab you in the back the moment the chance arrives to try and assume your position while they do next to nothing past their job description and even that has to be asked repeatedly of them.

That last kind of assistant I've seen plenty of at other bathhouses but feel fortunate that any assistant manager I had, came with a strong understanding of what needed to be done, the reasons why and yet were also able to achieve a wonderful work/life balance and most certainly had their personality.

Not all managers are the same either, myself included. Again, like any other business, there are also good and bad managers at a bathhouse. Some are overbearing who want to be the center of attention, they may even bring in a lot of attention to a bathhouse but when it comes to doing the work, they are lost little puppies, just with a coke habit that keeps getting worse to overcompensate for what he isn't able to achieve, and that includes a hard-on.

There are those managers though, truly dedicated to the work at hand who think long term and are not worried about putting in the hours needed to keep everything running smoothly and effectively for everyone while dealing with whatever bullshit may happening not only with customers but employees, other management and owners.

They may even be deemed the invisible ones due to the ease with which they can handle things without the fanfare but should be front and center and seen as a mentor to others.

If your bathhouse has a head office, count yourself lucky as they will help with the strain of juggling everything surrounding the establishment. Although it can feel like they are being difficult in certain situations, it can be because you are both in different business environments so it's a matter of understanding each other's logistics but they are the ones that also help maintain a business flow by making sure suppliers, maintenance work and other bills are taken care of and most importantly that you and everyone else is getting paid on time along with a myriad of other duties.

Now when it comes to the owners and who is connected with them, this I have always found to be the intriguing bunch.

Owners of bathhouses come in every age and background and are full of character, also both good and bad by nature, just pick the day.

Brian, the first owner I worked for, seemed to take me under his wing upon us first properly meeting. There was something very sweet and also very messy about him. He had seen and been through it all with playing in part a pioneer in the gay rights movement in the country to then having to deal with the AIDS crisis while also having his own health issues with HIV and running numerous businesses.

We seemed to connect because I never kissed his ass. Certainly, I got him whatever he wanted on a whim but because of all the businesses he owned and with that came a flow of money, he had a lot of people who all of a sudden wanted to be his best friend.

It seemed because I looked past that and was more interested to know who he was, we became quick buddies. I think he saw a bit of me in himself at a younger age, understood my ambitions for the business and my motivations. If I was worried about something, questioned something, or disagreed with something when no one else seemed to understand, I could be upfront with him as he listened and we dealt with the cards we were given without hesitation.

He was no angel but I liked that as he had an edge, although the one side of his hardcore party lifestyle would worry me and others at times. And like other owners I would meet down the road in the industry, Brian liked the acclaim in the community for having these unique companies, the so-called prestige that came with them, and of course the money.

The owners I would work with or meet over the years, whether in North America or Europe, came into the bathhouse industry in a number of ways. Many inherited the business from a former lover, some worked in the business, some took over the business when it wasn't doing well and an owner wanted out so they either raised the funds on their own or by business partnerships or a bank loan. And some owners have had a bathhouse venture financed by a husband/boyfriend/ partner but very few I have met already had the funds together to either start or buy a bathhouse already in service.

These owners might have come from a corporate background, bored with the 9 to 5 rat race, and just wanted to invest their time and money into a new business venture. Those are the ones that take it all seriously, watch the numbers and act accordingly, as it takes a lot of money and patience to get a bathhouse up and continued running.

You might also have an owner who may look like a brute but is actually weak when it comes to his efforts. You'll notice this immediately when it comes to their general business knowledge simply based on the fact that they have inherited the business from a former boyfriend down the line or somehow by luck got the cash together to buy a bathhouse.

Either way, fucking your way through a bathhouse doesn't come with the complete knowledge of running it, although some men at the bathhouses used to claim it does but really, that way, you just learn how to work your asshole to the best of your ability.

In my experience, when people start smelling the scent of money, it means a league of followers will start clinging to that person in anticipation of getting a piece of it for themselves.

If the owner doesn't have his shit together, he will slowly become convinced by his new friends (or even newer life partner) that this posse will be his confidants who will be there by his side to guard him of any bad people that might be after his money and/or business. And they will claim to help keep the money coming in with their intuitive business sense while trying to siphon as much off as they can discreetly, even if that only means getting a new Louis Vuitton bag and then leaving the owner behind. As it doesn't take much for some people.

Over time, once the honeymoon period has passed, and with any luck, these followers will fade away (yet a small segment will still come and go) and a proper team with some sort of university degree and accounting background will come together to help keep the company on its feet and moving forward.

The ones I knew and worked with over the years put in the hours with very few complaints. A few I knew seemed to struggle with having a personal life, more so meaning their sex life would be admittedly non-existent so they dedicated themselves to the work as at least they could be in a sexual environment and feel part of the team, they wouldn't even hook up in the bathhouse from what I knew and yet seemed happy enough which is still admirable.

Most of the time these can be very good people to work with as they are hopefully open to new ideas, will listen, and help decide what can be done to improve a situation or even a marketing idea while backing you up to an owner.

They will also have a legitimate office to work from and are available 24/7 like a bathhouse manager. You want them on your side but take note as they are also all about the money a good 90% of the time. Their main goal though for the money is to keep the business in operation with the main, and of course most important issue, the pressure to keep the owner happy so his parties, new houses, and vacations can keep happening for himself, his boyfriend, and whoever he lets tag along or even demands it of him at the moment.

Not 100% always the case but you will shortly find out while being a manager, that money is the main goal of what much of the business is about. Not always anything to do with LGBTQ equality or basic living wage and health concerns for the employees, even if the public promotions suggest otherwise. If your club is doing well, you must do better and it must be maintained daily. If it's at capacity, figure out how customers can spend more once inside or who can also be squeezed into the place.

A big sign there is trouble with the business is when an owner or manager decides to get rid of the list of men who have been previously barred from the bathhouse for various incidents in the past that could put the safety of others at risk, including drug dealing, fights, and threats, and are then allowed back in to thrive. That's your signal to get the hell out but make sure you are paid first.

We could be doing crazy, fantastic numbers, especially during Pride Week but then some manager somewhere will try to compare those numbers if not towards the numbers of the year before, then five years previous, and question why it isn't at that amount.

Or if the bathhouse did well, you could then have your bathhouse compared to one on the other side of the country with a much stronger and larger gay community cause somehow that should match or be better. It could all depend on who was on an ego trip that day along with not taking into consideration even simple things like weather, time of year, economy, or social trends.

It must only be record-breaking numbers, all the time. And even when you win, you never win as that was part of the game too, to keep you on your toes, but exhausting you in every way possible, as ultimately, you are replaceable so you better keep the men and money coming in.

There were even times where if you are doing a daily bank deposit, that they will watch the clock on it and could expect the funds to be deposited literally the minute the bank opens and God forbid you take more than 20 minutes to do it because of the lines in the bank because possibly the first thought that comes to in their minds is you are skipping town or something with the cash.

It probably did happen in the earlier bathhouse days if this could be some of their thinking. I've had that experience as I was asked point-blank on the phone while standing in the actual bank to deposit the funds what was taking so long and know of other managers that this has happened too so it's best to try and gain as much trust between everyone as possible.

They are exuding this kind of talk and pressure, not over an invoice that needs to be paid, but likely because an owner wants to purchase a big-ticket item or in some instances, an owner's boyfriend is in a panic to buy something. Things that would make you laugh about when it happens to you, you then realize money makes people act in some wacky ways.

The quirks of these owners always kept you on your feet as their whims seemed to be as unlimited as their imaginations. There will be owners who will walk into their bathhouse and either not see what you have been asking the funds for repeatedly to be fixed or updated. Or owners who see those things in the place and other insignificant things that need to be changed or taken care of and immediately while the idea of it is still stuck in their head. Everything comes full stop when they state something and until it is done.

It was always more beneficial to get anything new or updated in the bathhouse while the owner is visiting his venue because it can then be thoroughly discussed. Good owners will ask and even question what you want to try out or develop for the customers to enjoy and make it more appealing. But as always, it comes down to the dollar amount too, as they may have to run it by the accountants but the ones I knew, if they believed in it enough or loved the idea, it was going to happen no matter what.

You always have to keep in mind, it still depends on the cost as they don't want anything to disrupt the personal lifestyle that they have developed for themselves in the least and if anything, they want the way they are living to be expanded upon. Meaning, they want to keep the party and play parties going, buy a holiday home, hire escorts, spur-of-the-moment vacations, luxury shopping sprees, you name it and after all, it is their choice. Not always the case, but much of the time.

The owners of bathhouses I knew and know of on both sides of the pond will typically have a partner who is considered long-term. They will live together and the partner will be someone who they think without question is trusted and has their best interests at heart. Whether or not the partner has the same feelings depends on the relationship.

These longtime partners are for the most part the ones that have been with the owner since the beginning in some capacity. They know the owner's strengths and weaknesses and can have the last say with him.

This long-term husband/boyfriend/partner can be the louder one out of the two as a couple although, if they are smart, they are the quieter, more observant of the two. They should also be far calmer by nature, don't party as much yet are meticulous in the way they can keep track of who is surrounding them. They will make sure their home(s) feel like home while knowing full well where every penny is spent, and with who and how often as the owner might have copious amounts of lovers.

If an owner is a kind to live large and over the top, the partner will be the one who can reel them in and realistically set them back in place and keep them on track as the partner will want to know he will be protected first and for the long run just in case the owner does at some point break up with them or just frankly dies, because yes, with the big lifestyle, social demands, and parties, the owner ages and weakens rapidly and there have been times when the owner will then die well before his time.

People will be left shocked by the death, but secretly not surprised.

The main partner (as there can be more than one) can also be the driving force in many ways with the owner as to how the business runs, with who, and for how long. If they have an extensive history with the owner, they will be very close with those at head office and will know all the accounting numbers and will only spend just so much on themselves to not tip the scales and cause a stir and yet love telling anyone who will listen that, "He bought me a new condo in Mexico for Christmas!" Meaning for them both but letting it slip that it's for himself.

The partners I have known through the years can be good enough people to be around as long as you know your place and keep your mouth shut. One partner I recall liked to refer to their material things and what they were going to do next without touching upon any other subject in whole conversations except for when he was sizing a person up.

He also liked to brag to the bathhouse employees, of whom were working their asses off for them, of their trips and material goods without even realizing how he might have been making them feel if he even cared.

Then there are the constant comparisons. This one partner had heard that I liked to go on trips to Europe and tried to compare a whole continent full of culture and history to an all-inclusive resort they were just at, again, I just gave him a "wow" look and responding with how fantastic an experience that must've been for them, while again, keeping my mouth shut of what I really was thinking.

These partners overall though like a fine dining experience will claim to know the best restaurants in town, how to get a table, and where to buy the best shoes, blah blah. It was an act; you could tell they weren't happy but more so, vapid individuals.

Those kinds of men are what I refer to as being an "Agenda Gay". Overwhelmingly from those partners I knew, they were not into the drug scene for the most part but could do with a strong martini or two once in a while. They kept that nose of theirs clean as they had a lot of other sniffing around duties to perform.

They will seemingly be constantly thinking of what the owner has, what he can obtain from it, and how the show will run. He will make a small point of trying to get to know you just for his checklist, he'll be personable enough and yet will attempt to set you in your place subconsciously by reminding you of who the boss is and how much power he has and base it all on materialistic goods.

If you're new to the gay scene you may think you've just been schooled and your eyes will widen and your thoughts will flow. But if you know the game with these partners, you listen, smile, even agree but know internally what the real score is and how to move forward.

The long-term partner is more likely to have been with the owner right from the start, this can mean they can be close in age. They might have even known each other before the owner even had a bathhouse and will probably be with them for the rest of their lives because of this kind of connection.

At some point, you'll find out again through others at work that their sex life is pretty much dead and has been for years because the owner will have been sleeping with everyone at the baths but it's extremely rare that the owner's partner has had any sex at all as he will know his place on the pole and not want to jeopardize his future in any way possible but having left any blemishes. Nothing that might pop up in a nasty divorce case anyway.

After all, he just got the new condo in Mexico, he may have had an education of some point in the early days but when you have no real work history that can be found on a resume or LinkedIn, it can make life tricky as you can only claim detective duties for all the time spent monitoring not only his partner but the businesses, the managers, the employees, and the customers to sway the owner's ideas and plans.

With these owners and partners, they will be known within the LGBTQ community to some degree (especially the party scene) but when it comes to important issues, many don't like the attention or even shockingly sometimes the connection they have to the bathhouses (clutch pearls) so they will hide behind the company name and registered number and have an employee or manager answer on their behalf. Only the outspoken equality-driven owners will make a statement on something if asked in the media, the rest will routinely say, "No comment."

The owner and his life partner will know a ton of people but also prefer to maintain a tight circle of friends. When you first meet them, they will be testing you in a variety of ways to see how devoted you are beyond the business, how sneaky you might be, how trustworthy you can be, while trying to push what they think are various buttons with you and ask tons of background questions.

You'll be invited to all the private parties with them, yet expected to be right on top of things at work the next day and do a 16-hour shift. They might even try to persuade you to have sex with another fellow employee or manager, offer up that other person to you on a platter so to speak. More than once at various bathhouses I've had this happen, one owner thought I should sleep with another manager simply because he did a porn once. The manager was kind of handsome but not my type and it would've just been another notch on his belt situation so I just laughed the whole thing off. It's all tests plus I saw the porn and wasn't impressed.

If the owner and his partner aren't the very public, socialite types, then only those in the know find out who they are, and then you have to wait to be practically invited into their circle. It's up to you if you want to be a part of that circle though or if you think it's worth your time.

A good, smart manager though in my opinion knows how to stay clear of that lifestyle and knows their truth. I've seen it happen a million times where the ones that dive in on day one wanting it all, never end up lasting.

CHAPTER SEVENTEEN

Like many other people, not only in the gay community but in many walks of life, I've played around with a limited amount of various drugs and booze at parties.

Nothing major and certainly nothing that required needles or some concoction of drugs. It seemed to be only on rare occasions and in a social situation with one kind of specific drug or another depending on whom I was with or what party or event was currently taking place.

Alcohol I have used in the past thinking it would boost my confidence but as I get older, I've come to realize I am far more self-assured now, just simply based on life experience so by not having a drink before meeting new people or going to an event, I feel I am being my true self and it just works out better without worrying that I might be saying or do the wrong thing.

Living in France close to Monaco now for years, you quickly discover that wine is like water in the country, both plentiful and cheap. I have though seen many expats that arrive here and go all-in on the booze their first summer only to have to try and rid themselves of the habit later as it will start to bring on depression, weight gain, anxiety, and possibly a toll on their work-life. Not for all people, but you can easily spot it here for some reason, just add in all the heat from the sunshine.

For me now, there are many times I'd like a drink but tend to only do that socially at a dinner party, at a nightclub, or with a buddy once in a while. I'm always thinking of the next thing and like to stay on top of what's happening around me for my various luxury businesses which can involve a lot of strategic thinking for clients daily, so I prefer to operate with a clear mind to get things done.

During the pandemic, there were times I wanted a drink so I would cave and buy an occasional bottle of wine but when you are in a country in a lockdown situation with tough restrictions, meaning no bars, cafes, restaurants, nightclubs, or even shops open, it seems like a waste of time, money and who needs the extra calories?

As I get older, I still feel fortunate to have an abundance of natural energy and even more ambition (the beautiful, inspiring surroundings in France helps) so I find if I have a couple of drinks, the next day it takes a lot more to get motivated as I feel a bit lethargic.

Many years back in North America when I played around occasionally with an element of drugs while going out with friends, I found smoking pot just made me want to eat everything and it seemed where I lived the most popular drug at the time after cannabis was cocaine.

Coke could be expensive and although it gave me a rush of energy, I found it useless if I was just hanging around with friends gabbing even more about nothing in particular but if we were going out, it seemed like part of the process but thankfully for me, I never used it all the time, never even had a dealer for it. At the time it just felt like part of the fun of the scene and if we were going to a nightclub, it boosted the confidence even more, especially if you were dressed up in an outrageous costume to attend something like a fetish party.

This seemed common for many that went to the local nightclubs because the city, with all its beauty, could be very boring. Even at the nightclubs, it was always the same people so one felt they needed that added touch of excitement. Although in reality, the more you drink or do drugs, it does not necessarily make the party that much more fun as the night goes on, it just blows your money.

Sitting here in my home in France on a beautiful sunny, Sunday afternoon, I think it's time I divulge something more condensed here as it does pertain to this bathhouse world I was once in and is a part of my personal history and yes, I can see how naïve I was for much of what is about to be written.

The very few people that used to know of this secret in person, I haven't seen in well over a decade. The last I knew of them makes me feel sad for how their lives have turned out (and extremely grateful for what mine has become) as when I first became friends with them, they were young, bright, smart, smiling people with a great outlook on life and in the top of their professions to now be from what I understand, living quite tragic destitute lives.

When I first started working at the bathhouse, it was initially a part-time job on weekends in the role of a housekeeper, which although there were many hectic and gross elements to the work, I enjoyed the atmosphere and comradery of the staff and the customers and even brightened my world in many regards.

As part of the rotating work schedule that was set up, my hours could be from 8 am to 4 pm or 4 pm to midnight or midnight until 8 am which was fine to me, the hours seemed to breeze by because of all the details to take care of making sure the place was as immaculate as can be, doing loads of laundry, cleaning the rental rooms, disinfecting the steam rooms and general wet areas and helping customers at the snack counter, etc.

The first month and a half into the job, on one of my scheduled weekend shifts, I was working the graveyards as a housekeeper, it was busy but I recall this particular graveyard shift feeling a bit tired as I didn't get enough sleep beforehand so I just wanted to get through it all.

It was also on this graveyard shift that I worked with this particular cashier who was manning the fort for the night so to speak and at one point during the shift, he came into the laundry room where I was tackling a pile of dirty towels and sheets to wash and nonchalantly asked if I wanted a bump.

Having an idea what that was and assuming it was coke, I told him I wasn't sure, that I felt fine, and also thought I didn't want to risk somehow losing my job because of it.

Since there was only a couple of us on shift that night, he just casually said ok and told me where he was going to keep this small package hidden in the staff bathroom with the plastic tip of a Bic pen just in case I felt like it having my own bump and then he went back to the cashier post.

He had obviously had a bump himself yet still was acting normal just slightly more energized for the overnight shift so seeing he wasn't acting crazy on it, about an hour later I asked him during a conversation what exactly was in the package?

Turns out it wasn't coke but rather finely crushed crystallized meth.

Having heard the horror stories of gay men that I knew in the community and how deep they got involved in that cheap drug and how many basically lost everything, I was put off right away but didn't judge the cashier for what he decided to do. If anything, I was more concerned about him and a bit shocked that he was doing that specific kind of drug at work because of all the bad shit I heard about it.

Yet the adventurous side of me thought, this place felt like a party atmosphere, it would definitely wake me up, that I would try just a tiny amount and give it one go.

I pretended I knew all about it, as one does to fit in, and in conversation later told him I'd do a small bump. We quickly closed up the cashier and snack bar counter, headed to the staff washroom and I think he got the hint that doing a drug this way was new so he showed me how he would scoop a small amount on to the tip of the plastic closure of the Bic pen and snort it up his nostril, also saying a small amount can also be ingested by putting a touch amount from the pen tip on your tongue to swallow.

As we both giggled about it, I followed his lead. I had barely taken a small snort of the drug when he immediately told me not to tell anyone, especially the boss or he'd make sure I got fired first.

In my head I was laughing thinking, I'm new to the bath-house, I haven't otherwise done anything wrong but go for it. To his face though I just told him not to worry and seriously, who or why would I say anything? Then we went back to our work positions.

He continued to do his job as normal, for me there was no real feeling right away but within about 5 minutes I could feel this subtle rush of energy start to burst and I knew right away it was from the drug, so in my mind at least, I tried to appear as normal as could be and got a hell of a lot of work accomplished on that shift on top of anything extra that could be tackled.

Knowing that even aspirin can sometimes put me to sleep, the small amount of this one bump made it near impossible to sleep once I got home which I found frustrating so although I liked the sensation and especially the energy of it all. If it's that good and easy, I probably shouldn't do it again.

When that same coworker and I had shifts together after that, he would once in a while casually ask if I wanted a bump, no matter what time of day or night the shift was we were working but I would just kindly decline his offer.

Cut to a time in the future where I am now managing the bathhouse.

One random afternoon, I was taking a break from work knowing I'd be going in again for a second long shift that evening and was hanging out with a small, particular group of friends who I used to frequent some of the nightclubs with, especially if there was one of the monthly fetish parties where we would spend weeks before putting together the most outrageous outfits to try and top what we wore from the last fetish nightclub party.

For us, we never sexually played together, in fact, because this event was so heterosexual in nature, any kind of real sex acts were frowned down upon and could even get you kicked out of that nightclub. This event was more about dressing up and teasing everyone with your erotic look and for the time it was different and fun.

On this same day with these friends, one of them wanted to go to a specific suburban mall to pick up some new video game that he was into, so we all jumped in the car and headed to the mall. While on the drive there, one of them pulled out a little plastic baggy and I assumed it was coke until I saw it and then guessed it was crushed meth.

As they each took their turn at it, I was then offered it and by choice I decided to follow along and do a small bump, thinking of the long night of work ahead.

We got to this shopping mall, the friend picked up his video game, and then because a couple of the friends were hungry, we went to the food court and ordered Mexican food. I absolutely love Mexican food but at this sitting I could barely eat what was in front of me, having just no appetite for it.

This meth that they had seemed a little different from my

first experience with the drug, definitely stronger which had me just buzzing, telling them this while we sat in the food court, they started to tell me various tips and hints about the use of it as part of a casual conversation.

After the journey to the shopping mall, we headed back downtown to our homes and once I was dropped off, I remember just taking care of a lot of cleaning details in my apartment and even rushed to get ready for work, although there was no reason to either clean or rush to get ready.

Since for the most part, I could make my own work hours as long as everything was running smoothly, I ended up getting to work far earlier than I intended just to see everyone and was eager to complete as much work as possible.

General administrative work and especially accounting are always at the top of the list on a daily basis so once I arrived, I recall spending hours just getting to it all, making sure it was as accurate as possible, and worked ahead on other paperwork, orders, schedules, promotions, etc.

Being a coffee drinker didn't help as my body and mind were already rushing so even just the one or two cups added to the euphoria of it all.

In a weird way, I felt like I found a magic pill, and although it was just to be another one-off trip, that this cannot be good for me or anyone, after speaking to the accountants at the head office the next day, they were so happy to see how ahead of the paperwork we were and offered various verbal acclaims and encouragement.

Inside I knew I shouldn't but made the excuse to myself that I could handle it, that it would be ok to use once in a while to keep ahead of the daily paperwork that needed to be processed, that no one would know, and yet I also knew of what had happened to others that played around with it, but I told myself

I wouldn't be like them and would use it differently, thinking more work-related, as though that made sense.

My thinking was naïve at best and full of excuses, such as, if others can go about their lives and do it, why can't I? Not taking into account what a long-term effect it might have on my body and mind. It was like, the only reason to do it was to do an amazing, over the top job at work, almost to prove something to everyone. Again, naïve.

About a week later, the friend in the car that day that offered me a bump was also the one that would buy the drug for me. I called him and asked him if I could buy some from him or his dealer, just the smallest amount. Not even knowing what a general cost would be or how it should be used properly and how often.

In his voice I could sense some hesitation, so we set up a time to meet and when he showed up at my place with his girlfriend, he gave me a very small baggy of it, but first, he had a little chat with me about it.

I knew his own drug history and how he still seemed to manage to do well at his professional job so I thought I could too. Our friendship was more important than the drugs at the time so I listened to his advice. He was actually very kind and wanted to make sure I would not get carried away with it and told me how it could be used.

With that, the rest was up to me.

I didn't do the meth right away, I waited until what I thought would be a busier time at work with new projects that we were taking on to update the interior side of the business but more so to tackle the crazy amount of auditing in terms of accounting.

Looking back on it now, it wasn't about doing the drug to improve my everyday life, it was about staying ahead of work and giving everyone a good impression of how things were going but I was only cheating myself.

Even though I was really just a manager at this particular bathhouse, one always felt the pressure to set an example, bring in the best monthly sales figures constantly, all the while trying to be some kind of pillar to the LGBTQ community and provide the best bathhouse experience ever for the patrons. Overall, make everyone happy.

I loved this work but was sometimes so overwhelmed by the expectations, you almost didn't have time to think things through and just had to soldier on and evolve with everything being thrown your way. It was getting to the point I was afraid to take a day off, never mind two days off in a row for fear of missing out and getting behind.

At the time, I would only dig into the small baggy about once a week and by the same method of snorting a crushed piece or if that felt odd, I would even put the small amount on my tongue and swallow it which eventually led to me not being able to taste anything properly as everything I ate seemed to taste like licking a piece of metal.

The rush would lay in immediately, the work was then always done ahead of time, the acclaims kept coming in and my wallet started to get a touch fuller as all of a sudden simply because I never felt like eating, I didn't need to buy a normal amount of groceries that one would need in order to survive.

The next time I had seen these friends, my confidence level was shooting high and the first thing they told me when they came over to my place for a visit was, "You look great! But don't lose any more weight." And with that knowing look, I got the message.

I listened but in that same gathering they invited their dealer over, which I wasn't too keen on but once he arrived and we chatted a bit, he sold me a small baggy for about $10 while telling me that it was a slightly stronger batch so to be careful.

That same week when I went into the baggy, the amount I normally took seemed fine but not stronger. Not that I still had any real way to gauge any of it all, so I ingested a touch more.

Over time a once-a-week or twice-a-week habit turned into a once every two days to once or twice a day and it went on from there as my tolerance and desire for it grew.

This made my secret grow as I didn't have to contact that particular friend anymore to get some meth as I could contact the dealer directly and he would bring it to my apartment. I was on my own, but it wasn't the first time, just now I had a problem that was slowly making a new path of its own but I thought I was controlling the direction.

I had no desire for booze or food and basically lived on sweets. I have always had a normal body type and although I lost weight, I started to lose more, and combine that with no sleep I'm sure didn't make for a pretty picture.

All I did was throw myself into work and became very exacting in it, yet somehow putting on a calm and controlled exterior, or thought I was appearing as such. I would rarely see or even contact friends and family as I told myself I had no time for it, or if I did, I'm sure I must have talked their heads off in rambling, erratic conversations.

There were two people around me at one point, both women, who bluntly told me in the same week that I must be exhausted from work and to get more sleep because even my skin color was off. Which I did take to heart and knew was true so instead of stopping, I just altered how I did things in life a bit.

The other side was I became extremely horny and my work environment did not help in that matter. The very few people I would occasionally hook up with, we started to see each other more as I'd even give them free passes to the bathhouse so that we could have sex more often.

And it was starting to turn into very hardcore crazy sex where basically anything goes, my new desires meant I could not get enough of pounding ass or get pounded hard enough and I ended up sleeping with more men (or groups of men) than I normally would at any given time, yet also somehow knew not to make it known to everyone.

At the time it felt like some kind of sex cells were practically coming out of any pore every minute of the day.

I wasn't sure if it was the slight weight loss or my protective guard was down but I seemed to attract a lot more men as well, which meant more breaks were taken at work, so in breaking my own rules carrying on like that, the new energy to accomplish more started to lead to work piling up all over my desks and projects not being completed or even touched upon.

At the time I'm sure people must have known something was wrong or discussing it between themselves but no one said anything to me. I'm sure it didn't help that I made my life revolve around work so not really seeing friends anymore, people who could then see a difference in me to then possibly ask what was going on to see if they could help.

My behaviors and habits were slowly becoming either focused to the extreme and on infinitesimal details of things or erratic. I know my employees and head office must've been getting pissed off with me from time to time, and even with customers as well, but again, no one said anything to me.

Making money was one of the main things I kept focusing on, even if the paperwork was piling up, as my irrational thinking then was, they couldn't fault you if the money kept coming in were my thoughts. Yet that started to get crazy too at times,

I knew I needed to smarten up but was losing the sense as to how it could be done simply because I needed to first of all stop doing meth, then get actual sleep, eat something healthy and go from there but I couldn't figure out how or where to stop and start.

If I was mad about something, I could be very confrontational but more so in a smart-ass condescending way, or would burn up with my feelings inside about it and overthink everything to the tenth degree.

I was not well, yet all the false fronts I was showing or thought I was putting out there said otherwise, just a bit overworked and frazzled, that's all is what I would say. And let people know that I'll take a day off soon, not to worry.

I never became highly paranoid (if that is what is supposed to possibly happen), more so I wanted to show perfection as much as possible in everything I did, except for what really mattered, that being, myself.

One of the things my focus ended up changing and in which I became obsessed about was upgrading the bathhouse as I thought, a better, fresher-looking bathhouse brought in even more money. One of the first projects being repainting the hallways, being one of the many jobs we would try and do ourselves because can you imagine having an actual company come in to do it with half-naked men around having sex?

Once the hallways were done, each rental room was slowly getting updated with a new paint job, etc. With the establishment already being over 20 years old and with all the changes throughout the years from various renovations. A simple paint job was never a simple paint job as a lot of deeper cleaning and maintenance would have to take place first.

Of course, under the influence of meth as a stimulant, an absolute perfect paint job had to be done as I had almost a fear of someone commenting on how bad of a paint job it was so say for example a 4–5-hour job would all of a sudden take 12 hours to complete. That room had to be completely redone from top to bottom and as exacting as possible.

Although the hours were excessive and so were my efforts, no one complained but still, it shouldn't have been done that way as I didn't stop, to the point I didn't know what more than two hours of sleep in a row was anymore. A couple of times I even caught myself basically falling asleep with my head on the desk unexpectedly, so definitely sleep is what I needed.

Thankfully, reality hit one day. I was going to work as normal, and Kevin, the manager who previously ran the place and trained me, and who was still with the company just across the country now, was sitting in my chair when I opened the door to my office one morning.

I remember trying to stay cool about it all but shaking inside, he was a good friend and I was very happy to see him. Just that my office was completely filled with mounds of paperwork all over the desks and even piled on the floor that needed to be audited and processed. I sat on the chair on the other side of the office from my desk and could see he had been going through my paperwork.

With a welcoming smile on his face, and although I was in fear yet glad to see him, the first thing he asked me was, "How are things?"

I felt my heart into my chest sink and I basically started crying. Instead of telling him the truth about the meth use, I told him I was feeling overwhelmed with work even though I loved the job so much.

Looking at it though as an outsider coming in, it couldn't have made any sense. If I wasn't taking any real days off of work and was there all the time and things were managed before, why couldn't they be done now? The bathhouse looked great but my office told a whole other story.

He intently listened to what I had to say and calmly, patiently told me he could tell I was overwhelmed and it was one of the reasons he came for a visit. At the time our company was also in discussions with the owner/landlord of the building about the overall building renovations that were to be done with him and how we were going to completely rebuild the bathhouse alongside his project as we were in talks to take over the whole bottom level of the building instead of having just three-quarters of the space.

To this day I know Kevin on this visit knew the overwhelmed excuse was just an excuse. I've learned a lot from this man and one of the main things was patience and understanding and for that, I will always love him. He protected and stood by me and has had faith in me, even if we didn't say it in so many words.

That morning, after my little cry of both shame and relief, I pulled myself more together and we went on a tour of the bathhouse so that I could get him up to date on a few key things and then he told me to take some days off and do nothing but rest and he meant it, that he would manage the rest.

I agreed, gathered my things, said bye to the staff that was on shift, called a taxi, and went home. This was my sign to stop. Enough time and energy had been spent on this charade and meth bullshit, so I quit cold turkey by dumping what meth I had left down the toilet and getting rid of the discrete accessories that came with it, and deleted not only the dealer's phone number but anything to do with those particular friends.

I wasn't sure what was going to happen next, I just knew that immediately my body and mind needed simple rest and that I did for a solid seven days. Although I had to work on my sleep patterns, which are tricky at normal times when managing a bathhouse. The appetite and sleep overall came back naturally and quickly and there were very few if any instances in the way of cravings which I never gave into, I was lucky.

I looked at it all as a gift and a sign of a new positive start and even with the stress of work and life, things did fall into place again and I have this man, Kevin who stepped in to give me exactly what I needed with no judgment. It just felt like love.

CHAPTER EIGHTEEN

At a bathhouse, anything can and will happen when you have any large number of men constantly coming and going to the venue but that's what makes every day working in such a place interesting and challenging no matter what your job title may be.

Not only inside a sexually charged atmosphere can anything take place, but also directly outside of the space as well.

Bathhouses are usually quite large and are either part of a commercial development building or a stand-alone structure.

In my experiences, the bathhouses I have managed have always been part of an expansive commercial development building with this first bathhouse I worked at having occupied a large part of a basement level shared with the nightclub tenant next door in a three-story downtown property.

This meant that any smells or noise inside the establishment could also possibly carry into other parts of the building but we were fortunate to have a solid space with certain, specific sound barriers set into place along with an extensive ventilation and heating system.

In the bathhouse business, even though it is legal in the country I was living in, you want to be that quiet, unassuming, good neighbor. We happened to share a common and sizable entrance space with the nightclub owner next door, so we did know them and others upstairs as acquaintances in the property. If someone needed to borrow something or if you had a question about a technical situation in the building, there was always a kind neighbor to help.

Our particular building had a large number of tenants. On the main ground level were a clothing store and two Mom & Pop convenience stores on either side of the main entrance and behind those businesses, internally were a couple of offices and art studios, with more offices and work studios on the upper two levels.

As tenants, many of us were friendly and got along well with each other while also minding our own business. This particular building was actually known for its eclectic history in the city as it used to have a large dance hall at one time with our space formerly being one of the first bowling alleys in the city.

Outside the back exit of our venue, you immediately came upon the back alley where we had our own large metal garbage container that we kept locked and next to it there was also a general use, common metal garbage container that the rest of the building shared.

This meant that not only did you have to monitor what went on inside your establishment, but you also had to take care and be aware of common areas in and around the building as there were no caretaker, security, or concierge services.

Everyone got along so well that at one point, with the permission of the building owner who was also the landlord, we took it upon ourselves to update the large stairwell inside and common area shared with the cabaret next door with a new paint job and signage.

We had also noticed that the clothing store updated the front of their shop with a new paint job, followed by one of the convenience stores on the other end of the building, so with our own time and money, we offered and painted the rest of the front main level of the building just for the pride of place.

Business-wise things seemed as smooth as can be when late one March evening we could smell smoke in the space and as the fire detectors started going off, we quickly looked around while customers stared in awe not knowing what to do, yet thankfully stayed calm, only for us to discover that someone had set some cardboard and papers on fire directly against our back double, metal emergency exit doors with the smoke permeating slowly between the door closures and throughout the back of the bathhouse where our storage, laundry room, and the wet area was situated.

Since we had fire extinguishers right there, we quickly got the small fire out while the authorities were called. Within minutes everything was under control but as per procedure, we had to do up an incident report.

There was no real damage, only fire and heat markings left on the exit doors and we just figured it was some teenagers playing around or something in that regard. The fire department didn't take much notice either as it was a busy downtown location with lots of people always on the move.

When the month of April arrived, we noticed our competitor had placed a half-page advertisement in the local LGBTQ newspaper about the opening of his new raw play space just a few blocks from his main bathhouse business.

This meant to us, that being a small city, men will naturally be curious about the new play space and will likely go there a number of times to see what it's all about, so we factored that in as our sales might not be as high as normal the next couple of months while there was a new gay business in town and things settled.

To me, having a choice is great for everyone and if it helps expand what the community has to offer in terms of gay establishments then all the better for those that live and visit the city plus competition keeps your game fresh.

As expected, about the first two weeks or so after they opened, our numbers had dwindled a little bit but nothing really that substantial which even surprised us so we used this time to continue updating our establishment even more with small renovations such as decorative metal cladding, more mirrors, tiling, and various other small jobs to change things up.

Again, work-life seemed normal as can be when in May there was another fire outside in the back alley at the back of our space, this time it was in the general building garbage container that had been moved right underneath our large air intake vents next to the boiler room back door (these containers had wheels on the bottom for easier pick up by the garbage trucks and for people to move if necessary).

This fire was a lot bigger, to the point that by the time the smoke started to flow inside the air intake vents into the middle of the bathhouse, neighbors in surrounding buildings had seen the flames from the metal container and had called the fire department before we got the chance.

The fire department arrived so fast that they had the fire under control and extinguished within a few minutes. We just had to deal with the smell of smoke in the place but it wasn't that heavy and seemed to quickly dissipate as we took care of the airflow and thankfully no one was hurt inside and no one even had to leave.

We were fortunate that this happened in the morning, as it was our quietest time and when a deeper housekeeping cleaning system is in place to set everything up for the next 24 hours of business.

What was suspicious to us right away was when an incident report was taken, the fire officials recalled being at our same building a couple of months back, and when we checked the approximate time of each fire, besides being in the same location, the first fire incident took place at 10 pm, this second fire took place at 10 am.

Still, at the time, no one seemed to have an answer as to why or what to do except that the neighbors always had to make sure to lock the top of the garbage container shut after they unload their garbage into it. A couple of years later, City Hall made a new bylaw stating that all large metal garbage containers needed to be locked at all times.

What we did notice during May was that for some unknown reason, reviews of our business on the LGBTQ community online boards were all of a sudden multiplying, like easily 10-20 comments and discussions per day which were all consistently bad and even juvenile and aimed especially at specific times of when our bathhouse would be busy.

Yet glowing reviews were posted at the same days and times about the new play space that had just opened in April and the same kind of wonderful reviews were also written about the competitor's main bathhouse.

It was very biased and peculiar, so I started to save and print off the reviews because a definite pattern was being left online, and because of the very slanderous and even threatening nature of the comments, so we might have needed copies for our lawyers.

Reviews good and bad come and go with any business but these were so obviously set up like it was a public relations stunt of some sort going on. There wasn't much we could do about it as the new moderators they finally got on the website claimed free speech, yet that same company that set up the online forum system was also raking in a lot of advertisement dollars from the competitor at the same time.

It also all appeared as though the reviews were written by the same two or three people as the tone and comments were very similar each time. It was like a losing battle yet we didn't do anything wrong, if anything we were continuing to upgrade the establishment for patrons so we couldn't understand all the hate for our business and even some of our customers had their suspicions.

Most of the comments were how no one was going to our bathhouse anymore since the other new play space opened up. Our customer counts consistently said otherwise.

At times reading these reviews and comments would be infuriating as we were all working so hard at all hours and the improvements were not only expensive and time-consuming but our customer base was always diverse, happy, and loyal.

Thankfully early in June, we did notice that our client numbers were slowly going back to normal, even exceeding expectations. With a bathhouse, it could still all be tricky to try and predict how the business will evolve.

Also because of our geographical location in the country where during the summer months, people want to be outside more, going to the various beaches or men left to go on vacation somewhere. Our history always indicated that during the summer months, business tends to slow down a little. Knowing this was part of our background, we just continued with business as normal.

As June progressed, there was yet another fire, this time it occurred in about the middle of the month and in the evening, and on the main level inside the building is an artist's studio at the back facing the alley, which was directly above part of our main wet area where the toilets and one of the shower rooms, boiler room, porn room, and steam room were located.

Yet again, we could slightly smell smoke but not as heavy as the other times and we weren't sure where it was coming from (we even wondered if it was our imagination because of the last fires) we could just hear the building alarms and when we went outside and checked the back alley, everything seemed to look normal on the surface.

The fire department showed up immediately, we don't know who called them but we were thankful. Since we did not have keys for the main level glass entrance door into the building, they had to break it open, and as there were only a couple of other office doors in that long corridor, but seeing some smoke coming from the end of the hall that's where they headed directly. A woman inside the studio was for some reason not letting the firemen inside her space until they somehow quickly convinced her to open the door.

We were told later she was cooking something that burnt, so that is where the smoke was coming from so without a lot of fanfare, they got whatever the small fire situation was out. This still had a few of us concerned and worried throughout the building now.

Word the next day around the building was that the woman was a drug addict who also hadn't paid her rent, no one had any idea when or how she was able to move in, many assumed she just took the space over from the previous tenant who upped and left. She was cooking or making something with a kind of hash oil on a hot plate in the studio so the fire was the last straw when the landlord found out. The legal process had to take place to remove her, even if she was a squatter, so she had been given an eviction notice, which in the city meant she could still technically reside there for the next 30 days.

Then things changed once again on the morning of July 3, 2003.

I had just finished an almost 14-hour overnight shift where I had been doing some accounting and preparing everything for the upcoming weekend while also doing some small weekly maintenance jobs.

At around 6:30 am that morning, feeling exhausted, I wrapped things up for my shift and called for a taxi then said goodbye to the cashiers as one was going to be coming on shift and the other was going to be leaving so they were about to start their shift change in a while. Since the cashier's office was situated across the hall from mine, I told the cashier coming on to call me if he needed anything.

The taxi arrived practically the same time I got upstairs and to the street and being tired, I was glad I only lived about a 6-minute car ride away. Once home, I literally went straight to bed.

Then my cell phone rang at about 7:14 am, it was the cashier who sounded panicked and confused. I asked him to slow down and tell me what's going on. He said he wasn't sure just that they smelled smoke and that it sounded like all the fire alarms in the whole building were going off. What should they do?

Although he was ahead cashier who had been working there for years and knew what to do in an emergency, I think he just didn't want to do the wrong thing because now the time had come to act on the procedures and his nature was to be very quiet and mild-mannered.

I told him to just make sure everyone is out of the place and to get out himself, that I would be there as soon as possible.

It was a weekday and at that time in the morning, there were maybe 2-3 customers in the place who all safely got out with the head cashier and the housekeeper on duty at the time.

Immediately after getting off the phone with the head cashier, I called a taxi again and looking out my living room window of my apartment building high-rise while getting dressed, I could see a lot of smoke in the distance downtown which was shocking, to say the least.

I rushed downstairs to the front of my apartment building when the cab was just pulling up. Got in, and told him the location I needed to get to as fast as possible and he took the best route there, thing is, as we got closer, the amount of smoke in the air looked worse and traffic was getting busier as it looked like streets were being blocked off. It was like something you'd see developing in a disaster movie, very tense and scary.

I got the cab driver to drop me off as close as possible to the location and ran the extra couple of blocks towards the building in a state of shock, confusion, and disbelief as everything was looking so chaotic. It felt like a bad dream and I kept telling myself that everything will be alright, just make sure the guys are ok.

The street where the building is located was completely blocked off. Power was apparently out on the street and in surrounding areas.

I was able to find the head cashier right away, he was subtly crying, shaking, also in disbelief, and acting like he'd be able to walk back into the building and get back to his duties right away. He proceeded to me more of what details he knew about the situation but that thankfully everyone got out ok.

He was actually worried as he had left the money in the cash register which frankly who cared about that and that although he closed the cashier office door, he couldn't remember if he locked the main entrance door so that bothered him, but that was just how he was thinking at the moment. Us and those around that worked in that building seemed to have the oddest concerns and comments, I think it was just the shock of it all. I just kept thanking God that no one was hurt as far as I could tell.

At this point, the area was packed with fire trucks and other emergency services, and we kept running into other tenants which reassured us that more people were ok.

Many of the building tenants were just showing up for work for the day or came in earlier because they also got a call about what was going on downtown. Everyone was just stunned at what was taking place in front of our eyes. And because of the age of the building and bylaws at the time, there were no fire sprinklers built into the structure of the property, which might have just done a lot of damage if there had been sprinklers setting off but at least it would have helped stop the fire from the beginning.

With the number of people watching this fire, it was causing more confusion and stress for the officials fighting the blaze. Everyone kept getting pushed back and further away for safety reasons. And that's when a big explosion occurred that sent shards of glass and flames out of the front of the top floor of the building. There was a large photography studio in that space so people I talked to assumed it was his chemicals that were stored and used for his work that caused the explosion.

We were told later that this was the biggest fire in the city's history and with the most fire departments in attendance. The huge plume of black smoke could be seen from all angles on every side of the city.

There was nothing we could do. It was so heartbreaking in so many ways, the lack of sleep didn't help either. I tried calling our head office numerous times but I think with all the power outages and the downtown core is in chaos, the calls kept getting cut off.

Those of us tenants must have spent most of the day there; trying to see what you could from the other side of the various barriers anywhere close to the building. You didn't know what to do next or who to speak to or if you should stick around anymore for some reason. There was no handbook for this type of situation as it was taking place or after the fact.

What did seem instinctive was to take photos, which many did, and there also happened to be a film school directly behind our building so you better believe those students were documenting anything possible along with the hordes of news media that showed up to the incident.

Hours later the fire was out but the city as a precaution with the fire department had the building, or what was left of it, torn down by a demolition company to do what is called a "loss control", meaning the building fire had taken over too much of the structure to save it so it was best to try and protect the surrounding buildings as much as possible and stop any spread of the fire.

After seeing everything starting to be demolished into a huge pile of rubble, I kept gathering as much information, phone numbers, and business cards as possible from those I knew who were associated with the building or even on the block.

I remember getting back to my apartment at some point, dealing with non-stop phone calls now that the service was working again with many people who were calling to see if myself and the staff, and everyone else were ok. But the other side of that was the same amount of phone calls from people trying to find out the latest gossip which I was not going to put up with at that time as I was more concerned about the safety of everyone else during this traumatic event.

What then also started to happen while the smoke was literally still settling was employees and I were getting calls and emails from customers we knew or somehow got our information wondering if we would be open that night, as crazy as it sounds.

It didn't help to see the news repeat information about the fire on all the local TV channels every few hours and for days afterward, it was like a stab in the heart every time. I also couldn't stop crying about the whole situation as it was all just devastating yet I tried to stay strong for the employees and the others affected.

I don't know what it was, but the remarks, suggestions, concerns, and comments coming my way and to the employees at the time were unusually strange almost as though people just didn't grasp what happened. I think it was because if they weren't there in person to see what had taken place, they were getting second-hand news or like us, just couldn't believe it.

One of the first calls I made when I got home was to head office since there was so much static or lack of signal on my cell phone when I was outside near the point of the fire. The person in charge of accounting at the time kept asking about some of the random paperwork and could I fax any of it to her right away?

I was stunned hearing that was her main concern at the time and had to repeatedly tell her, there is no more bathhouse, there is a pile of rubble, there was a fire, there is no business, there is no building, there is no paperwork to gather and certainly no fax machine to send it from.

She had been with the company for what seemed like a million years, so she was probably just as shaken by the news. Once she saw the actual news on their side of the country on TV, the next day she was more understanding and shocked so gathered ourselves and helped each other to try and take charge of the situation as much as possible with more help coming from the rest of head office and Kevin who always had sound advice.

My phone did not stop ringing day and night, nor were the number of emails coming in. It felt like I had to accept every call coming as there was word out that I had died in the fire, with the same rumor going around that employees and customers died so there were those that were worried, those that wanted to gossip, but also it could be a city official of some sort trying to call me.

Overall, the day was one of the longest, strangest and saddest ever and when I did try to get some proper sleep, even a nap, that wasn't going to happen as my mind was to wound up with everything that had taken place, so around midnight, I hopped on my bike to try and process it all while going to see the ruins of the bathhouse for more perspective.

I could see from blocks away that the street was still blocked off, most of the street lights were out surrounding the area and certainly, all the other businesses in the area had no power. It was eerily quiet after earlier seeing the chaos of the day.

There was really no one around except for a solitary security guard standing on the sidewalk next to the pile of rubble that was sectioned off by a hastily placed chain-link security fence.

It was weird to see how the mix of the businesses was all shuffled around on top of each other, there was no way a person could just go and walk on top of it. It smelled of smoke even if you couldn't see any and in many places, the parts of the building glistened from the water that had been poured on it by the reflection of what lighting was available around the site.

Our business was in the basement level, yet part of our gym equipment was somehow at the top of the strewn building pieces a couple of stories high. Just so many odd things to see while dealing with waves of emotion.

When I went around the block and headed down the back alley on my bike, I was surprised to see a few tenants at this time of night who had parked their vehicles behind the now crumbled building and who told me that people had already been coming around trying to steal metal and anything else they could from the rubble and that the one security guard on-site wasn't much help.

That's when the tenants that were there also started to tell me more about what they had found out had happened with regards to the fire since earlier that day as we started to piece together everything.

After some discussion, we decided to team up the next day with the other tenants so that everyone could take turns on watch at the site as this incident that happened wasn't going to go away anytime soon.

As I said goodbye, I rode around the other side of the block and took some more photos of the smoke-filled rubble then headed home and attempted to get some sleep.

Very early that next morning I was woken by a phone call from the main accountant at head office. The situation was even more real for her now so she was helping to take control along with the other staff members at the office so we could proceed as best as possible.

We all started to take care of a lot of administrative and insurance issues. While I consistently gathered as much in-formation and evidence as possible, made myself available for any authorities if they had questions while being in consistent contact with the owner of the building, the only thing that was weird at the time was there was basically zero help from City Hall to answer even the most basic of questions.

Although I didn't know it until later, this could be because there will of course be insurance claims and possible lawsuits so no comments or guidance could be given which left many of us in limbo for undetermined amounts of time. Yet it still felt like there should be some kind of city official to help provide some guidance in these situations.

Day-to-day life drastically changed because the responsibilities had as well. The employees also didn't know what to do with themselves as basically, they were out of a job now, which naturally because of the shock took a day or so for many to realize.

Many of the employees, like our customer base, would ask me questions the first week and even a month later as to when and where we will open again? Customers would say they still had free locker or room passes or a half-price coupon and how could they use them? Or could they sell them to us which was a wtf moment?! Every conceivable reaction and comment came not only my way but also to the now-former employees. It all made for an extended, highly emotional time for us.

As for opening a new bathhouse, it's not as though 5000 to 10,000 sq ft spaces are readily available by a landlord for what is basically a sex club to start a business. As frustrating and even outrageous as some of the comments and questions could be, I tried to reassure people when we have answers, they will have answers.

Certainly, anything that was going to happen for a new bathhouse wouldn't be done overnight, given some of the comments that suggested otherwise. But 28 years of business brings a lot of loyalty, history, and memories for people so that had to be taken into consideration as well.

Some of the strangest and saddest times were when myself or even my employees would tell me how they would go into a grocery store or some random shop and customers would approach us. The customer would get sad upon seeing one of us, wonder how we are and some would even start crying about what had happened, or get mad and confused about it all to then start blaming everyone and everything, then they would at times add to what gossip they had heard about the situation much of which we really didn't need to hear as a lot of it was obviously bullshit.

Since the employees had lost their job, with the help of head office, we helped get their unemployment benefits coming in as soon as possible and paid out any kind of vacation pay, etc. Anything to help support them. As time went on, many assumed, even if told otherwise that a new bathhouse would not be opening right away, to take care of themselves and try to find other work in the meanwhile.

Many of the now-former employees didn't know how to restart their lives so I helped them with their resumes and any work connections I might have had available and we all rallied around each other for support. We felt like a family so we were constantly in touch and I still am in contact with many of them to this day.

After some discussions with head office, it was decided that I would stay on as manager since I was also on the board of directors, my new duties were to help with any and all insurance and legal issues that might arise, while we were considering if we should open a new bathhouse.

Lots of things were up in the air, we just had to wait for key answers from city officials, insurance agents, and lawyers while trying to figure out how to move forward and be ready for whatever else was to come our way, which at this point felt like it could be anything at all.

For myself, as bad as the situation was, on the positive side, I had been able to slow down a little from running a 24/7 business. I had time to reflect, research, investigate and plan more now that I was able to get proper rest yet it was all still an adjustment.

Although the future seemed uncertain, I felt strongly about what I needed to do. I also got a little more than obsessed with what had happened with how and why. In a way, I now had the time to find out answers, at least to some of the questions I had as too many things seemed suspect.

The other tenants and I started working together at the site, we took turns day and night gathering information and evidence to help each other, dispelling rumors (of which there was plenty), and shared what we could to help each other navigate a mess like this while trying to rebuild our lives and livelihood.

People that had seen the news about the fire felt bad for us, some tenants managed to gather small amounts of monetary donations for themselves which is good as many didn't have insurance and lost their livelihoods too.

The fact that we had to practically live outside the building for at least a month or two that summer was frustrating and just kept your mind on what had happened. As we tried to deal with officials who were not always the most helpful or forward with answers to questions.

To top it off, the demolition company that was hired to take care of the site to slowly remove the debris had been running what appeared to be a routine scam.

The owner of the demo company appeared all polite and sad about what happened the first day or two but then he became threatening shortly thereafter when he found out we wouldn't be leaving the site like so many others had before in similar situations.

This commercial building that contained much of our lives

was very large, as I mentioned it was three stories high and was located close to the middle of the block extending from the sidewalk to the back alley and was very deep and wide with a long history as it was built in 1908.

The owner of the demolition company was basically a one-man operation and frankly, an asshole who occasionally hired day workers or truck drivers to help him on the job to haul stuff away, whatever he thought was valuable was then pulled off the trucks at a site far outside the city and sold privately for him to make a profit on.

Part of the responsibilities for many of us tenants was that we had to gather what we could at the time from what was left of our business to help mitigate the losses for insurance reasons. Although our insurance company was also doing their own investigation, they seemed pleased with all the additional photos and videos of how things were progressing that were also readily available to them.

Looking at the rubble, this wasn't mostly a charred property. Many areas, such as ours had been intact with no damage except the water followed by the demolition. Once they had the main upper floor section of the fire out, the place was torn down as part of the demolition so that people wouldn't try to enter a partially burned building afterward as it could have then led to the city getting sued if anyone got hurt.

This demo guy was supremely pissed that we were around the site for the most part of a 24-hour day. To him, anything he came across was finders' keepers and we were to find out later he kept a lot.

There were times when it would practically take tears from a former tenant if they could spot something they owned as he shifted the pile and even then, he would begrudgingly climb out of his excavator that he had set up in the top middle of the pile of rubble, pick up the piece of property and fling it into the back alley where it would get more damaged or pick it up using his excavator if it was too heavy an item and instead of placing it down gently, lift it high and drop it into the back alley destroying the property found.

At the same time, the demo man was pulling his antics on a daily basis, we were slowly able to at least get a better idea as to what happened that initially caused the blaze and moments afterward.

The short version is that the woman who had started the fire in her studio was illegally living in the business space. She should have never been allowed to do that but with the housing crisis and cost of living in the city, many survived by squatting this way.

We think she might have presented herself as an artist or even took over the place illegally from a friend and just used the bathrooms in the common areas as a place to try and keep herself clean. She was apparently always unassuming; no one including myself noticed her or had known of her before either.

This older woman had once again that final morning, we were told, attempted to cook with hash oil on her hot plate stovetop. Although we were also to find out she was known locally as a crack addict and was concocting some kind of drugs in her studio at the time and it again started a fire.

We were to find out later on, she had been previously kicked out of a rooming house where she also started a fire for this exact same behavior before coming to our building downtown.

The fire department showed up again to our building that fateful day, they got the fire out, and this time she claimed she was making popcorn...at 7 am in the morning. We were also told this was the same excuse she used at her former rooming house. Since we didn't know her name, people just started calling her, "Popcorn Lady" in reference.

Once the fire department officials thought the fire was out in her space in our building, they then brought in air blowers to help push out the smoke.

The problem is, because of the building's age and subsequent renovations throughout the years by various tenants, Popcorn Lady's studio did not have a properly closed-off ceiling in her place, just wooden rafters that ran the length of the building.

When they started blowing the smoke out of her place and down the long hallway to the front open door and also out the back door, embers from the fire that were still burning had gotten in between and along the long rafters of the ceiling and deeper into the building which then started a fire between the ceiling and the floor above while trickling into other workspaces.

Once the fire department realized this, and with the fire hidden from their views, it had spread to other unknown sections of the building which started smaller yet still uncontainable fires throughout those rafters and seeped through the upper floors and vents.

The explosion that blew out the front windows of the top floor unexpectedly onto the street was from the fire and heat between the rafters under the photographers' studio floor which also stored the chemicals in his workspace. After the explosion came more airflow into the building, growing the fire substantially.

But to see the fire report after it all, of which much of it was redacted, and which took an extremely long time to get and that we had to practically fight for with lawyers, you would think someone simply dropped a single match.

A good year or so later, what I could read from the piles of binders full of redacted information pertaining to what had happened at and surrounding the fire while I was at the lawyers' offices, the report certainly told a very sanitized story from what could at least be pieced together since much of the facts had been blacked out.

Back at the demolition of the building one morning, the owner of the property next door offered to let some of us use his roof to look down into the site itself to get a better idea and take photos of what was going on as the demo man seemed obsessed with the center of the building site with no real progress being done on any other area.

We found out why as soon as we got up there.

The demo man had cleared down into the building to where the bathhouse gym area was and utilized the large floor space after removing anything left in that room. Then, anything he could find of value he would place into the large cleared fitness area and work around it while digging around for more belongings he thought might be of value.

The day we happened to be there was a good day, he didn't even realize we were on the roof until some tenants spotted some of their stuff and were yelling at him to stop. What we caught him doing was, he had found some of the business owner's safes in the building and he was literally rolling them back and forth on the floor to try and break them open with the excavator.

That really set him off on a rampage since he got caught. People couldn't take enough photos and videos of what was happening. Once he calmed down for two seconds, he called the police on us, stating harassment on the job and that it wasn't safe for us to be on a patio roof terrace.

The police took our side but for some peace on the site, most of us came down.

I didn't like the demo man for what he was doing but knew that yelling at him and just being an asshole like him, in general, wasn't going to help anything, so I just observed and took notes plus photos that I shared with others that were affected by the fire.

The demo man thought because I was quiet and never yelling at him, I wasn't upset with him so a couple of days later in conversation with me, since he really didn't know the kind of business was being run there only that the location was mine, he asked what all towels were about that he kept finding on-site.

When I responded that the business was a bathhouse, I still don't think he got it. But when he mentioned the floor area in the gym, he said he ran into some hardwood booths in a row that were almost impossible to break down into pieces to haul away.

He asked what was there, thinking it was some kind of small storage room or perhaps phone booths. When I told him, it was a large row of glory hole booths, he was shocked and didn't know how to respond to that one and seemed embarrassed he spent so much time trying to tear it apart, then the idea of the place was coming together as he started to find all the vinyl mattresses and pillows, boxes of lubes and condoms, sex toys, etc.

We had three safes in our own business, one built into the floor that was empty and I'm not sure if he got the other one next to it, which would've had the overnight cash drops and receipts but I assumed he got that one.

There was also a small safe in my office, that held the change floats, expense cash, and whatever else was about to be deposited or saved.

One day, close to the end of the demolition process. The demo man had gone for lunch, and a former upstairs tenant had noticed an item of his had fallen into what used to be my office area a floor below street level.

It was so weird seeing my personal items like t-shirts and shoes in the broken rubble next to strewn files and what was left of office equipment. I wanted to get to our stuff but we weren't sure how?

Spotting another opening close by and literally risking our neck, we somehow squeezed and crawled our way down towards my office where I was able to get the tenant's fallen belongings and some random nostalgia keepsake stuff.

My clothes I left behind and any other personal belongings as they smelled badly of smoke and of all things, fuel. I managed to get some bits of paperwork and for some reason, I got some rental room keys also as a keepsake.

The office safe was badly damaged on the outside with what looked like oily chemicals, probably hazardous, same with any computers. Being emotionally hurt by what I saw, as much as I wanted to try and save more stuff, it was just stuff and it was damaged and I thought it was best to get out before being discovered in there.

During this devastating period full of heartbreak and emotions, the rumors were rampant that the competition in some way had something to do with our business being destroyed.

Sometimes I thought that was possible, sometimes not. It would be continually pointed out to me by people as to how and why (typically with the same story), some would also note the history in the city of which appears a number of bathhouses in the past were all somehow removed from the gay scene by fire or otherwise in some manner.

The city does have a shady history for such a remarkable place so who knows?

I could let that information and the coincidences eat me alive, which it did for a short while since I had so much time for reflection.

Realistically though, slowly as any element left of the business site was being cleared away for good, seeing the process daily was hard but once it was done, I would still go back, just to squeeze through the opening in the chain-link security fence for the occasional visit of a now-vacant lot and walk around the area just to reminisce but more importantly plan ahead.

CHAPTER NINETEEN

Since the bathhouse was now destroyed, while dealing with all the administrative and legal issues surrounding it, and after the initial shock was over during this time, the rumors in the community now we're taking a turn as to when and if a new bathhouse was going to be built somewhere either by us or someone else.

Whenever the former employees or myself ran into one of our past customers, half the time these men would tell us how they were now going to the only bathhouse and play space left in town.

They would tell us how that bathhouse and its other new play space were now busier, simply because there was nowhere else to go.

Whether we asked or not, in conversation many of the customers would tell us in confidence that they disliked the place for various reasons, mainly because it had little to no sexual ambiance, prices to get in were raised right after our demise, yet they were being charged with every nickel and dime possible for anything else on top of the rates such as if you wanted a fresh towel or even having to pay for the deposit of a towel when you checked in.

Apparently, they'd still get the one free condom upon arrival otherwise you had to buy more condoms or bring your own, basically little things that men took notice of so they felt like they were being ripped off on almost every visit and didn't know when that would end. Even though it's just a bathhouse, for many of these men it was an important social activity and it was bothering them that with no other options, they felt that they were being taken advantage of because of the current situation.

A majority of the complaints (not that we could do anything about it) was that the employees at those bathhouses were constantly rude and overall, it was just not a welcoming and fun place to be, so many of the customers were anxious for us to open a new bathhouse somewhere.

At the time we still didn't have answers as our insurance was taking longer to come in and legally, not financially, we couldn't do anything until that was cleared. This was mainly since so many people were now suing City Hall and various officials along with the owner/ landlord because of so many factors with and surrounding the fire.

What also made things difficult was Brian, the owner of our bathhouse had recently died, and with his estate still being dispersed and settled, that left many more decisions up in the air.

While this was going on, one of the last, newer employees of the bathhouse that had been hired at least a year before the fire, a soft-spoken individual, who had become good friends with one of the head cashiers at the bathhouse, suggested one evening when we were all hanging out that he might know of someone that wanted to open a bathhouse, an investor.

We knew who the "investor" was as the two of them used to have sex at the club on his time off when the investor friend was in town. After that bit of a laugh, we really thought nothing more of it.

In a bathhouse, for those working in the business, regularly you end up being approached by people with their dreams of investing, becoming a partner, or owning a bathhouse. Many of them assume because they have been to one a few times, it must be quick, easy money, and take little effort to operate.

The whole bathhouse idea can be based on having fantasies realized and for many owners that can be true, as there are many who, no matter what they look like, just have to tell someone they are the owner and it will be like having your choice of goodies in a candy store. It's not always a 100% guarantee that the owner can have who they want, but dangle the carrot long enough and it will at least gain them some new admirers that will make up for the ones that say no.

It wasn't unusual for regular and new customers weekly asking myself or the employees how having a bathhouse is such a great idea, that they were going to build one of their own while adding how they will also do better than us.

Or, could they invest in ours when we didn't need or were even looking for investors since business was good. This is not to say we are the experts either, in our case, Brian had bought the place from someone else, built it to what it was and we were just there continuing to make it work.

Right after the destruction of the bathhouse is when even more inquiries came in from people wanting to, typically as a group of buddies who came up with the idea while standing in a bar one night, start a bathhouse, which also means more hands in the pot.

In speaking to most of them, it was all about the money they had in their head they would be making from the start yet they also didn't want to put a lot of money into it (if they even had any) but thought it should happen and be a glorious looking palace of a place.

The discussions were interesting and the ambition and innovation were wonderful but with no real plan (and especially money) it wasn't going to work, and never did happen with any of them.

Later that week, Neil, the former employee of the bathhouse, wanted to meet with me and his investor friend Frank about the possibility of opening a bathhouse. For something to do I figured why not, so we met for coffee where Neil tended to stay his quiet self with his face only lighting up when he spoke up about his design ideas while Frank spoke more about money for the possible project and type of property, etc. I liked that he seemed genuine and asked some very good questions pertaining to all the financials first.

Frank seemed more serious about it than all the others, and not being one to hold back, I was heavy with the questions, he answered as best as he could, and to be honest, I was a little hard on him but if he was certain about this, things were only going to get tougher.

At the same time, I asked Kevin for his advice on this possible business opportunity to which a good portion he also hammered in the costs, ongoing financials, the work and was quite blunt about it possibly failing.

Since my own life was in a bit of limbo, which looking back explains a lot of my thinking at the time, decisions with head office finally started to come to light pertaining to us possibly developing a new bathhouse.

The owner Brian, of our bathhouse, had left a lot of his estate in the will to his brother who was also always more of a silent partner. Since they already owned a number of businesses including bathhouses in the city where they lived and with us now being gone, plus the insurance taking forever and other issues.

The brother decided to simplify things and not reopen a bathhouse in our part of the country, even with potential commercial spaces being found and with assistance from our building landlord who owned other properties in the city. It was just going to be too much for them to take on from across the country and I sadly agreed, as it would also be too much to do all on my own.

It was tough to hear but at least myself, the former employees, and whoever else was interested had an answer and I was still kept on for some time to continue to handle any of the former business administrative issues and dissolution.

I was also offered the opportunity to move to their part of the country to continue working with them but at the time I didn't want to leave where I was living as there had been enough upheaval.

The whole situation of how things happened was still an emotional time and looking back I let it affect me more than it needed to and in many ways and because those supportive individuals at head office weren't physically around, there was plenty of things they did not witness daily or just didn't take seriously mainly because they weren't in the city to truly experience firsthand what happened during and after the fire.

It was understandable as their routines didn't completely change because of a bad day as they still had fully operational businesses to manage and structure where they lived on a daily basis, so I think in many ways it was easier for them to move forward.

I too should have been moving forward more for my own sake, as it felt like because this is a small city I was just so strongly associated by others with this former establishment and in many ways didn't feel I was allowed to move on from it all. It felt like I was branded by the LGBTQ community in a sense at the time and I was feeling stuck.

In day-to-day life back then, not only for myself but for the employees, every time we stepped out onto the street it seemed someone would approach to discuss most anything about the bathhouse at all.

How they missed it, the gossip surrounding it, the talk about a new bathhouse, even questioning us as though we might have had something to do with the fire, everything imaginable came our way but very rarely were we asked how we were feeling and were we doing ok?

Looking back, I would have done many things differently but you get older and hopefully learn from life's ups and downs.

And now that I was more available and always up for a new challenge, Frank and Neil started to want to discuss a new bathhouse even more now so I went along with it all to see at first how it would all possibly develop.

Frank's plan was to keep his job in the mining industry he had been working in for decades, which was very sensible. And at one point during one of our meetings, he had shown me the proof of funds for a smaller sized venue (you've got to start somewhere) and if more funds were needed, he stated he could get it.

We were all being a bit naïve about this, and I was probably still shell-shocked combined with my love of working in a bathhouse, and I missed it all and didn't want to lose out on this new business venture. Frank just wanted to invest his money as part of his portfolio but I knew he was also in love with Neil, even if he didn't say it that openly in so many words.

Frank also had a strong, calm demeanor and liked to think important things through which to me came off as being a patient individual, and for this, most of all he was going to need all the patience he could muster.

Neil didn't come with much work experience at all being in his mid to late twenties, he basically showed up in the big city one day, heard through a friend about the bathhouse, and applied.

Back then I had some reservations about giving him a job at the bathhouse at the time because he was so quiet and I was worried he might run off in the middle of the shift in shock by something he might witness, but he ended up being a dedicated worker, willing to do whatever work task was needed and opened up more as an individual with everyone as time went on and had a great attitude.

During any meetings with Frank, whenever Neil spoke up, it was only about the big dreams of how he was going to design the whole place which seemed frivolous for the most part yet he was also the kind of individual to actually read the small print in any contract.

My gut instinct was still very unsure about the situation so I just told them one day, if you are serious about owning a bathhouse, start getting the legal and administrative paperwork together and I'd help where I could with trying to find the right venue and we'd move forward from there.

I had also told myself if things started to go badly, I'd give them a couple of chances and if it was still bullshit, I'd be gone.

Frank had an apartment in the city he shared with a work colleague but was usually on the road, out of town for work. Neil and I would keep him updated and we slowly started to work together more.

Frank and Neil had also decided once things were really underway that Neil would outright own the bathhouse, which seemed crazy even then but that Frank was the investor who still would have a lot of say and that I would ultimately manage the place but also be there through it all to train Neil on all aspects of the business so we could work together building up the business.

They would talk about the big dreams of how much we would all be making and promised me the world. I would remind them that the business will have to grow first and would state to them the realities which would be hard for them to hear and would even be denied at some points, which would then get my guard up with concern.

As in life, one can have all the stop signs in front of them with all the warnings required but still, find a way around where you think you want to be.

Neil, really had no idea about business basics as I was quick to find out. And Frank automatically put Neil on a very generous payroll plus expenses (it must be love) while any pay I got was basic and pathetic, to say the least but with big promises documented.

I still proceeded to guide Neil with the initial set up with government forms and registrations, along with setting up a business bank account, and while on his own, Neil managed to find, of course, one of the highest-priced legal firms in the city to continue to legally set up the business.

Once Neil could see how the paperwork was making things more of a reality, he became both enthralled and overwhelmed with it all and wanted what felt like a million copies of everything yet never kept any of it in order even once I sorted and tried to maintain his filing for him.

He also started contacting the lawyers over things that weren't relevant or required day and night which of course cost every time he called them. We had to explain to him they were not his friends and that the more he played around and wasted time, the less money would be available for the bathhouse.

We just took these actions by him as being very new to the business world and excited but once you kind of laid down the law with him, he would then take notice, at least for a day or two so you had hope.

In looking for a bathhouse property, any of the potential places I had found during the first year after the fire were now already leased out during what appeared to be a business boom in the city.

I was also soon to find out property hunting would turn into an obsession for Neil. We were a good match that way as I love properties too but for me, I was more realistic, for him it was more about building upon a relic or finding something far too grand in scale.

In many ways it was good he was so obsessed as he wanted to search and look at everything and for the most part, kept an open mind, but if he did find something that really caught his interest, Neil would at times be so intensely focused on it that he wasn't thinking about the practicalities of it all, the options that would be required for such a place and even the price as he thought it would be magically paid for monthly.

We knew there wasn't enough money to outright purchase a property, also because of the way buildings were constructed in the downtown core, anything that was perhaps a stand-alone property was rare and very old with an owner who was holding out for a development company to come in and pay him big money to purchase it so they could tear it down and build a new high-rise of condominiums.

We would come across some excellent properties available but then we would run into the issue of considering the neighborhood in general or neighbors in the building itself and how they would feel about a bathhouse being near the same property with men coming and going at all hours of the day and night. Most importantly though was if an owner would even allow for our kind of business to be in the building, even if he didn't know really what a bathhouse was, the word "gay" would sometimes be enough to put an owner off, and even then, how does one really delicately explain the purpose of a bathhouse to a straight, practical stranger?

Many factors had to be considered for a property, location, close enough or within the gay community, safe, welcoming neighborhoods, areas in the city where regulations would allow for such a business, and how quickly and economically a site could be converted into a bathhouse.

We had set out the accounting work for how many rooms and lockers, supplies, employees, etc. were needed on average for a new bathhouse to be profitable but if Neil got excited about a place, all that would go out the window so you'd have to reel him in again or have Frank discuss it all with him and remind him of the task at hand.

It took a couple of months of searching either on our own or with the help of realtors, of which we'd have to explain to them what the business was and in turn, the realtor would either not help us find anything or show us unsuitable places or the realtor would be after a lease commission and try to manipulate us into quickly signing on a place without any approvals or due diligence being done.

It ended up just making more sense to research online ourselves and go out literally on foot and then contact the realtor from the signage in the window for more information or the property management company at a building that seemed to have a possible place.

Then property obsessed Neil contacted me very late one night, all excited about a potential place he thought might work that he came across on an evening stroll. I Google mapped the location from the address given to get a better idea of the building and it already looked like it had potential compared to the others.

The next day when we went to take a look at it, from what we could see through parts of the large windows that weren't covered with a reflective foil, that it appeared to be a big property like a former business with various offices and maybe even a large store of some kind at one point that was now filled bits of hardwood flooring piled high and old office equipment everywhere.

It also happened to only be two blocks from where the former bathhouse was located, I instantly liked that as it was still downtown and would be a familiar area to our past customers.

And although I was more enthused about what I saw, even without inspecting the inside yet, I still didn't want to get my hopes up and was having some reservations due to just seeing the amount of work that we would first of all need to have approved by the city and the property owner, along with the time it would take to do the work and most of all, the funds.

But to stay positive, I mentioned it couldn't hurt to see what was in there so we arranged with the property manager to have a visit.

We got in to see the inside of the site the next day. The building caretaker and the manager in charge at the property management company showed us around.

Once inside the building at the entrance from the street, there were some makeshift offices near the front of the interior and we were told the place was 5000 square feet, which is a great size to start with for a bathhouse in this city. And that the floor to ceiling height was about 20 feet which looked great, but my first thought was trying to control the sounds from the sexual acts that would be emanating in the space but music that would be playing non-stop and a functional wall layout could help as partial sound barriers.

The floor was original, like from the 1950s and hardwood, well past its expiration date, with other layers of flooring underneath and big chunks were also ripped out, but we were told it was a cement floor under it all which is excellent.

The middle area of the site was empty except for some random office furniture that seemed to be stored there and at the back were public washrooms that were retro, again, from the 1950s.

Most of the walls looked solid and thick with brick and cement and so was the ceiling except for where a former large stained-glass window used to be that was now boarded over by wood and plaster. This whole space was the biggest section of the commercial development building, taking up 1/7 of the whole building and with its entrance off the street. The rest of the building itself was 6 stories high and was constructed in 1925, all brick and cement with an amazing original marble entrance and stairwell near the elevators.

We loved the place right away as it looked like it had lots of potentials but it was also going to need a tremendous amount of work which means possibly more money to be spent if we were going by the way Neil was managing the funds anyway.

We were told the property had been different types of businesses throughout the decades, one of which being a large garage, then grocery/department store followed by a small factory with offices and one of its last uses was as a porn studio. That last part told us that they must be open-minded as a property management company.

The people that were showing us the place seemed very liberal-minded and since we couldn't hide the fact of what we thought the property could be used for when they asked, we told them that we used to work at a former bathhouse a couple of blocks away and we were looking to possibly open a new one. This seemed to go over well. It also helped that they remembered the fire and even knew the owner of the building.

This site had not been used for a few years and so they were open to options and ideas. In showing us the property, they mentioned it also has a basement level of the same size that was currently being used for building storage.

That was interesting to hear as a possible further development option and you could see where someone had covered up with flooring where the original opening to the steps to go downstairs was located, so we had to go view the other area by making our way through the inside common area hallways in the building.

Once inside this storage area, it was poorly lit, but all gutted down to the cement walls, floors, pillars, and ceiling. Only the cement stairs remained with a very small section being wooden pallet storage units.

This would mean down the road; we could possibly have a 10,000 sq ft of space in total to expand the new bathhouse after it starts to make a profit. You could see Neil's eyes light up immediately.

CHAPTER TWENTY

After the viewing, we were both thrilled with thoughts of the property we just saw and with all the potential it offered. We were practically jumping with excitement as we made our way back through downtown.

We were told the next day that more discussions would have to happen but that we could have the main level of 5000 square feet of space or just the lower basement level if we wanted also at 5000 square feet or both spaces.

Naturally, Neil wanted both levels right away. I was fine with having either floor and mentioned if we could start with one level and then eventually move into the other section as the business grew, then that might work out well. We had to let Frank know first and crunch the numbers.

Practically overnight Neil had drawn up numerous massive design options, some quite outrageous and not practical in the least, some interesting with possibilities to build upon. All the power to him for being creative but my concern was getting this all going and not running out of money partway through or possibly having to cheap out just to try and make a go of it while in operation. That would be the worst as knowing how many of us gays can be, as we'd spot and point that shit out right away.

After going through various design ideas and taking care of all the accounting work, especially since Neil had now convinced Frank that we should have both levels of the property which I still had some concerns about, nonetheless, a meeting was set up with the property manager at his offices. It went well, he asked a lot of questions and also along the same lines I had about money, making sure there was enough and that the place would have to be viable.

This all still took at least a month of negotiations and also required Frank to be a part of the ongoing meetings too since he was the financial backer, with that, in due time, with a lot of legal paperwork, a rare, very long-term lease was set up with contingencies set into place with city hall permissions and an unusual and very lengthy rent-free period to get things under-way. The property management company I found to be more than fair, thorough, smart, and generous, with no complaints from me.

Now that the deal was on, several design ideas were still being thrown around by Neil, in some ways to save costs but in many ways that would blow the budget right away and even just in a specific area of the bathhouse.

With this type of business, we had to find an architect with a strong interior design background who understood that this venue would need to be gutted on the main floor and take into account all the massive plumbing requirements for the wet areas, heating, general airflow and air conditioning of the ex-pansive property, extensive wiring that would be required, and who could continue to work closely with city hall given the na-ture of the business and have us up to code and definitely on a budget. The architect couldn't be shy to ask questions or listen to what could be a considered strange requirement due to the place being a bathhouse.

We got a potential design layout mocked up ourselves with rental rooms, wet areas, storage, technical and mechanical rooms, office, cashier and housekeeping areas, common play spaces, etc. while trying to stop Neil from changing the design every two minutes.

After interviewing a few architectural/interior design candidates, including one or two individuals from the former architectural firm I worked for, it was either too much for them to understand and take on, or some other candidates were shocked because of the kind of business and refused to work with us. Yet some were all in but wanted to charge the moon and the stars because of this particular business and wanted to somehow stamp their egomaniac personal touch to it all.

Probably because it's a small city, somehow Neil managed to find the same architect that did up the design for the raw play space the former bathhouse competitor had opened. We thought at least this architect/interior designer would be open-minded enough to meet with us and if he's designed this kind of business before, all the better.

Turns out he was behind the design of the competitors' last main bathhouse and his other newer play space. He didn't have a hand in the initial design of the raw play space as a previous first group of owners had been putting that together before running out of money but did help with setting the rest of it up later after the bathhouse owner took the project over.

It actually felt strange to meet with him at first because of his knowledge of the competitor's bathhouse businesses but he only touched upon that briefly and kept things professional. Still, Neil insisted he sign a non-disclosure agreement (which the architect it turns out also had to sign one with the competitor) and invited him to come to view the site, once there he too saw the potential and it helped give him a better idea of what needed to be done and how the design process would go.

He looked over our combined design ideas, had lots of questions and concerns, and was very upfront about what city hall expects to pass inspections which were appreciated, if not a bit disheartening at times for Neil but the architect was now on board and I felt more confident about it.

Besides getting paid well to do his job, I don't know to this day how the architect had the patience with Neil but he did, especially at first when we'd hammer down a final design ready to submit to city hall for approval but then Neil would throw a wrench in it with middle-of-the-night changes but eventually, after some stern conversations. Neil let it all be submitted for approval.

Sixteen weeks later, after some back and forth, the plans with city hall were approved. In the meanwhile, we took a chance and gutted the property as much as we could by ourselves since we were in a waiting pattern.

It was dirty, even dangerous at times, and a tremendous amount of work but it gave us hope and inspiration. Although I was soon to find myself in the property on my own because Neil would be shopping for things for the business or sitting around dreaming up more design ideas which led to us being behind on all the prep work.

A freelance project manager who was recommended by the property manager was also hired to keep things on schedule and budget, and even though he cost a lot to have around, he did keep us on track and in turn saving us money.

The approval also meant more legal work was needed to be done and estimates from various construction companies were slowly coming in.

When we signed with the construction company, we were told work would be done on a budget, but only just, we did have some extra funds available if required and we were given a reasonable timeline.

As with any construction job, especially in a place this size that had to be gutted and built again throughout as very little could be salvaged, the costs naturally came rolling in as issues came up. Parts of floors had to be jackhammered away for additional plumbing requirements, a new layer of the concrete floor had to be laid, with the HVAC unit being one of the biggest expenses as it also had to be craned on to the roof of the bathhouse near the stain glass ceiling.

I knew the timeline was going to be extended right away. During the prep work alone Neil refused to have us get in even a couple of extra workers to do demo work or even patch and paint, with promises that he would help out but within an hour or two of getting his hands dirty he would suddenly be done and disappear no matter what.

A pattern was starting to happen with Neil, that no one could figure out and especially if he was needed around. If you couldn't reach him by phone, if you went to the site, at times when no one else would be working, such as late at night, he would be there doing bits of what he thought was work which would just make more work for us later or he attempted to lay out chalk lines for rooms from the floor plans that he would get fixated on. At the end of my patience at one point during the construction. I saw him move a long chalk line for a wall 17 times by millimeters.

I and others that knew him, even on-site workers from the construction crew at times would calmly ask him what he was doing. If he was trying to implement a city-approved change, add a new amendment to the plans, or just in general ask him if he was ok. Typically without a response but a focus on what he was doing.

Things were about to get brutal and we've only just begun.

Although it felt like we had all the time in the world, we didn't. The pressure was on and the longer this process took, the more life goes on with less hope of gaining most of our past customer base back, if at all, which honestly, we were already well past that point when we began. Yet there was also a feeling that it wasn't so much of a worry as people in the city, especially in the gay community, always seemed to be hungry for more entertainment venues.

At first, the discussions between a small group of us were to keep this whole new bathhouse thing a bit of a secret. As excited as we were, one reason being was, we would then be consistently asked when the new bathhouse would be open, what the place would look like, and be composed of extra "expert" advice when there was already a lot to do to get things finished.

That idea went out the window right away, as word quickly got out within the building containing the venue where the new bathhouse was going to be opening.

Practically right after signing the lease, there were some gay individuals with their own offices upstairs attempting to become best buddies with us and dying to get a peek inside, who then told two friends who told two friends and so on.

One such individual in the building came into the site through the basement level when we left a doorway open to the common area hallway as we were having a meeting.

With barely an introduction, he interrupted the meeting and rapidly told us he was glad a bathhouse was going to be right here and then proceeded with his list of ideas of what we should and should not have, one of them high on his list was a room should be designed for people with a scat fetish (meaning shit and play with shit).

The look on our faces didn't stop his enthusiasm for the subject. He thought this was something very much needed as it was missing from bathhouses these days. He thought there should be one or two rooms that could be rented where men could shit on or with each other to then play around and have sex.

He then continued with how the room should be constructed, that there should be shower or tub vinyl lining on the walls with a drain in the floor and a hot and cold water hose. Yet he had no idea as to how or who would have to clean that all up afterward. Even with his insistence, he was eager for us to practically have it drawn into the plans that second. I just smiled and casually thanked him and said we'd put it on the list of ideas.

And then I jokingly added, "Although I don't know if an employee could be paid enough to clean up a room like that continuously? And what would the other customers think of the smell?" As it seemed to be the one part, he didn't think through, but as often as he could from that day forward, he sure did try to sneak into the site and rattle on about it or stir up some gossip.

At another stage of the construction, he wanted to apply to work at the bathhouse, so I just asked him for his resume as a part of the conversation and he got deeply offended by that suggestion. He mentioned he has had his own business office in the building for years and in none of the 15 years of his career has he ever had to produce a resume.

During the construction process, depending on the type of work going on, sometimes doors would be open for fresh air or as easy access for the workers so those passing by on the street could see inside and at times random strangers would just walk on in and around without permission (even with signage stating otherwise) so then we'd have to gently walk them back outside and let them know that for insurance reasons we couldn't have visitors on site.

It got to the point we'd have to do this with those tenants in the building as they thought since we are all in the same property they didn't need permission, the visiting would also take up time but it was mainly for safety reasons as we couldn't have just everyone coming in.

Being the kind of person that certainly doesn't mind working every day especially if it's something I'm passionate about. And although my agreement with Neil and Frank at the time was to take a smaller salary than normal until the business was in full operation. I felt that the more I could to help get us all to get one step closer to completion and opening date, the better. And that it was always good for someone to have a presence on the site for any questions or concerns the construction crew or anyone else might have so that we could move forward.

I was also feeling though that I had to make up and back Neil up for what he wasn't doing because as time went on, he would either be in the place working on something that wasn't essential to pass a hurdle to move ahead or he was starting to show up at off-hours when everyone was gone as then he might not need to have an answer for any of the crew, which would also put us behind if he, say, had to sign off on something.

One of the habits he formed if he was on the site was, if things got too busy or heavy with responsibilities, he would then either disappear to the office the property manager was letting us use upstairs in the building for free or just disappear from the area altogether and had then gone shopping for either himself or purchasing random things for the venue that weren't even on the must-have list.

At first, I couldn't understand what was going on, but as the pattern grew and was taking shape, to the point those working on the site could also see what was going on.

I knew he was quiet by nature and so I tried to be empathetic. In speaking to him on our own, he would seem to be relieved to express how he was feeling about things, even cry or be angry, or he would completely shut down altogether and not say a word and just stare at a wall or myself like a zombie.

Between ourselves, we would try to work out together what he could or could not handle, the stress and expectations were too much (which would then make me wonder how he would even operate a bathhouse) so I would offer to take on even more responsibilities because you could tell the basics were even becoming a heavy burden for him.

This was already not our first big conversation like this and I just wanted to get this construction business done and for us to be open, and as naïve as I was about it, I kept having faith in it all and with Neil but my concerns were increasing on how this would work out.

Making him feel better though and him putting in any efforts at all after one of my hopefully motivating talks, would only last for a day or so, then it was back to the routine he developed for himself.

More than once I was ready to drop everything and walk away, but at the time I thought, this project had come so far, if I leave now, with my luck they would open, be a success and I'd be left mad at myself with nothing to show for all the efforts. Thankfully today my thinking is no longer like that but when you're in the middle of it all, it can be hard to see things from another perspective.

This all led me to be the one who was internally and constantly frustrated at the site, trying to do my best in making sure things were getting done and at times with or without Neil's approval on how something should look or be completed simply because no one could find him for varying lengths at a time.

Only to come into the site the next day or to find him that night in the place tearing down what took a team a day of construction to complete. Mainly because he thought a wall wasn't straight by his expert measurements, or if he thought a wall was off by a quarter of an inch...yes, a quarter of an inch. And that wouldn't be the first wall that would get torn down, wiring and all.

This told me something more was going on than just the stress of the project or he just flatly didn't know what the hell he was doing and had zero respect for the fact that someone, not him, has had to work hard to pay for the project and his constant changes, it also showed no respect to the workers onsite as.

At one point we lost our project manager simply because he was just that frustrated with Neil as he kept messing with the project schedule and everything else. Before he left though, the project manager made sure to tear a strip off of Neil before he quit, even with a large amount of money he was getting paid, the hassle just wasn't worth it to him.

The construction crew would get so pissed off at the antics that they would at times also disappear for a day or two and work on another building site so then me, Frank (from whatever work location he was at) but rarely Neil would practically have to beg them to come back.

After the final time that happened, the team leader of the construction crew came back and told Neil in front of everyone, any more design changes, will be added double to the bill, Neil listened by didn't seem to take it seriously and of course, after a few days, the changes started again, so then the invoices increased, quite substantially and although I didn't like it, I couldn't blame him, plus I really had no say in it all.

It's understandable that in any construction project changes will be made once you see the new design, function, or practicality, it's to be expected. But Neil started taking it to an extreme, destroying or changing things at least a few times a week, when he decided to come to the site.

Now Neil was starting to disappear for longer times, perhaps two to three days at a time and he would never answer his phone or respond to emails, no matter who you were or what it was about, it was I think now a way he thought he was protecting himself by disappearing.

Only if Frank was in town would Neil be around like nothing happened, and would be on his best behavior with a completely changed demeanor and especially if he was doing a walk-through of the site to show Frank the progress made while putting on his best appearances.

At this point though, many working on the site knew this was bullshit and even became protective of Frank because of the money he was dishing out so they would chastise Neil right in front of Frank while the rest of us stood back and watched. This started to happen so often that both Frank and Neil would kind of laugh quietly about it and move on, which was just weird.

I was worried about everything so much at this point that if I got to speak to Frank or both of them in person, I would take the opportunity to voice my concerns, to which nothing would come of it besides the odd promise. If Frank was working out of town, I then started to either call or email him to keep him updated, as he seemed to respond better to that kind of communication.

With Frank's job taking him on the road more because he needed to make more and more money for this construction, their time apart was starting to grow.

We were now well past the initial free rental date for the bathhouse as per the lease agreement and were supposed to be paying a hefty rent every month for a venue that was still being constructed. Thankfully after some discussions with the property manager, once he saw the amount of work that still needed to be completed, the rent was lowered to try and make things easier but not for much longer.

Even those working on the site could not believe how long this project was taking compared to other construction jobs they had been on and increasingly in the LGBTQ community there were questions as to why it was taking forever to open with many seemingly just giving up hope on it happening at all.

During this time, Neil ended up giving up his apartment because all of a sudden now he wanted to save costs and moved into both the site and slept in the office upstairs. He tried staying with me but that lasted a night as he fell asleep on the sofa in the middle of the night but left food cooking on my stove and almost burnt the place down.

In a way, as strange as it was for him to move to the site, it made it easier to find him for work that needed to be done or approved, at least at first.

Myself and others that knew him also had some additional worry past this construction fiasco, because although he was a tall man with a seemingly normal body mass, he had begun to drastically lose weight, stopped shaving which made him look gaunt, and since he didn't have a real kitchen to use, he would just get ready-made food from the local grocery store or he'd be inhaling fast food from the shopping mall that was just down the street. As long as I could see he was eating, that helped lift some of the worries with everything else going on.

Neil was never the kind to play around in the drug world as far as I knew so to me it wasn't drugs that were making him lose weight drastically, it was just this new stress-induced lifestyle. Mutual friends and I used to do everything we could to make sure he was eating proper meals and sleep normal hours, but as a grown man, he seemed to not listen and just keep to the structure he set up for himself.

One day out of the blue though, everything was about to change yet again. I showed up at the site on Monday morning at my regular time to find Neil was there, actually in the venue and doing real work. He seemed more alert, on the go, happier, and just more optimistic which was a pleasant surprise, even the construction crew that was around seemed more positive about everything.

This brought a smile to my face and yet finding it unusual I casually asked him what's going on? He just kept smiling and shyly gushed a bit while focusing on the work task at hand.

Then around the corner comes this much older, big man behind me, who then bypasses me while holding a small tray of paint and a brush and asks Neil some random work-related question then walks away. I curiously asked Neil who that was as we didn't hire anyone and we always had the same crew on the site?

He blushed and told me it was just a friend, so kind of thinking nothing of it, I went back to what I had been working on to see them both at various times during the day practically all over each other.

Letting it go but also thinking, what the fuck now?! As it was weird enough to see his complete change of attitude (although more positive), and I was protective of the property (and Neil) because of all the work that had already been put into it, so just who was this strange guy?

Neil's actions that day were obvious to everyone on site as these two were definitely together and I kept thinking, what about Frank? And how the hell did he find the time to meet someone when we have all of this construction business to take care of that we were literally living and breathing day and night. Then again, he was disappearing a lot, so at some point during the day when this new man went running an errand, I asked him who this person was?

His mood instantly changed and he got slightly defensive and even in my face over a casual question and then stated it was his boyfriend and that they had met online.

I was stunned in more ways than one but got the abrupt message to let it go.

The next day, kind of the same situation. The crew said Neil was there when they arrived and was already working away with this new person. My first thoughts were, ok? This is good but it's a weekday, does this strange man not have his own job? As he looked to be in his late 50's.

That morning Neil was still in a great mood and was finally cordial enough to introduce me to this man who, in my mind, was going to be nicknamed Moose. Moose seemed laid back, helpful and it was looking like he was getting along with everyone on site. It was refreshing to have things running more smoothly with less daily bullshit for a change.

This new routine wasn't going to last though, as more noticeable changes were coming.

In this situation between Neil and Moose, I figured it was not my business to tell Frank, even in fairness to Frank for all the ongoing efforts he was making, it was a tough spot to be in but I just thought, these were grown men.

Late one morning though one of the workers answered the site phone and it was Frank looking for Neil. The worker innocently blurted out to Frank, "Oh, he's off with his boyfriend somewhere?"

Inside I was like...oh fuck, yet I was glad Frank knew.

Within minutes Frank called me on my cell phone and asked what was going on. Knowing what he meant, I told him he better talk to Neil about it as I'm already taking on more than I should be.

When Neil came back with Moose from being out shopping most of the day. They came waltzing into the site holding numerous bags of new clothes under each arm, while wearing some of their new summer wardrobes, with fresh haircuts to match, and all I was to discover later, on the company expense account for a company that wasn't even in business yet.

Once settled inside the site, Neil finally checked his voicemails to then found out what happened from Frank's messages. Neil turned red with anger and proceeded to yell at those of us within his radius about it.

That's when I calmly flat out told him that he needed to take care of his personal business with Frank, we are all just working here for the both of them so leave us out of it.

From that day forward, the tone with Neil continued to change and not for the better, the attitude and overly-inflated ego from not only Neil but now this Moose character were astonishing to witness.

I don't know what he told Frank but the feeling when seeing Frank on his next visit shortly after is that he appeared to have accepted this new situation. Maybe it just came with experience given his age and he went back to thinking of this as being even more as a business investment now, especially because financially he was so deep in the red thanks to Neil's erratic spending habits. You could see an almost mournful expression on Frank's face like he didn't know what else to do.

I know legal agreements had been made between Neil and Frank for the business but Neil would not allow me to know to what extent until I pressed Frank about it and he then showed me the documents. Frank was simply a silent investor. Neil did his homework and made sure to have the fine print done to his requests in their contract.

Things started to escalate further with Moose, whenever he and Neil decided to show up on-site they would walk around on some kind of power trip. It was shocking at first how blunt and outright rude Moose would be and I would gently talk to him about how we were trying to get work done, the construction staff have a crew leader, it's not his place to talk down to a construction crew member or demand something and if he had a concern, he should discuss it with Neil first (or try Frank) and we'd go from there.

Even though at this point Moose was just an asshole who stopped helping with any work altogether on the site, I thought it was best to just let him think he's boss as you could tell he had anger issues.

The first couple of times Moose tried to pull an attitude with the site crew or even myself, he would listen and even once in a while apologize but that never lasted long as his true self began to open up and more often.

If things felt uncertain before, there was even more uncertainty now as he started to make everyone feel like they were walking on eggshells the minute they came into the worksite.

In a discussion during this time when I could get a moment alone with Neil, I asked him what was going on because he was starting to use Moose as his mouthpiece for the things he'd never say. Neil then gave me a cold stare and had the nerve to say I should start listening to his boyfriend more as he has some good ideas and anything he says will be a benefit to the business.

Arching my eyebrow, I gave him a look and said, "Ok, sure."

As there was no changing his mind now, he was part of Moose's game plan.

If you know me, I'm all for new ideas, I like to push new limits, take a chance, and am not afraid to try anything and love a challenge but this Moose was bringing absolutely nothing to the table. He continued to be disrespectful and condescending to the workers on site, to me, even to the property manager who was wondering who this strange person was at the site and who already had some serious and legitimate concerns because of how far behind work had become.

Moose became consistently rude on the verge of threatening if he didn't get his way, everyone that came into contact with him would walk away stunned. With that, some of us took it upon ourselves to do some digging, which took little effort, and it turns out Moose was an unemployable ranch hand, let go from his previous jobs generally because of his behaviors and with more than one past boyfriend claiming he was an abusive individual both physically and mentally which got me and a few others concerned.

Oh, and he had zero experience working in the bathhouse industry or really any industry at all for that matter. From everything we read, he drifted from dead-end job to dead-end job and boyfriends.

Things were falling into place and making more sense now. Since Neil and Moose met on an online dating site, Neil had also previously mentioned that on the first date, Neil showed him the business site, and in my opinion, this is when Moose saw Neil as an easy mark as he showcased a massive 10,000 sq ft business and so Moose was now attempting to carve out a position for himself and thinking $$$.

One day, while the custom bed frames were being built and fitted into each rental room, as it was about to get underway,

Neil and I were discussing the height of the bed frame.

Initially, Neil marked the base of the bed too high on the wall, so I told him that remember, we have to take into account the thickness of the foam mattress with the vinyl cover plus any bedding and pillow on top of the bed to which Neil agreed but who was standing behind us in the doorway? Moose, who piped in what height he thought it should be and he was rather rude and insistent about it.

I was over this fucker, for weeks Moose had been badgering everyone over every little thing, along with underlying threats and with Neil already holding up progress, we now had Moose to add to the equation.

Without skipping a beat, I turned around and asked Moose sternly, "What are you basing this bed height on?!" "Cause as far as I know you've never even been in a bathhouse, but now you're some kind of expert?!" Followed by a, "Aren't you new here?"

One of the construction crew members was close by and literally covered his mouth from laughing and he later thanked me for telling Moose off, but of course, Moose had an answer-back and practically tore my face off to tell me. I literally thought his next move was going to be with his fist to my face he was so angry.

After I rolled my eyes at him, and since he didn't have a real answer, I walked away and went off the site to get some fresh air, and when things felt calmer, managed to speak with Neil one on one and we figured out the most accurate bed frame heights according to plan so the workers could come in and do their job.

At one point during these tense times, when I was able to catch Neil in a good mood. In passing, I half-jokingly asked him, "How does Frank feel about all of this?" To which Neil replied, "Frank's just an investor, he knows the situation, and besides Frank has a wife and grown kids of his own so there is not much he can do about anything, if he wants to make his investment back, he has to keep following through with the deal."

Which again told me everything I needed to now know.

Frank having a wife and family was new to me as we had now known each other well over a year at this point and there was never a mention but I can see him keeping this kind of secret too, given his generation and expectations in life.

One thing for certain, after those last private discussions, if Neil was around, close behind him was Moose.

This was getting stranger by the day and an extremely tense time while trying to build a business on top of it all was no easy task.

CHAPTER
TWENTY ONE

The only good thing I could see out of the Neil and Moose situation was that, because Neil thought he was happier, he was taking better care of his health and putting on a normal amount of weight, even a little extra if truth be told but this was far better than his skeleton weight level before. At least the man was eating.

Now though, their honeymoon of sorts was coming to an end, Neil and Moose started to both pull disappearing acts again or they would do half days. And any lunch hours were always 2-3 hours long, sometimes they would show up in the middle of the night and do their own form of work on the place and every weekend was a long weekend for them and they were not to be told otherwise by anyone.

In the meanwhile, they had also got a new place to live together, because apparently there was some sort of situation at Moose's current home so it wasn't going to work out, and again, it was all some secret as to where they were now living but it turned out to be a massive condo, in a new building with all the amenities you could imagine.

This was to them considered an "expense" through what funds Frank was still able to keep providing.

At this time most of the main construction issues were being finalized, we were close to the finish line for opening, this alleviated some stress and stirred up the talk around town again about a new bathhouse in the city.

The work that still needed to be completed, although quite extensive was now more cosmetic.

Neil somehow managed to get a small team of painters come in who were friendly and did a great job, I was to find out later by one of the painters that Neil put an ad out on Craigslist and hired them to come in to paint the maze of hallways and numerous rooms and that he would pay them under the table. The painting though quickly came to a full stop near the end of the first week when it came time to pay them as Neil could not be found.

This turned into another drama in itself and not the first time as throughout 75% of this project, if Frank hadn't transferred funds or not enough funds were available since Neil was always overspending and blowing any budget, more than once he would leave the person or group of people high and dry after work was put into the site and they then not getting paid.

This is when he would run off and hide even more for longer periods of time and I would be on the phone and emailing Neil who would never respond or if I managed to get Frank on the phone while he was on the road, he would then do everything in his power to get the funds in. The problem would then be trying to track down Neil and practically hold his hand at the bank to get the funds for whoever was owed or for him to even write a check.

I lost track of the number of times this would happen and because by all appearances I was the one closest to Neil, people would then come down on me as to where he was and where their money owed might be.

It was absolutely embarrassing on every level and I took even more notice when my very basic small salary was not being taken care of so I could also get paid. More than once I would have to chase him down and since Moose was on the scene, then I would be made to feel like I had to practically beg for my pay while being questioned by Moose about my worth. Even then I knew it was wrong, I still shake my head now about how much I was putting up with at the time.

I was on the last of my nerves and losing the sense to care anymore as I was made to feel repeatedly by Moose that I knew nothing, and Neil inevitably sided with him. One day the talk from Neil would be how they were practically broke, the next day he would be flush with cash and shopping for themselves after Frank put in a fresh deposit at the bank.

The concerns about being able to financially open, even with everything coming into place was becoming more questionable.

And while everyone else was working to get things ready, Neil considered it part of his job to spend hours online looking for decorative items to buy and very little of it related to the operation of the business.

Neil took no interest at all in learning more about the running of the actual business, assuming he'd be making big money the moment he opened the doors so it would all be taken care of for him. He would regularly state this if he was looking for an excuse of some kind.

An example of his efforts was one afternoon they brought in a very basic-looking light fixture that cost $700. Not a decorative piece, no real reason why it would be required or with even a particular location for it in the space, just that he liked it.

When it came to buying something like a cash register because having any type of computer online cash/debit/credit system was too scary for him to imagine, he would spend time going to various second-hand stores and would end up buying not one cash register but several old, basically useless models that barely worked but he thought should somehow be pieced together, again, at least until the money started flowing in.

For the most part, anything that was on the list of essentials from the beginning for the bathhouse was becoming less and less essential. Even down to locks for every locker, towels, cleaning supplies, the basics to him he couldn't see a reason for or if he did get something required, he would purchase three times the amount which would be far more than required. And Moose had no idea in the first place of what would be needed so he was no help at all, if anything he was nothing but a hindrance.

To get around town for these shopping trips, Moose had his own, very old, used sports car that kept breaking down, nothing to write home about. It basically had the power of a sewing machine but was set on wheels.

With the opening of the business about to take place, they couldn't have that, after all, they felt like they had to look the part (for whatever that was), plus taking taxi's all the time was too expensive if the car wasn't working. So again, in secret, until they felt like showing it off, they went out and put down a deposit on a very expensive Range Rover.

Though for all the efforts of a show they were putting on for others, more cracks were appearing and it was becoming even more transparent to everyone.

I and others tried in every way and with every amount of patience to stay friends with Neil, remind him of previous fun times, anything to stir memories and bring him back to the person we knew and loved in many ways, but he was too far gone now.

Neil was now losing weight again, and for some reason, he decided to grow a beard which just ended up making him look even more gaunt.

When he had a new deposit of funds, his outlook and energy were better but if the money ran out, trouble would start from every angle.

With these ups and downs came tension between Neil and Moose, always loud and dramatic with lots of yelling and things being thrown. It was obvious to everyone, what Moose thought he was getting into wasn't paying off as soon as he thought. But when it was good between them, they ruled the world so don't you dare show or say anything different.

For myself, I tried my best to keep everything on track and everyone happy, I took on responsibilities I shouldn't have in the first of all because they needed to be done and Neil simply didn't feel like doing it.

My life became very stressed because of the ongoing situation, and any time I'd come into the site to do work. I felt very much taken for granted, ignored about business concerns and the opening date while being constantly called everything under the sun by Moose either to my face, alluded to, or even in claims to other people that might have come on to the site.

When it came time to discuss and finish up my work agreements for when the place was in operation. Forget it. When I gave the paperwork to Neil, without reading anything, he passed it on to Moose who made a mockery of it. It was bad enough I had to beg to get paid, even part of my current salary.

Since my work agreement was now on the table, and Neil telling me in a moment together that I was still needed, I stayed around. This though aggravated Moose as it was obvious, he wanted me out with the opening of the bathhouse being so close.

Any moment and excuse he had, if I was on the site, he was coming at me, claiming I wasn't putting in any real efforts and saying I was useless and that I should just get out. The yelling was enough from this unstable man, more than once I literally thought he was going to just take a swing at me with a hammer to the back of my head one day or something, he was increasingly becoming unhinged and on the verge of being physical in his aggressive state.

Moose did not want me there at all and in emails and calls with Frank keeping him updated on a daily basis without holding back, Frank would practically beg me to stay as I would be, "rewarded immensely for all my efforts."

With Neil becoming more like a zombie again showing zero emotion, and friends telling me forever to leave, one day I finally just grabbed my personal belongings and quietly left.

I came home, felt sad but also had a sense of relief, I let friends and family know I was no longer associated with this place, along with the local LGBTQ business community I was close to, the property manager, and anyone that had or still did work on that site as I didn't want to go down with that ship when I had already sunk enough.

Within a day or two of leaving, I was trying to move forward while reflecting on what I had given to this bathhouse of what was a couple of years too long of literal blood, sweat, and tears.

I was getting emails and text messages from all kinds of people about the shit show that was apparently taking place at the site. Plenty of which I found amusing, frustrating, predictable, and sad.

A couple of months after the initial drama had passed to what I had been privy to, I was feeling better about life in general and even got a new job that actually paid well, on time, with full benefits, and in a completely different field.

One evening, after work relaxing at home, I opened up the

local LGBTQ community paper to see a huge advertisement about Neil's bathhouse having a grand opening with an actual date.

My first thought was, how did he afford that advertisement as he was already in arrears with the media company? And the second thing I did was laugh, yet I also had a bit of concern and curiosity.

Naturally, I was alerted to this news again along with the ongoing gossip from people in town. I listened, but my gut instinct said the opening night will be busy with those mostly curious as to what took so long, but also knowing all the small details that still needed to be taken care of in the business, things won't be managed well.

The customers will be happy about a new venue in town but then quickly disappointed and lining up with complaints so it wouldn't be long until they closed for business.

The time for their opening night came and went, if a friend or former customers I knew from the bathhouse days approached me on the street or contacted me personally, I would get all kinds of updates, even the property manager and building caretaker would contact me or ask questions with concerns over things I no longer had access too.

During a shift at my new job about a month after the new bathhouse opened, I got a text message from Frank, he was in town, could I meet him for coffee? It sounded urgent. I hesitated but being curious I agreed to see him the next afternoon at a coffee shop near the apartment he shared with a co-worker.

It was actually good to see Frank the next day, he seemed happier which was nice to see yet knowing his financial situation due to the bathhouse, the feelings were of uncertainty.

He had gone through the trouble of baking me a banana

bread loaf which was also not like him while putting on a positive front. After the small talk was over, he got down to it.

Frank let me know he was out of town while the first night the bathhouse opened was taking place and from what he was told at least, it went well, it was busy and they were running off their feet to keep up.

But at the same time, they got lots of complaints about things not working, cleanliness, the range of porn, the costs to get in, numerous lock issues for doors, thefts, lighting, you name it and the complaints hadn't ceased since.

Neil was down to his last $1600 and that's what he opened the bathhouse with, Frank was working double-time to try and infuse more cash but he also had big concerns with Neil because he did not look healthy and the fighting between Neil and Moose got so bad that the police had to be called not only to the bathhouse but also to where they lived numerous times as there were now physical altercations between the two.

Neil was currently living at the bathhouse again, sleeping in one of the rental rooms as Moose had kicked him out with the police present at their last fight yet Moose was demanding Neil continue to pay for the condo rental.

None of this surprised me, from there in the conversation, apparently, Neil felt I had back-stabbed him in a way because I left the bathhouse project but Frank told me he sorted Neil's ass on that one quickly.

With Moose gone, Neil was hoping I would come to the bathhouse to see him, and Frank flat out told me he wanted me to come work at the venue again to which I laughed and shook my head no. Even with his promises to back pay me and give me a top salary with bonuses.

I knew this was coming, and what the meeting would be about and reminded Frank of everything that went down, how unreal it was, how fucked up the whole situation is, and that this bathhouse will not last.

Frank actually agreed and then begged me to at least see Neil, that Neil had missed me and as a friend and could I at least touch base. I told him I'd think about it.

Frank proceeded to email me over the next couple of days and promised me the world, I knew it was bullshit and nothing would come of it but in a way, I wanted to see for myself hoping to get some concrete answers rather than hearing the gossip of what the bathhouse looked like open, plus I was bored.

I called Neil, he answered right away, he was quiet. I asked him if he was ok, after a moment, he said. "No." I offered to meet him at the bathhouse the next night which seemed to make him feel better and he kept thanking me.

Stepping into the bathhouse the next night when it was now open felt different. First impressions stated it did have the aspects of a bathhouse walking in, which I didn't expect but thought that was good.

It took a while for a cashier to show up at the window and when he did I recognized him right away as being a late forty-something, local odd jobs type of character who I knew to have a good work ethic but a bit cagey. I told him I was there to see Neil and he buzzed me right in.

Neil was in the front lounge area. When I saw him, he looked exhausted so it felt natural to just give him a hug. He was still quiet at first but seemed open to talking about things. I flat out asked him how everything was going. Neil let me know how things started out, that it was hard, confusing, demanding and he didn't realize you have to also keep some kind of momentum going, that he was feeling overwhelmed and tired, didn't know who to trust or in general how to move forward.

Neil also made sure to tell me how he and Moose broke up, apparently, they had many verbal fights which turned physical right away to the point, he got kicked out of their condo with the police being involved so he was now living at the bathhouse in a room as he no longer had the office upstairs in the building to go to and that Moose was in contact with him and demanding all kinds of things from him.

After I left the bathhouse during the project, Neil was mad at me because he still felt he had some protection from me for not only the business but in how he was being treated by Moose. Of whom had also started up with his crack habit again (which was news to me) but it explained why they could not be found for either hours or days at a time, and the constant erratic behavior.

Neil started quietly crying, felt alone and hounded by Moose, and just didn't know what else to do. To take him away from the situation for a moment, I suggested we tour the place so he could show me, perhaps proudly, what changes have been made and overall get an idea of what it all looked like now as what appeared to be a not quite fully functioning bathhouse business.

It was a Thursday night, before 9 pm, there should have been lots of men cruising the corridors. This was certainly not the case, yet there appeared to be a lot of laundry to do, the cashier and snack bar area looked very sparse and not very secure as anyone could have slipped in behind or over the counters and taken whatever cash that might have been around, or keys for rooms and lockers, etc.

With the lights being lower now to a seductive bathhouse level compared to during construction, the ambiance was there but it felt like plenty was still missing or unfinished. The wet areas looked great, same with the steam room and dry sauna.

The rental rooms looked comfortable and like you'd expect in a bathhouse with a fitted sheet and pillowcases and even the blacked-out playrooms and glory hole sections looked good, even if they were missing some key elements such fuck benches or slings.

Knowing how money was spent though, it showed immediately in what was visually available but yet also what was missing. And any customers who have been to a bathhouse before would notice quickly and were not shy about making suggestions or listing complaints to the staff, Neil, or online as a review.

I warned them all from day one, that there will be lots of expectations for a new bathhouse, if you don't have all the necessary basics covered and more, the tide will turn against them, and after barely a month that is exactly what was happening. There is an unspoken element to the gay community that states, if they are spending their $10 for a good time, you better have it all together and more. Just because you are opening a gay business does not automatically mean long-term and immediate support.

Excuses for not having things set up right from the start (for whatever that might be) by telling people you are a new business and that you will implement everything as money is made and time goes on will not cut it, as cruel as it sounds.

And it was already showing here, on this evening, with a space of 10,000 sq ft, there were maybe seven customers aimlessly roaming around.

Nearing the end of my visit, Neil asked if I would help him. I told him I was still owed pay from before and that I put up with a ton of bullshit in the past on this project. Neil acknowledged that, I also told him I was happy enough for now in my new job and that he had quite a mess to tackle that I wasn't sure if I should be coming back. Which he seemed to understand as well.

We said our goodbyes and I went on my way, to come home to an email from Frank practically begging me to help them out, at least a little, and how happy Neil was to see me and for us to be friends again.

Here's what this fool did. The new job I had was great but I needed an edge and I don't know if it's because I got used to the conflict or if I was the kind to fight for the underdog or both but I let Frank and Neil know I would come back, but only to a small degree and with some strict measures set into place.

The first thing I wanted was my back pay owed, which they partially came through with immediately so at the time I let that go and took it as a sign of what was to probably come.

I also agreed to only come in when my time allowed as I was already working a full-time job and that anything that needed to be done when it came to the administration of the business would be followed through and there would need to be some very serious staff training done. Neil would have to get himself together, listen, and adhere to the new structure to be set into place along with some other key issues in the business.

They both quickly agreed to that, so at first, I came in a couple of nights a week, and then before I knew it, I was back about 4 nights a week while still working my other job.

I walked into a total shit show the first night back. It was astounding how quickly the bathhouse when downhill from my visit with Neil.

The so-called employees Neil had kind of hired were the last people you would want for the job or any job for that matter.

Their noses got out of joint quickly when they were told I

was coming back to help get things better in line, and even when I explained to them, I'm not taking over, just helping out for a little while. I was now a threat because they had already seen Neil as being their new target for their agendas to use for everything they could. And Neil wasn't acting as an owner and employer but rather gave in to their random requests and demands without question as he thought of them as his new friends.

The cashier that had let me in to see Neil the first night, really got upset as he thought he was walking into a management position and was already being paid as such at least until those checks stopped.

No legal employee paperwork had been done at all, and anything to do with taxes was an afterthought. I was soon to find out these so-called employees were making up their rules than to top it off their work hours, writing it on a piece of paper for Neil, and in turn, he would write them a paycheck for what they claimed they were owed. No confirming their hours worked, no income tax, employee benefit deductions, or anything of the sort dealt with first.

Observing the rapidly declining situation, there were very few customers. They might have a rush of people come in near midnight on a weekend, but when they discovered there weren't many men to meet and play with there, it was like they'd just jerk off on their own and leave.

There were maybe a handful of employees, who considered themselves friends of Neil who would just show up and claim to be working out of the blue. The ones who seemed more regular as staff to the business all had various motives and were quick to try and triangulate a situation between each other and Neil, it was even attempted on me by a so-called employee but I sorted him out soon enough and I kicked him out of the club.

To add to it all, Moose was still in the picture, not in the business, at least whenever I was there but still hovering over and demanding what he thought should be coming his way.

This was at a time when the government had recently announced, mainly for tax purposes, that anyone living with someone for 6 months or more in a year, could be considered common-law spouses, so they could take advantage of any tax benefits and whatever else came with that spousal partnership.

I found out Moose was using this to his strength in every way you can imagine and was claiming he was going to sue Neil for spousal support. It's funny to look back at the desperation of that old man now, but because of his threats in the past, Frank ended up paying Moose about $25,000 to go away, which seemed to do the trick...for the trick.

This was the true final time for me, I was seriously wasting my time, no money owed was coming my way but they payout the asshole Moose. I knew the bullshit was going to happen again. It wasn't even about the money; it was the challenge to try and salvage the business which well before then had no hope in hell.

I left quietly again after one last time in a total mess of a bathhouse, but when begged to come back by Frank, I had some harsh words for him and bluntly told him he wasn't ever going to recoup his investment, to wrap it up now.

For the most part, I was left alone by Frank and Neil (who apparently felt I had no loyalty to him), I would hear the rumors about the bathhouse but wouldn't act upon anything, why bother.

It got to the point that they had asked the property manager to invest in their business, of which he rightly didn't do, then they came to me in a roundabout way to invest with them numerous times, which I didn't do. The nerve.

The caretaker of the building had let me know that there were no employees in the business as Neil couldn't afford to pay them anymore or give them items from the bathhouse in exchange for payment, which led to more issues.

Neil was then attempting to have straight nights which really didn't work out well in the least but what did come of that was pimps in the neighborhood were paying Neil a cut so that their clients could bring in prostitutes and use the rental rooms.

Any comment or review on the place online was not very kind and would say mainly two things. That there were no customers and that the place had become a crack den.

While that was all happening, for a business that easily cost almost $1.5 million dollars to build, Neil was selling items from the club in a feeble attempt to pay the rent on this massive business property. To also save some hassle for the local pimps, he let some of the prostitutes actually try and live in some of the rental rooms, while he continued to live in the venue.

It was all just a matter of time now when I got a frantic call from the building caretaker to rush down to the bathhouse. I was at my job so that wasn't going to happen and the caretaker knew I was long gone so I was curious why he thought I should be there, to then find out bailiffs had arrived and were taking whatever wasn't locked down out of the bathhouse. This also then appeared in the local gay press and when asked if the bathhouse was being closed down, Neil told the reporter that it wasn't, that he was updating the place.

The new locks on the doors after that though told the rest of that story.

The last time I saw and heard from Neil and Frank was the last time. I have no idea of what happened to them except for, of course, the rumors. I assume Frank went on with his work life and knowing they both owed a great deal of money in the city, and Neil's personality, I was told Neil went into hiding, left the city, and was last living with his elderly mother in a far off, small town.

CHAPTER
TWENTY TWO

Now that the drama with that bathhouse fiasco was over. It was the last I would be contacted by Neil and Frank and with time for reflection, a lot of lessons were learned.

Even with the uncertainty of that time period, there was still a lot of predictability about it all, I could see what was going to happen, and then it did. I should have walked away a million times but I also think we sometimes go down certain paths with a glimmer of hope, even when we know better inside for reasons yet to discover.

I was happy enough at my full-time job, the people I worked with were wonderful and normal as can be, it was nice to be in a work atmosphere where people got things done and there wasn't so much gossiping and backstabbing, it was actually something I had to get used too. I never dreaded going to this job so I must have been happy enough with it and if I was asked to work overtime, I always accepted as I was used to working in a 24/7 environment anyway and like to keep busy, and at least I was asked and had the option to say no.

The only small issue I ever had with the job was, even with every day being different in terms of tasks and client situations, it wasn't challenging enough for me. I would stay because it was safe and predictable and I probably needed that at the time. Yet I knew it was going to be a stepping stone of some sort, something to fill my time while my entrepreneurial spirit worked on other plans. I needed to be on the fringe of something and striving for more.

I didn't have to wonder and wait that long as after Frank and Neil's bathhouse was shut down, one afternoon I was contacted by the property manager of the building the venue was located in.

Rumors in the community had moved on from the various theories about why the place had closed for business, to then what would or should go in its place and exactly who might be stepping in.

The downtown crowd was always full of talk with little action behind the words given the fact that it's such an expensive city to live in and there really aren't a lot of people that actually have the deep pockets required to introduce a venue such as a new nightclub, pub or even another bathhouse to the community. No matter how much of a front they put on to others that they are loaded with cash.

Since I had always been on good terms with the property manager and could be relied upon, he was wondering if I could get together with him and the building caretaker at the former bathhouse site.

Knowing I wouldn't have to deal with Neil, Frank, or Moose again, and being very curious as to what the place looked like after its final days, along with what they wanted to discuss, although I had an inkling, I agreed to meet with them.

With what had taken place, it felt strange to go back to the bathhouse a couple of days later. Cringing memories came flooding back as I approached the building and even more so when we met outside the front entrance and went inside.

It was nice to see the property manager and building caretaker again, they were always friendly and to the point which I appreciated.

Stepping into the bathhouse you got an immediate sense of abandonment, that things did not feel right and did not end well here at all.

Once through the front security doors and into the main entrance and lounge area, things immediately looked unceremoniously stripped out, disassembled, broken, bashed, and banged up. It still had the semblance of a bathhouse but felt very barren and like someone had to leave abruptly.

Even though the property manager and caretaker had been in the place a few times since closing, they stated it was still weird for them too as they saw the progress from day one to this now sad ending.

As we talked, we slowly walked through the venue, where they would point out things that had been changed not according to plan and could even be considered a safety hazard as we passed by various damaged areas.

It was quite shocking to see what reeked of desperation and utter confusion. It was as though Neil was trying to dramatically change the design of the space, which was a habit of his anyway, perhaps to try and entice new clients but in turn, he was removing key elements and playing with the soul of it and it also easily reflected what must have been his mindset at the time.

Other impaired areas could have been done by customers given the type of clientele he was apparently catering to at the end as it otherwise didn't make sense. There were holes punched into walls, doors practically ripped off of hinges, lighting fucked around with, and many other things broken or ripped away.

The main interior walls and rooms through the maze of hallways were intact but you could also tell changes were made that would go against any fire regulations and code.

You could tell Neil had sold off pieces, even the banks of lockers which is what customers need to store their clothes when they don't rent a room so not sure of what his idea was there on how that would work but he obviously needed the money.

It looked as though he had been selling off almost anything possible and then the bailiffs stepped in to take out what they could in the rest of the place. Overall, the main building structures and segments required of the bathhouse were left but it was down to the bare bones now except for lots of business paperwork, personal items, and garbage strewn in rental rooms piled high and left behind.

The property manager and caretaker didn't hold back in what they had to say, much of what I was hearing about at the end of those bathhouse days appeared to be true.

They were stunned at what had happened the last couple of months and weeks and I knew how extremely generous and patient they had been with Neil. It all ended simply because Neil and Frank were in such arrears with the rent, of which Neil was warned and received notices about frequently they told me. During the last time I tried helping them out, they were in denial that the business was about to be finished. Even though I was told Frank had handled the rental situation but it was just more secrets, bullshit, and lies.

The only way out for the property management company was to evict them and they said their main worry during that period was that someone was going to get badly hurt in the place or something would happen to the building in general while those days of eviction counted down.

In the same breath, it was mentioned that it's now all in the past. And with a positive smile, they both stated that they were looking forward to the future.

After the walkthrough of the space ended, we made our way back to the main lounge, we had all gotten to know each other better throughout this particularly strange bathhouse building process and they knew my work history; with them, I was always the one easily accessible when Neil and even Frank were off on one of their disappearing acts.

Then, without hesitation, they asked if I know anyone in the bathhouse industry that might want to take the place over?

I knew this was likely one of their intentions in us gathering for a meeting and I had an idea immediately; it might be a long shot but it couldn't hurt to find out. I told them to give me a couple of days, that it was fantastic to see them and that I would reach out to a number of people I know. For myself, I didn't know what this would mean with my future, but if you don't ask, you don't know if you never at least tried.

On the way home after the meeting, I was thinking of a million different ideas and plans but knew the key person to contact for at least some feedback was Kevin.

I knew Kevin was busy with managing a new bathhouse in the city where he lived, as he had mentioned how it was a tough process getting everything together for the construction of the business, but now that it was in full running mode, things were good.

Brian, the same owner that had owned the first bathhouse I managed also owned a couple of bathhouses where Kevin lived, at the time it was one of the reasons Kevin moved back to his hometown city. This way he could help Brian by taking on the responsibilities by managing the bathhouses as the owner at the time wanted to slow down and retire.

After our owner, unfortunately, died around the first time our bathhouse was destroyed by the fire, the owner's brother who was a silent partner later sold the larger bathhouse to a company as an ongoing process of simplifying his own business operations.

Kevin then got on board with the new owners and took on various roles (as you do with this kind of job). They basically gutted and rebuilt a new bathhouse to their brand and standard, so Kevin and I were both dealing with everything to do with the construction of these places in a span of a couple of years and close to the same time. Once construction was completed he became their bathhouse manager for that city's location and he seemed to enjoy it.

Since Kevin and I were longtime friends, I had been keeping him up on all the happenings of not only the first bathhouse and the fire incident and the ongoing issues after that as a way to once in a while vent. I'd ask him for advice and it was just nice to talk to someone that knew what this whole bathhouse business was about, so I kept him completely updated with this last bathhouse project.

When I got home, I emailed Kevin to tell him about the meeting I had with the property manager and caretaker at the site of the former bathhouse.

To add to that, being a bit of a history buff and thinking it might come in useful as part of a historic time in the city with the LGBTQ community, I knew this bathhouse had not done well and was closed because of poor business decisions. But I thought if it might be my last time in the place as I didn't know the full intention of the meeting, I would at least document with pics taken with my phone of what the place looked like in the end, as I had kept a record of images throughout the duration since before the construction anyway.

In the email, I mentioned to Kevin everything that was discussed in the meeting as I never held back with him. I also attached the photos I took, so that he could see how things were left but that the majority of the main aspects of the place were still intact.

I didn't know much about the bathhouse company he was now working for, just that during their construction, like myself, Kevin was putting in a ton of hours but at least getting paid and he seemed to also be rewarded for his efforts, he was happy and that they seemed to know what they were doing and got down to business.

At the end of the email, I told him that I didn't know what their current situation was having just built a bathhouse, I assume they are busy now that they are open, but that if they were looking for another business in another city, this place would obviously need some work but the property manager is fine with another similar business coming into the building and the property is available.

In Kevin's response back the next day, he was surprised by the photos, yet not really given Neil's handling of things from what I kept him updated on, he even reminded me how he predicted the closure. He seemed a bit on the fence about everything but intrigued. I knew Kevin wouldn't have an actual definite answer and discussions with the owner of his bathhouse and team would have to take place so he'd get back to me.

That was all I needed to hear. I considered approaching other owners in other cities (not that there is a lot of choices), but their bathhouses were not quite as up to par when it came to standards.

A few days later, after more emails, photos, calls, and discussions of interest, things started to move forward quickly.

Kevin and a few top members from the head office of the bathhouse he was working for arrived in the city, we met with the property manager and we all had a tour of the space. Lots of tough questions were asked, including to myself in regards to the whole bathhouse construction process, and without a lot of fanfare but plenty of due diligence on both sides, plans were slowly coming to fruition.

When both sides saw the possibilities and got some more background knowledge. Meetings started to increase, more emails and conference calls were held along with some nail-biting situations and fingers being crossed. With all that, a long-term lease was signed and everything started to change rapidly again.

Arrangements were made for Kevin to move back to town and for us to be on board to be the prime personnel to renovate the facilities for us to open. It meant I would have to give notice at my job which I was sad about yet felt confident in my decision and about the world I was heading back into as this extensive team seemed to run their businesses like a finely tuned machine, had years of experience behind them in numerous cities and Kevin and I would be able to work as a team with our own bathhouse to manage, that last part was an absolute joy to me.

Getting into it all immediately, I was nervous at times as so much was new and we seemed to have to take on not only what was in front of us, but keep updated on the other bathhouse functions too and I didn't want to make mistakes.

Some of the team from head office could be hard asses and blunt but I was used to that, the only thing that was confusing on occasion was there were so many top people surrounding the owner it could be difficult to know who to go to or who to take an answer from, as they all had a history in the bathhouse industry and each of them with their varying personalities wanted to run the show their way even if they say you are the boss of your place.

Thankfully though Kevin was there as a guide and helped with giving me more background on everyone and on what to do so I just tried to take everyone's advice, ran plenty by Kevin first, yet was also expected to speak up about my experiences in the industry and just evolve with everyone and everything happening as it would all, hopefully, fall into place.

We now had the bathhouse space, but it certainly wasn't a turnkey situation by just putting a sign up out the front that we were open for business.

Again, the legal paperwork had to be set up with the registration of the business, insurance and a tremendous amount of the venue was to be upgraded, so more designs had to be professionally done and that meant approvals would be needed from city hall once again which was another minimum 10-week process.

During this time, once Kevin was settled back into the city, we spent our days helping to take care of all the administrative paperwork, do what small construction upgrades we were allowed, set up contracts with all the suppliers for things like professional cleaning supplies, bedding, and towels, obtain office equipment, etc. But most of the work was project managing the site for the renovations and the very long list of items miscellaneous and tedious things that needed to be done.

In the midst of all of this, I also went to a couple of their other bathhouses for more in-depth and hands-on training to learn more about those particular businesses in those cities which gave me a much better understanding of their brand and how the operations ran as we were close to opening ourselves. Those were long, busy days with very little sleep but it was good to put more faces to names and they were very patient and helpful in many regards.

It all certainly answered more questions I had and prepared me for what was about to take place with our establishment as it had been a hot minute since I was in a truly functioning, busy bathhouse.

Back at our bathhouse, the heating and air conditioning systems were being fine-tuned, new water systems were installed for better, more reliable functioning, and a dry sauna was introduced next to the updated wet sauna.

One big thing that we definitely required was to have a jacuzzi installed. City Hall had stated at first it wouldn't be approved as they were trying to stop them from being introduced into any new developments because of how frequently they had to be maintained for health and safety regulations.

No matter how much pleading, it was on the cusp of not happening, especially for a bathhouse business but we also knew how much of a big draw they were for customers.

As the countdown approached for us to open, I had kept my best friend in town updated on some of the progress of the bathhouse and told her, it was looking like the city wasn't going to allow for us to have a hot tub.

She happened to work in the main office of the big stadium a couple of blocks from our downtown location. This stadium held all the big concerts and sports events and she mentioned how that seemed weird we weren't allowed a jacuzzi as the sports team just had their huge locker room renovated with two new jacuzzis installed next to each other and by chance, this was even noted in the local newspaper about the team having their locker room completely upgraded.

With this information, I told Kevin and the team that this might be a way to convince those in charge at the city hall. Since if this sports team were very recently allowed two jacuzzis and were in the same vicinity as us, why couldn't we have one that is highly monitored? We could even possibly get the exact same model since it seemed approved by the city?

We proceeded with it right away and our argument worked, it was a bit funny how it happened, so once that gave us the approval, we ordered the same jacuzzi and got it installed. Although not grand in scale like the company was used to in their other bathhouses, it held quite a number of people and was very easy to drain and maintain.

As our opening deadline approached, more items on the checklist were getting done like the upgraded music, sound, and video system that was state of the art. We still had to of course watch spending but if it was in our other bathhouses and was reliable and part of the brand, we had it too.

That included a 100k worth of fitness equipment, a number of the largest and best flat-screen TVs available, a completely online check-in and out computer sales system that let us know dates, times, lengths of stays, over time, customer counts...you name it at any time of the day or night and an online floor plan of the space to do more tracking. That alone made working life much more precise and easier to manage.

Paint colors and lighting is something many don't seem to take into consideration, especially in a large social environment as it can at times be all about those subliminal feelings and perceptions.

Knowing this from building the previous bathhouse, it was continued and enhanced even more in this new bathhouse. A subtle pink undertone in light-colored paint actually calms and keeps a person relaxed along with enhancing body colors next to it no matter your nationality.

Instead of using black paint, we used a particular shade of brown in most of the corridors that also enhanced skin tones, followed by, of course, low lightbulb wattages, and in our case, we used a number of yellow-hued light bulbs and I have never seen so many dimmer switches installed in my life than in this place, on top of what was previously installed in all the rental rooms.

Each rental room had a flat-screen TV and we had wired in at least 30 different channels of every porn genre imaginable for a client to choose from in their room when they weren't already passing by some form of porn on the big screens in the hallways and lounge areas.

One of the main ideas was to add as many elements of attractions as possible so that once you are inside, you weren't really given a reason to leave. As a reference again, it was a bit like Vegas, with tons of vending machines selling every kind of food, beverage, sex toys, and lube, and a bank ATM machine was installed.

Even if you didn't feel like having sex, it was just a great place to get away from the outside world for a few hours. Hit the gym, sit in the jacuzzi or steam room, watch a recently released movie or sports game in the main lounge or take 10-20 steps in any direction and watch porn.

It was a tense and tiring time but the thrill of opening soon and at a pace I never felt before was exhilarating.

As the date approached, more of those from head office and the other bathhouses, along with the owner and his posse were arriving to make sure everything needed was already in or about to be implemented in the bathhouse.

Everyone was working both day and night to get it all going, some were playing around or not contributing much, but I had obviously experienced this before so came to expect bullshit games as part of a power-play or more often because they were trying to leave their mark on the venue.

It wasn't anything one couldn't handle and I still felt very confident in the direction we were going, just one of those things you took notice of as many of these people, I was either just being introduced to or were already building a working relationship with at the time so it was beneficial to know what everyone's work ethics and quirks were as then you knew who to work with more to get things accomplished.

CHAPTER TWENTY THREE

The next step to opening the bathhouse of course was to hire employees to come on board. To me, we needed to have good people that weren't into playing games having experienced enough of that already.

Thankfully we lived in a city that is a cultural melting pot as I thought it was important that the team should project a strong sense of diversity represented for our new customer base as they too tend to come from every background imaginable.

What I didn't want were men that would-be players and with the amount of time I had already spent in the industry, there could be plenty, and of course a few who will still slip through the cracks.

We were about to be what I considered the top bathhouse location on this side of the country and I wanted people that would be happy and proud of where they worked. It was also thankfully coming to the point in society where bathhouses were finally more accepted as part of a social scene and nothing to shy away from, that part I had to be more open to because of what had been instilled in me for so long beforehand.

With that, at times men that work in a bathhouse can be categorized generally into a few types of employees. And much of this I was hoping we could try to change what was seen as the norm in the industry (or gay community) as I wanted us to stand out on better ground for the long haul.

Like in any business, some employees are just trying their best to make it in the city or flat-out survive in the world. In a bathhouse, there will be honest, down-to-earth, unassuming yet handsome men who are responsible, sensitive, empathic, and just want to do a good job. Those are the men to be valued as part of the team as they also tend to get along so well with the customers and fellow employees and management.

Employees that are working part-time at a bathhouse for extra cash and are usually working this job while also going to university or maintaining another full-time job. With that kind of work ethic, you sometimes wish they would be the ones you'd also hope would go full time due to their work ethic.

There will be those men that are working like crazy and will ask for or accept any overtime hours they can get as they need the money while they use the rest of their energy trying to figure out how to make a better living for themselves overall. Their position may be that the place is a stepping stone until they find something else. Just like people from any other work environment and it's to be expected and they can still do a great job.

You'll also come across men that don't want people to know they work in a bathhouse simply because of what the place conjures up for the general public or how it might affect their private life. Completely acceptable. After a while, you'll notice their guard going down more after seeing how many everyday patrons check-in and out all the time and they also tend to still do a good job. They'll just tell their family or friends if asked that they work in a fitness center or something as it comes across as safe and normal.

This next group of men I'm going to describe is an obvious sweeping generalization of a type of employee that can be prominent in the industry or more so as I'm sure many of us have met in the community. We could at times see these men coming from a mile away with their motives, maybe not at first but for sure when they think the coast is clear.

These are the ones that are clean cut with gorgeous model looks with a buff body but that can be lazy when it comes to working. They may not be the smartest but they are eye candy for the customers who might hope they could nab them for some fun on the side, so you might hire them, or are told to hire them but you know they won't be around long.

While they are on the job with their muscle God vibes, you hope they aren't also dabbling too hard in the booze and drugs, especially with the party and play scene as you'll soon find out if they are, even with the approval of the head honchos, they'll be trouble for the bathhouse.

When the employees and customers start complaining about them, then it's time for them to go.

These can be the employees who will put on a terrific, well-rounded front when they first start, but then after they receive their first or second paycheck and they think they have a handle on how the place runs, is when things start to turn for the worst.

If they've been partying in their spare time, they'll start either arriving for shifts late or want to leave early with a flimsy excuse. They'll be flustered and frustrated easily due to lack of sleep from doing who knows what?

The customers that would show up before just to be around him during his shift, will start to lose their admiration for him and maybe even complain if he's been rude to them or pulling off some bullshit in the club.

These, in my experience, are a dime a dozen men, that tend to be the people that will show up in the big city with even bigger dreams with a deep desire to be accepted to what is considered to be locally the A-1 Gay scene.

Some of them tend to learn late that looks don't always win, it's having cash that talks. They will have numerous, rotating roommates in their basement suite or a one-bedroom apartment which will be their little secret for never hosting and most of that crew will probably be in the same position and they will pretend they are friends at least until someone better comes along.

These can be wonderful men with good hearts that also don't necessarily fall into that segment as long as they have some direction in life and aren't all over the map or influenced by what those deem essential in the LGBTQ community, materialistically anyway.

You'll know who they guys are from the start when you look past how flirty and handsome they are, as even during the interview process they will tell you they need to have the whole week off for Pride, yet they will also want to party in the bathhouse during that time and can their friends have some free passes?

These guys can be a lot of fun, especially when they first start working in the bathhouse, just over time you'll notice or hear from other staff how they aren't pulling their weight during a shift by not completely cleaning rental rooms properly, always on their phone or letting basics like letting the laundry pile up.

If they start to take their job more seriously, things can work out otherwise you just know by the telltale signs when things might be coming to an end.

With this new bathhouse, I was hoping and planning with the help from Kevin that we'd form a great team and have little to none of that last kind of employee who will just add to the drama and work.

We had placed ads in the local LGBTQ media and online for the positions we were looking to fill, those being of housekeeping clerks and cashiers.

At first, the resumes and people applying in person seemed slow or were just not suitable at all. The candidates that did show up in person came across as enamored by the place just from the changes in the entrance alone if they knew the short history of the location.

With us hiring employees also came those that I either knew from the other bathhouses I worked at as past customers or those that worked for the competition also applied, which was all fine.

Some of the men that applied also thought it would be a quick way of making money on the side and thinking given the kind of business that they could be paid under the table. Not happening.

Then some expected you to hire them, without a resume, simply because we both knew each other in some capacity so they should just be handed a job.

All in all, we ended up gathering a good group of men to help open the bathhouse. You could see them take to their positions during training with enthusiasm, lots of questions and curiosity, excitement, and even nervousness but bonds were formed without hesitation. Since they started to do training well before opening, a natural support system was developed for each other as who knew what would take place once the doors opened for business.

Word on the street was, from what I could tell, favorable and optimistic about a new bathhouse coming onto the city scene.

What seemed to be different this time around is we didn't appear to be overwhelmed with a ton of people just trying to find out the latest gossip about the place or what they could also get out of it, nor what was good about it or bad about it.

I think because there were no secrets to hide. Only that we wanted to pleasantly surprise everyone when they came into the bathhouse to see how fresh and new everything was and how every little detail was in place along with how effectively all the aspects about it functioned.

The only thing I would ever see on social media, yet we took no notice about it as we were confident in our position was some people didn't like the fact that a big bathhouse company was coming into town as it took away an element of it being independently owned. My thinking on that was, who as an individual can afford such an enterprise in this town? Please stand up.

Others on social media were also trying to start a competitor's war on who would have the better bathhouse. And we hadn't even opened yet. Those comments were juvenile and competition is good for everyone as far as I'm concerned.

With us about to open, marketing was already underway and done a lot different than what I was used to or even allowed to do half the time due to budget restraints.

This meant I was about to be put under the wing yet again by who was considered the main marketer of the whole company, Colin. When Colin arrived in town and we got to finally meet, he was nice but I could tell he was also sizing me up.

Colin was the kind of person that did the job he was supposed to do efficiently and by whatever whim those higher up might ask for, he had a long history in the business, knew everyone with their strengths and weaknesses, was open about himself but only to a point and liked to divert the conversation if he didn't know what to say or even how to act socially in a moment.

I felt we got along well for what we needed to do but also felt Colin was a bit of a spy of sorts and because of his length of time in the business he could come up with whatever story he chose to tell to the right people if necessary. Colin was also looked upon differently because he wasn't in the thick of it in the business with customers every day, he had his unique position and the ear to the right people if necessary.

To me, at the time we seemed like friends, maybe because I was still new to the company though we both still had to figure out the trust thing as one does in the industry. You could tell Colin had his moment in the sun and was just that bit more needed around because of his length of time already knowing the ropes, he was considered a fixture in the firm, so to speak, and knew how to kiss the right person's ass.

Colin was handsome in a nerdy way, socially adept to a point but I always felt like he needed a good hug and cry. I don't know if he ever even had a boyfriend but he was a sweet guy.

In terms of his work, you could tell he basically remembers producing graphics on a VIC-20 computer and became enthralled with the visuals world and took to new programs and applications with ease and built a solid, if specialized genre portfolio.

Colin's first visit was probably longer than necessary, I kept thinking his hotel bill was going to be huge for the amount he was needed and he certainly worked what hours he chose to do but did accomplish everything on time and by demand if necessary.

He worked for the company but it also seemed like he was an independent freelancer by the way he talked, and that this was one of his clients, yet as far as I knew it was his only client.

Upon meeting Colin, he was slightly quiet at first, I think because of the key individuals who were surrounding us but when we were one on one, he was more personable and asked a ton of questions to get to know more about the city, who was who, what nightclubs and bars catered to what particular crowd, etc. Which was fantastic and I told him what I only knew at this time since I wasn't frequenting the nightclubs a lot anymore as I had become bored with it all.

I was going to have to get back into it all though, part of which I kind of dreaded because it could be so predictable but got back into the feel for it all, and I was looking forward to introducing myself to the owners, managers, DJ's, along with their clientele to let them know about us being a part of the LGBTQ community.

On his own, Colin checked out the competitor's bathhouse (he thought it lacked a lot), plus some of the local bars, restaurants, and nightclubs.

Then it was our turn to go out over a couple of nights. I could tell compared to where he was from, he found our city a bit provincial and I agreed with him there, so he thought our promo scheme was going to have to come on even stronger, which again I agreed as the crowd, no matter how leathered up and tough they could sometimes present themselves were very cautious in many ways in terms of what they did socially.

I set up meetings with owners or managers beforehand to let them know who we were and about the business and that we would like to have a hand in sponsoring events if necessary. Or more so show up during a nightly event at a bar or nightclub and speak to patrons to introduce ourselves (which Colin had me do since he was technically a visitor to the city).

Doing some of this could be unnerving as Colin would so intensely watch me approach men to tell them more about the bathhouse opening and hand out free passes that I was worried about making mistakes. I even told Kevin about it the next day as Colin was just so up my ass about it (yet he certainly didn't seem to be a social butterfly in the least) and yet he expected it to be done his way with his exact words yet that is not how people spoke or approached others in our city and speaking to Colin directly about it went nowhere.

Anyway, the deeds were done, we went out at all hours of the night while I still did my work helping set up the bathhouse during the day but it was very good to get to know exactly who was who more in the scene as an update and we were all able to work forward together from there.

And Colin was very helpful for whatever we needed once the business was in operation. I still felt there was a bit of a wall built up between us for some reason but as time went on, I valued him more as a friend and in the end, we actually became good friends.

During this time, an important part of setting up the bathhouse for the opening date was to have a community health nurse involved.

When AIDS struck the gay community decades ago, many things to do with the bathhouse industry changed drastically which meant such a venue would have to learn to evolve and help educate their patrons.

Depending on where you live and who owns your neighborhood bathhouse establishment, many times LGBTQ health awareness initiatives are either slow to roll out, implemented by the city, or sadly not at all.

Bathhouses are a lot of fun, basically, anything that you can imagine takes place in such an atmosphere. That doesn't mean that you can just let your guard down though for the sake of not only yourself but others but sadly many still do so the best we can do is educate ourselves and others.

One of the things I liked about the first bathhouse I worked at was the incentive started by the owner Brian that condoms should always be free and available throughout parts of the club in bowls on tables or as the case when smoking got banned inside any business premises in the city. We used large ashtrays that were mounted on the walls in the maze of hallways and easily converted them into condom holders and they were ideal in places such as the entrances to the communal playrooms for someone to quickly grab.

This was in the late 1990s, and as you'd expect men would grab handfuls and take them home or whatever, as odd as it was to blatantly see happening at the time, you didn't give it a second thought as it was about safety first if not in the bathhouse, then hopefully elsewhere.

Brian also happened to own one of the biggest adult sex toy warehouses in the country so when weekly orders were placed to be shipped out, boxes holding thousands of condoms were always top of the list and it used to actually freak us out a bit if for some reason we started to run low on them if a new shipment hadn't arrived yet or was late as we didn't want to run out of condoms.

This all sounds normal but at the time there were plenty of bathhouses that would only give you one condom package with your towel and room or locker key when you checked in, if you wanted anymore, many owners would charge exorbitant amounts for just a few condoms which put off many people and put them at risk.

As time went on and attitudes changed, many bathhouses either on their own or with the help of local community health centers collaborated, and space was actually set up within bathhouses.

Back at the first bathhouse, we had a very kind and good-looking health nurse come in once or twice a week. We'd give him a rental room, make an announcement along with putting up signage that a health nurse was available and where if they wanted to meet with him for everything from obtaining counseling to answering safe sex questions and even getting a flu shot.

Initially when the second bathhouse was being constructed, we set up an area specifically for a health nurse to come in but from what I understand it was never utilized much, if at all, because of how badly things were organized with that owner.

With us about to open, we kept the same confidential office and area in mind and enhanced it tremendously and by chance, I was able to get the same health nurse to come on board with us once we were open. It was wonderful to see him come back and things are full circle and continually up to date with customers, even small seminar meetings were to be arranged for anyone of any gender interested in attending.

This was one of the most positive things to see, having safe spaces for members of the LGBTQ community to come in and also have group meetings about any topic imaginable as health covers more than just your body, it's also your state of mind.

CHAPTER TWENTY FOUR

Our deadline for opening the bathhouse had arrived. We had most of everything we wanted to be completed and ready to go except for some small added touches. Any other changes necessary would be made once we could see how customers interacted with the establishment with feedback from them and employees as well.

Still though, with our very fresh business permits and approvals in place, we were good to go and planned for a soft opening.

That late afternoon word was out on all forms of social media and advertising plus through the usual gossip on the streets.

With us to help hold down the fort were some members from head office for both support and to monitor how we would do in every way possible. The atmosphere was one of a mixture of excitement and nervousness for us all, even if everyone didn't show it.

One or two of those from head office didn't seem to be sure of what they should do with themselves so they ended up adding more work for us or seemed to get in the way. It appeared to be the way they just handled things, maybe even testing us out, but it was still good to have them around.

Feeling all kinds of emotion, I wanted to support the employees on the front line as best as possible as you could tell they too wanted to make a good first impression to everyone that came through the doors but we all reassured each other things would be fine.

With that, the doors were opened and those already in line started to check-in for their first time in the bathhouse. In the beginning, it was friendly, regular, everyday men, very under the radar yet happy to be amongst the first inside and full of smiles while they explored the venue.

As the evening arrived, more people started to check into the bathhouse and this is when things started to get interesting, not just for the night ahead but for the whole first few days.

We found people either got right to their own business right away in terms of hooking up, while others roamed around in awe of the venue and were eager to chat and congratulate us all. Things were ready, but not 100% so we let those know in conversation with us that more was yet to come and to tell us what they thought about the venue. All indications dictated though those men were thrilled with the establishment.

And just like with the first bathhouse too, those men that were looking for a special rated time period showed up on the dot to pay their lower set price for a room or locker, all fine and to be expected. This was another good indicator that I was in my hometown city.

Then the characters started to arrive. Those you would also expect in a bathhouse at any given time but it was fascinating to observe these men come in while everything is shiny and new, scouting out the place, with or without an agenda.

When customers started to get a handle on the bathhouse, they seemed very pleased with all the renovations and many felt like they found their own piece of man play heaven. As expected, there were those as well who had to throw in their two cents even with the couple million already spent suggesting what more we *had* to have in order to make it *the* bathhouse as the go-to spot. Like there was much choice in the city.

It is always great to get feedback both bad and good to see what we can work on. There was the occasional feeling though that anything someone didn't like and was very vocal about seemed to come from a place of perhaps jealousy or envy, you know, that bitchy queen know it all talk, but amusing.

Any of the one or two complaints we would soon find out, turned out to be something they thought they could personally add, meaning they wanted us to hire them to do their own special lighting techniques, sound system (which at least 100k was already spent on), those kinds of big-ticket items, along with how we should hire them to do our promotions, etc.

And even with having over 30 channels of every genre of porn to select from, some would complain that it wasn't enough so you knew early to just gauge everything for what it was at the time and engage with them politely and accordingly.

What was an absolute joy was seeing customers that used to go to the first bathhouse I worked at, we all got a few years older but it was nice to have familiar faces around again. We'd have some hugs and laughs and reminisced about the old times. Kevin seemed to like this aspect as well as it gave us all a chance to touch base and rekindle past friendships since he was back in town, plus because the location is only two blocks away from the first bathhouse, as word got out, more of that former crowd started to come to our venue.

The members from the first bathhouse were the ones most impressed with the upgrades and loved the whole ambiance and were so much fun to have around.

With that came the rough and tumble crowd who had

taken advantage of the Neil and the venue itself previously, some of whom were surprised first of all that they would have to pay to come in and then bold enough to still expect the same things they were getting from Neil basically for free like deluxe or VIP rooms. Another side of that was some of the men wanted to know if they could rent a room by the month using their welfare checks. Those to were to be expected and easily dealt with as telling someone no correctly can go a long way.

And although we were already fully staffed, once men got to see the place in person and how much fun people were having, some of the men would walk up to the front counter or stop us in the corridors and flat out tell us we had to hire them on the spot or ask for a job while they were wearing just a towel wrapped around their waist and not treating the bathhouse like a real working business environment, just expecting what they wanted on demand.

These were the kind of individuals we wouldn't hire anyway because if they could slip into a job that easily, then they think they'd know how to run the rest of the show to get what they wanted and do a half-ass job in the meantime if they even showed up or worked a full shift at all.

Along with having a good crowd of men in attendance, making for a fantastic first few nights, we also had various LGBTQ bar and restaurant owners trickling in who were impressed with the bathhouse. It was wonderful to chat with them in person and I loved being a liaison to see how much more we could start working together in the community.

Then too came a few nightclub owners and managers or their employees with more to follow during the weekend before their own establishments opened for business. Some were checking out the place on a more business level as we too had a top-of-the-line sound system, dramatic lighting, and ambiance.

With that, some were wanting then to set up a much stronger business connection literally simply from what they saw once they stepped inside without even exploring the place as they were that impressed. Some could walk in with an attitude, or not, but nothing that ever phased me or us, and once they got a better sense of what we were about, it was a pleasure to work together more.

Circuit party event planners we had already been in contact with, so they started showing up as well and loved what we had going on. The top event planners in town who were established were the easiest to work with once we opened, they had a strong following, were organized, and had the best intentions. We would supply them with whatever they needed, be it free passes, door prizes, sponsorship, whatever. In turn, we were on guest lists and/or given free tickets. Not that many of us had time to attend no matter how much we wanted to.

The ones that were more of a hassle were the wannabe promoters trying to break into the event planning party scene and who were trying to have a hand in managing absolutely every element of it possible which then made things mismanaged on their end while expecting the world in return.

Half the time it was like these individuals were not even doing it for the party or community, but trying to make some quick cash with hopes of also becoming a celebrity of sorts while not having to hold down a regular job, which even the top promoters were still working elsewhere. If they made claims about giving back a percentage of everything made to charity, we'd really have to check them or their motives out or give them a one-off chance because more often than not, nothing would get donated and the funds would all go to themselves leaving suppliers and charities dry.

Last but not least, and very much expected due to our city having a reputation, practically worldwide, of being a very liberal, laid-back drug haven - we had the dealers showing up the first night and from then on to some magnitude.

They'd arrive ready to set up what they thought would be their new territory and thinking we won't know the game.

As undercover as some of them thought they could be, they were easy to spot. I was still in the same city of the previous bathhouses and being great with faces, it was easy to recognize many of the men and they at times seemed more surprised to see many of us still around which could throw them off their plan, at least at first.

As the weeks moved forward at the bathhouse, both new and familiar drug dealer faces gradually kept discovering the club for the first time and at all hours. As each of them made their way in, each of them also stood out like a sore thumb.

Their eyes scanning the place for their own security concerns and because the venue was 10,000 sq ft in size over two levels and with small upgrades and changes still ongoing the first few months. Staking their claim and trying to swing deals without getting caught was a testing period for them to say the least.

The bathhouse had a shortlist of rules in bold text posted on signage in various parts of the business, many men were glad of it as it showed we would be a safe space to play and they didn't want to fuck up and be barred for some reason not known to them. On that posted list of rules of was stated any drug use or selling drugs means being automatically barred, not that it swayed dealers a whole lot if they were desperate for a deal and if they could at least get a score in first.

To be honest, this was more of a public relations front to ensure people of their safety and we tried our best to curb any dealing or partaking in drugs but men are going to sneak them in, no matter how much you try and stop it. Dealers will do what they can anyway. You felt little in the way of back up when you found out a couple of those in top positions at head office or otherwise also liked to partake while they played so depending on who and what was going on, we both monitored the situations but also had a blind eye to it all too.

What was different at this bathhouse compared to the last two I was at was everyone had to get a membership which meant they also had to show a form of valid government iden-tification, this put off some customers at first but then they agreed to it when they found out why. With dealers, it was a different story if they were desperate to sell, after a ton of ques-tions asking what and who sees the membership information, they would then hesitantly become a member. Which would also help us keep track of how often they were in the club, length of stay, etc.

The memberships were used as a form of security for ourselves and our customers. If an individual did something wrong and was barred, it would then show up on the com-puter screen with the date and brief reason why. It could also be removed or overridden (whether or not that should happen, would depend on who decided that and why). The membership also offered benefits such as a free pass after a certain number of visits, gift bags, prizes, etc.

Since all of the money, debit, and credit card transactions were online in our system, this also meant managers, owners, and head office officials can sign in and see who and how many are in the bathhouse and on waiting lists, etc. Owners and managers can go to a member's account and upgrade them by putting them ahead of a waiting list line, upgrade their pass or revoke everything and bar customers like a head cashier or clerk could do.

The bathhouse was mapped out on the screens with what rooms and lockers were where and who was checked in, how often, and for how long. If there was a waiting list for a room during a busy period, the mapping notified us when an attendant had finished cleaning a room, making it available so that notice would go up on specific screens in the bathhouse and customers waiting for a room could see their locker key number flashing to come to the front desk with their belongings and switch to their rental room. It really was part of a safety check system and valued for keeping everything running smoothly for customers and ourselves.

Still, the professional-looking environment and process were enough to rattle even those new to this particular place that thought about starting some trouble.

Our customer counts were not super high to capacity that first week until we hit the weekend hours, which didn't surprise me as it seemed typical of the city where people waited until others went first to get their feedback whether online or in person, then they made their decision to go so our numbers slowly went up from there and we were able to start forming a customer base.

The slow growth was good though as it gave us time to take care of things in the bathhouse we perhaps didn't consider amongst everything else going on, the staff were busy but not overwhelmed so they learned by experience and routine better. And we were able to acquaint ourselves with the patrons coming in on a much better, welcoming level and pinpoint those that we were going to have to keep an eye on.

Any dealers coming in from the beginning were to a relatively low degree and manageable. It was the ones that assumed they were part of the A-1 Gay scene with an attitude of being untouchable who could actually be the messy ones and who could mess a lot of people up and cause issues. Even if not removed from the bathhouse right away, we were certainly watching a few who already were on the verge of being barred.

These so-called A-1 Gays were the ones that men clamored around for some reason, mainly based on looks or if their face was nothing to write home about, at least they had the muscular body or vice versa. A strong segment of these men were also the ones overdoing it with steroids giving them no neck and more of a thickness yet they considered themselves to be the Muscle Mary type.

These kinds of men would arrive late at night and either want to be introduced to one of us in management right away, pretend to form a friendship, and pretend that you too were now part of their scene simply because you both briefly met each other.

Or they would be higher than a kite checking in with their buddies, yet slightly paranoid while their mind was reeling while checking into the biggest and most expensive room possible while half of their friends scrambled to get enough change together to each rent their own locker.

Once these men came in for the first time and had met me, from then on, they would ask the cashier at the window to get me if I was around, then they would proceed to ask for a free pass but only for the best VIP or deluxe room. If I wasn't around, they would once in a while demand a cashier call me at home or wherever I was (no matter the time) to confirm they must be allowed in for free, which was ludicrous, and talk about having no self-pride.

A portion of these men though continued to pay for what they wanted on their own. It depended on how well their level of drug dealing was if they were cheap or not if they thought it was owed to them or to try and cover the game they were playing. Each situation and person were different yet the same by their core.

Although these men were pieces of work and for the most

part predictable. Sometimes this was all just part of how things went in a bathhouse. They did bring men into the venue, hot men, and a lot of them were some of the most handsome and well-defined muscular men you've ever seen. Just with a personal issue or two that they were trying to handle all in the name of the party and play which over time, could make them not the prettiest to be around anymore.

These particular A-1 dealers would have the place buzzing, quite literally. Men were always doing something sexual while being naked anyway, but when they're flying high, any inhibitions left in a private bathhouse atmosphere were slowly stripped, again literally, away. Even those not partaking in the same activities could then also get coerced into the action so one had to be careful in what one got caught up in.

With these prime dealers, we would observe them frequently as more than once myself, and the employees would have to deal with a possible incident because of their actions. It wasn't a whole lot, but once is more than enough.

Within the first couple of weeks of opening, one so-called A-1 Gay event planner who also happened to be yet another underwear designer wannabe (both fronts), a total steroid king with two small heads and a known drug dealer had enticed a young, beautiful man that was new to town and just looking to fit in who then became an easy victim by getting the chance to meet this individual and his little group in the bathhouse.

While in the office, I was told by staff that they were worried about a guy who got in with this crowd and was acting very lethargic. Checking in on it immediately, the dealer was already attempting to get ready and leave the venue and his buddies had all conveniently dispersed. Apparently, people were a bit intimidated by this dealer on reputation, and his steroid looks alone, I wasn't. I point-blank asked him what's going on while an ambulance was called and an employee and I were taking care of the customer who was now practically passing out.

The dealer claimed everything was ok, so I demanded to know what his "friend" took, which was apparently a load of GHB. The dealer, still trying to nonchalantly leave the scene, mentioned he'll be fine, just let him sleep it off.

It was more important for us to take care of the patron affected by the drugs and since the ambulance attendants showed up right away, while they took care of him and brought him to the hospital, the dealer had checked out.

Turns out the customer who overdid things with the drugs ended up being ok as he contacted us later to thank us for the help. It had certainly put a scare into him and it was months until we saw him again but he reassured those of us that with how bad things got for him, he wasn't going to mess around again.

The dealer though, without hesitation showed up the next weekend when I was working an overnight shift and totally acted like nothing was wrong. Since I knew at some point he might come back, I spoke with management about barring him temporarily from the bathhouse but because it was early days for us, I was told to give him another chance.

When this A-1 dealer was first settling in, I walked up to him in the main lounge and asked him if he remembered me. He claimed he did, and in conversation, I tore a strip off his ego and made it very clear that he was on watch. No more bullshit, that just because we are the new guys in town doesn't mean we don't know the score. He appeared very stunned to be spoken to that way and toned it down that night but of course any other visits after that he still played around and pushed limits so he was one we had to watch.

With everything happening those first weeks and months, we were definitely on the ground running.

CHAPTER
TWENTY FIVE

With the bathhouse now fully in operation offering anything one would require to enhance your experience; more and more men continued to discover the venue that seemed to be filled with activity both day and night.

What came next being in management and even for some of our employees was that all of a sudden we didn't have to wait in line at nightclubs or bars anymore, not that some of us running the show had much time for it, but we tried. We did have the direct connections set in place with fellow LGBTQ business owners and managers but it seemed even without that, all one of us had to do was say what we did or where we worked to a bouncer, and without hesitation, we were let right inside.

As a form of gratefulness and public relations, those same people in the community that had direct access to us also of course got VIP passes to the bathhouse, along with free passes to hand out to whomever they wanted, etc. All just part of doing business.

During the opening weeks and even months, we were handing out a lot of free passes for lockers and rooms just to help build up the business and customer base plus it's to get men into the habit of coming to the bathhouse.

Being a small city especially if a weekend was approaching meant men that normally wouldn't give you the time of day on the street were all of a sudden hovering around until they could find the right person whose ass they were going to kiss. Which typically meant Kevin or me, or an employee if they thought they could get something for free.

Having experienced this before, we knew it was going to be coming well before opening day. Funny enough, all the ass-kissing never seemed to come from hard-working, happy-go-lucky average men, only from those in the scene that again, considered themselves to be part of some clique of A-1 Gays which every city seems to have in their communities.

A small percentage of these men would have a professional background of some sort and were daringly handsome men with all the charm and sense of humor but when it came to real-world stuff, they tended to ignore their personal, almost transparent issues as long as possible.

I knew a lot of these men in passing for years and can appreciate an absolutely beautiful man, but I think especially because of the industry I was in; you end up seeing every body shape and size along with dick lengths and widths imaginable, both day and night that, at least for me, made me more interested in the actual individual as the rest starts to become a blur.

Knowing what was coming next from this group and their intentions, all of a sudden they hoped I would be their new A-1 best friend, I let them play this out to a point. I let them do all the talking as though I was their new buddy, curious to see how much time and effort they put into it all, and just so they could get some free passes or better yet a VIP card.

One on one, the guys could be so sweet, genuine, and forthcoming, but even if there were just a few of them together, they seemed to try and outdo each other with wit and looks yet came off as the same. It was amusing, to say the least, and pathetic at the same time, and something a few of us at work would joke around about, as with or without free passes, they were still showing up.

Some would full-out ask for free bathhouse passes with barely a hello or an introduction, since I guess just asking for what you wanted because you were good-looking works?

Most of the time though I was constantly contacted at the club or they would somehow get my private number or email and I'd be invited to some random gay's birthday party or an event, so I guess this could be considered the payback for being with that crowd if that was what truly interested me.

Don't get me wrong, many of them got passes, part of the job was to get men to come to the bathhouse so it was no big deal. It was just interesting to see how far some of them would go for something that wasn't expensive. And it happens to all of those in management to some level, how you want to play it back is up to you.

My popularity (for whatever that was) with this specific set of gays became part of the job and I took it as such, nothing more, nothing less, and thankful that I had my true circle of friends in my life.

I now look at this as a time as a way of setting me up better for my current work-life since these guys were and still are very much like the influencers of today. Teasing the world with their looks and expecting this same world to give to them anything they desire and for free but providing very little if anything at all back to anyone.

Everything has to have a balance and with a bathhouse, it didn't hurt to have them inside the place with their good looks and hard bodies. In that case, everyone wins.

Every day customers used to tell us in conversation, these A-1 Gays might ignore you on the street any given day, but if they are all heated up because of the surroundings and ready to go, get them in a sling or part of a group scene in a playroom and anyone can have them. Also, in the dark, no one is ugly. It was obvious we working there weren't the only ones who noticed this happens.

One thing I liked to do was if a customer came into the bathhouse that regularly paid to come in or it was their first time and they didn't put on a big show about who they were and liked to keep things under the radar, especially if they were the absolute sincere and kind to those around them. I liked to discreetly offer them some free passes on the way out so that they will come again. It's another form of relationship-building to those least expecting it and they seemed to be far more appreciative of the gesture.

Over time you learned to go with your instincts about a person and in this form of business, your gut can tell you a lot about each person walking in the door.

In the bathhouse world, all of this was expected. Handing out free passes is going to bring in some vultures. It was just a matter of balancing it all as we were still trying to run an actual money-making venture.

With the bathhouse being a very freeing environment and a fun place to play, you wouldn't believe how many people you meet that don't also consider your work to be a business at all with employees and bills to pay. We'd even have to remind some of them that, especially if they had the nerve to not ask for one free pass, but expecting a handful.

You also had to be careful because if you knew they had a shitty, low-paying job but looked hot as fuck and wanted to get some action in the club, that was all fine to give them the odd free pass. But if they started asking you for extras and other peculiar favors on top of that, that's when the red flags would go up. You'd find out more about the individual as you slowly got to know them and half the time it would turn out they had an addiction issue developing and/or they were in financial trouble.

Many of us have seen it happen with popular A-1 Gays a million times sadly this way, sometimes simply by pissing off their group somehow so then, they were cast aside on their own. As their looks didn't keep them in their club this time.

They had it all going on and then slowly were losing everything, no matter how much intervention took place. Soon they would show up in the club but not acting normal just needing a safe, familiar environment, standing alone, internally stressed and worried about where their life is headed but hoping they can attain a bit of whatever they had back. Many would be looking for a mark. Someone that might be a decade or two older could then maybe help them out financially in some way, perhaps by being their companion.

If the individual who is now a set target was flattered by the attention and maybe even got to fuck the guy (they'd be eager to tell us about it) or maybe they were just happy enough that someone might be genuinely interested in them, if not on the first visit but maybe by the third or fourth meet-up. Once again, thinking it might be love, the gentlemen would inevitably end up giving them money, at times they wouldn't even be discreet about it while standing at our ATM machine.

You might not hear about the transactions right away, but suspect things are going on, these are grown men making their own choices though so it was also their business. It would only be an issue if a verbal fight started between them in the bathhouse at some point, then the sordid truth would come out or one was trying to get the other one barred for some reason.

Then the guy that got played would just learn his lesson and tell everyone that came through the door and the staff about it all. The taker would then disappear for months at a time, to sort his situation out or would end up being in an even worse state.

And yes, at times men, even on a whim, would want you to bar someone from the bathhouse simply based on their looks or if the person rejected them. It was extremely rare we would do something like that though without the actual individual doing something huge that we knew they shouldn't do. We wanted to be fair to everyone so being one-sided and suggesting we bar someone wasn't going to happen.

Overall though, much of this is to be expected as with how the running of the business was done as well. There was always a lot to take on and every shift was certainly a busy one. The things I loved most were you couldn't really predict what was going to happen or what duties, many of them new, I would have to take on but I adored the challenge of it all.

Even if it was frustrating at times since we had so many people above us, it could be hard to figure out who's rules should be followed and I didn't want to step on any toes.

You were expected to lead with your own experience and initiatives, yet don't. Even Kevin seemed confused about what we should do at times when asked so we would then do the best we could as we were managing the venue and tended to work with who was perceived to be the top manager at head office.

Although we felt confident in our decisions that were thoroughly thought out, once in a while we'd still feel like we had to hope for the best outcome since with so many in upper management, you weren't going to be able to please them all and this was at times just with the basics.

Again though, everything was fine, you just had to evolve with whatever direction was taking place that week or moment, and best of all, the employees took to everything in stride with a couple of new staff members coming on board as well.

Since we were in a major city, one of the things that could make work even more interesting was when the occasional celebrity would come in to play.

During my time working in bathhouses, the city had been known for decades as the place where any number of Hallmark Channel movies and random TV series are shot along with big Hollywood productions that would end up, at least half the time grossing big money and it was a boon to the economy on a year-round basis.

Movies and TV shows filmed in the city were chosen due to the diverse locations that are typically reminiscent of other places in the world but it's mainly because of the lower costs and tax credits.

In any case, many film and TV productions were filmed either on the block where the bathhouse is located or within a short walking distance away. This meant we'd get the random celebrity checking in for some action either during the day or after hours.

Any celebrities myself or the employees encountered over the years, I'd say at least 80% of them were still in the closet. These guys knew what they were doing in a manner that suggested it obviously wasn't their first time.

The celebrity would tend to come in at hours when it wasn't overwhelming busy, do their business quickly then leave. Unless you were good with remembering faces, since everyone has a towel wrapped around their waist, and with the lights always being set low, you might not even notice who they are while hooking up with them in a playroom or cruising the maze of corridors.

There were celebrities though that would come into the baths at peak times, they'd mix and mingle so easily with the crowds and being half-naked, you still wouldn't even know who they are even after you might have had some kind of sex with them unless they told you, simply because it's the last person you would ever expect to see.

If I was able to recognize a face from somewhere, even subtly, out of curiosity, I recall discreetly a few times going to look at the recent check-in list and then going into the office to confirm online who it is but even then, I wouldn't let the employees know until after the person left unless they too recognized the guy.

One or two of the employees if they recognized a celebrity would be all excited so then I'd have to talk them down and remind them to be professional but typically the staff didn't even have to be told much on how to act if a celebrity of some sort comes in.

Most of the employees were also too busy to care that much anyway and they treated everyone the same, never trying to chase them down in the venue or see what they might get up to. They had a sense of decorum about it all and would really only chat about it later amongst themselves. Acting this way meant that the celebrity would also come back on numerous occasions because they wouldn't be hassled.

Besides film and TV celebrities, politicians would regularly come in, and many famous writers and sports stars of every game and competition.

Some of the celebrities were fine if they were recognized by other customers and it wouldn't turn into something overwhelming for them. Or there were times when a celebrity wouldn't even try to disguise who he was in some way. Those men kept their heads held high and had sex full out wherever they wanted and didn't care what the other men knew what they were up to.

Once in a while those would be the ones, we would have to keep an eye on a little more, especially if the place was busy as they would be the first to overdo things and get into some kind of trouble by dipping into drugs or booze they might have snuck in or been sharing and then their demeanor would change.

It also wasn't unusual for certain celebrities to come in on a regular basis once the first one or two times made them feel more confident about the place and if they were on a long production shoot in town. After only a few visits you could almost set a clock too when they would arrive next as they would come in at an exact time, like say 6 pm during an early evening special. Ask for a specific room due to its location where they felt safer from the glare of the spotlight and stay for an exact amount of time that is anywhere from 37 minutes to 3.25 hours.

Hopefully, the ones that stayed for the least amount of time managed to get some fun in as rarely would they be seen in a communal shower, at least from what I have known as they'd quickly get dressed and practically run out of the bathhouse. These were mostly the men still in the closet and from the looks on their faces leaving, seemed to have some guilt for even being in the place.

We had others too who would be in highly-rated TV sitcoms at the time that tended to play a best friend role to the star of the show who would come in and certainly had their own way of doing things.

One actor who I always assumed was straight. A tall, dark-haired, good-looking, strong man but not with an overly muscular build, would be shy upon the first arrival with his baseball cap down low and then within minutes inside dispose of that persona and almost expect to be fawned over.

He always rented a locker, as none of us ever remembered him renting or even playing in a room and he liked to get a blowjob from multiple men at a time, preferably if they were of Asian descent and in one of the most open areas of the bathhouse as possible.

He started to gain a different kind of fan following when he came to the bathhouse and the ones that happened to be there when he arrived would get excited in anticipation.

When he thought the time was right, routinely in an intersection of corridors and always in a spot that was perfectly lit, he'd lean the back of his shoulders against a wall, push his hips and hard dick out, and seemingly en masse, the men would be clamoring over who gets to taste his dick while he massaged and flicked his nipples.

The men weren't allowed to do anything else with him and he wouldn't even touch them, he'd just continue to flick and pull on his nipples. If one of them stepped out of line or tried to get in on that action that he wasn't attracted to, he'd either shake his head no or flat out, but kindly, tell them he wasn't interested. Anyone passing by was certainly allowed to stop and watch the show though.

Another actor who used to be a regular loved his kinky shit when he came to the bathhouse. He was also in some big-name sitcoms over the years either as a friend or co-worker in long-running parts and would also play leading man roles in various other shows. He was always very nonchalant in his demeanor, friendly, with a strong jawline, dark blonde hair and a solid build, great smile, intense blue eyes, and very observant as though he was always on the hunt for something.

Whenever he came to the club, it appeared as though he had set up dates with other men as they would always arrive together or meet up in the venue. This actor would rent a deluxe room if the VIP rooms were already booked and made sure to keep the door to the room wide open so basically anyone could watch and possibly get in on the action.

Thing is, if you wanted to participate, it could only be with what he had in mind, that being mainly anything to do with feet. He also had a kink for the use of anal beads of all sizes, which is was how he liked to warm up things, if he was in a mood to get fisted though, which was basically every visit, he was in the sling without hesitation and loved getting pounded (literally) by a goopy, lubed up fist while gritting his teeth, breathing heavily and sometimes yelling, "Fuck man! Oh God!" as he looked at the ceiling. Which would attract more attention in the venue as to what was going on in that room.

What really got him going though was when he'd either get on all fours on the bed or in what we would call the "pencil sharpener" position with his ass in the air, while his head was buried in the pillows while having someone, very talented, balanced on one leg over him while inserting their other, again, massively lubed up foot as far up his ass as he would allow.

Just another day at the bathhouse.

It just goes to show, you might see these men on the gossip websites or in some big public relations push as being a straight, macho man who for some reason still hasn't found the right girl yet.

Could be because they are busy getting their kink on at a local bathhouse, which can take up a lot of time. For us, to each their own and it was always engrossing for many in the venue.

CHAPTER
TWENTY SIX

Things were going well at the bathhouse. Even without all the fanfare, we seemed to be capturing the desires of a very diverse audience of men that enabled others to find exactly who peaked their interests.

We also had a variety of theme fetish nights every week that enticed those that were attracted to everything from the twink crowd to those into leather and a lot of bear events were already underway with more added to the schedule as that seemed to be our core base at the moment.

Suggestions on what theme we should come up with next was always accepted and to add to all of that, we had the top DJs in town playing sets both during the weeknights and without skipping a beat, on the weekends.

At any given time so many men were interacting both sexually and in general socially with each other that it made you wish outside of the bathhouse, we could all get along so well.

The bathhouse certainly didn't lack entertainment yet even if you just wanted to check in and get away from it all, the place was so big, you could just find your own little corner to relax and zone out for a bit or make new friends.

One particular crowd that was always fab to have around were those that worked in the airline industry as they always made sure to stop in for a visit at some point when they were in town. From the many we met, if they had an overnighter, instead of resting in their hotel room, they always were ready to hit the bathhouse, sacrificing sleep for the scene before catching their next flight out as that's just how they seemed to roll.

With their work backgrounds, the men from the airlines tended to be very friendly; and being well-traveled, they knew what they were aiming for with a good amount of confidence with only a few waltzing into the bathhouse with an inflated ego. They were always wonderful with the staff, are conversation starters, enjoy a good laugh, respectful, and like to get down to all the playtime they can muster up.

With that, we had one particular airline steward that comes to mind.

Imagine a man that is both strong and tall who looks like a Greek God. He tries to be understated in his initial approach to checking into the bathhouse, but he has already garnered everyone's attention just by stepping into the lobby.

He's been to the bathhouse a couple of times before and arrives every time the same way, by being a bit shy yet subtly aware his natural beauty makes him stand out, almost as though it's too much and a curse that can be tricky to manage at times.

The employees that checked in this Greek God were trying to be cool about it while you could practically hear their hearts flutter. Supermodel wouldn't even be a big enough word for him. When he finished checking in with his quiet demeanor, carrying a massive overnight duffle bag, he headed directly to his rental room on the lower level.

With this guy, with very little difficulty at all, people were mesmerized with how gorgeous he is and would be willing to give him anything he wants without him even having to say a word, simply by how beautiful and desirable he looks.

After he settles into his rental room, he leaves to cruise the joint, and doesn't even bother with traditionally wrapping a towel around his waist, and why would he?

Naked, his smooth, dark olive skin seems to have a slightly shimmering glow all over his tight, delectable body with his naturally defined muscles. Just absolutely perfect in every way. Even his dick, while flaccid was still engorged and large with the veins slightly protruding with the head of his penis practically throbbing. It's probably one of the best cocks you've ever seen. You'd offer him the world just for a touch or a taste of his skin and he still hasn't even said a word.

Even for those of us who have seen it all in a bathhouse, this man was quite extraordinary.

The Saturday night he arrived, the bathhouse was in full steam, patrons were busy cruising throughout the club while the DJ played all kinds of hot, erotic music while he was also naked behind the wheel in his booth. While porn of every variety was playing on the big screens under the dim lights.

Walking around naked in a bathhouse is no big deal at all, if anything it's appreciated by quite a few men yet also barely noticed for being such a normal thing to do.

The first hour of the Greek God's arrival, he was doing his thing, which from what we could tell was really nothing more than roaming the halls and taking showers while hordes of men were following him around, almost obtrusively so, hoping to grab his attention and get some action.

Having sex or even talking to anyone seemed to be the last thing on his mind, which is fine if that's what he wanted to do and it just drove the men crazy. What then started to make the Greek God stand out even more, besides his amazing, finely tuned body and stunning good looks as he had gone back to his room and began to carry his big duffle bag around wherever he went almost as though he'd lose the world if he somehow wasn't connected to this bag.

One of the housekeeping staff on the floor noticed this as peculiar and alerted us. Although the patrons didn't mind, the way he was unendingly carrying the bag could mean a variety of things. He's perhaps dealing drugs, carrying booze, sex toys...whatever it is, good or bad, it was unusual as he wasn't taking it to another place in the venue or had met anyone from what we could tell so he wasn't just taking his bag to that person's room. There was a paranoid element gaining momentum to what and how he was starting to act.

Once I was updated more, a couple of the employees and myself casually kept an eye on him. He wasn't doing anything wrong but gut instinct said something was up.

Especially since, men as beautiful as this, unless with friends they have checked in with, tend to prefer to hide in the background as much as possible. This way they can pick and choose even more discreetly who they intend to have sex with, as they might not want people to know what type of men they really go for in fear of being judged for it, and never stick around long after unless they want more than one hook up.

As time went on, the Greek God was roaming the hallways at an almost marathon pace while going into the toilet stalls a lot, he was also going in and out of his rental room more frequently which is a big sign something was up.

Before long, we noticed he then became more sluggish, to the point he was letting men feel him up and grab his cock while he tried to keep his pace in the corridors yet would also physically be leaning against the walls for support at times as he tried to keep moving. He still wasn't finding whatever he was seeking and he was avoiding going through any of the more common areas like the gym or lounges, anywhere with brighter lighting.

By this time, the customers were also noticing something was off and many of them came to us about him, half with worry that he wasn't ok and half completely fascinated with him and were wondering how things were going to end. When we would try to find him; it wasn't that hard to do as he had so many men following and trying to get a piece of him.

Turns out he managed to meet a regular customer who is normally protective of the goings-on in the bathhouse and who approached one of the employees as he was leaving for the night, telling us the Greek God just walked into his room as he was getting ready to leave, seemed off and wouldn't leave his room and this patron just wanted to check out and go home. I then went with another staff member to check on the Greek God.

The Greek God was now gone from the room he walked into, and a couple of customers could tell what was happening and pointed that he went back to his own room down the corridor. His door happened to be slightly open with the lights off inside so I knocked as I slowly entered the room while the staff member stood in the doorway as back up. The Greek God was sitting at the edge of the bed, in the dark, with his head slouched forward and facing down as though he was exhausted.

Immediately I asked him if he was ok, he kind of acknowledged me. Then beckoned me to sit next to him, for safety reasons I refused and just kept a casual conversation going with him until he tried to fondle me and basically tried grabbing my crotch.

As extremely tempting as he was, something was off and on a busy weekend night, it's best to get the situation taken care of as soon as possible otherwise it will take up the evening focusing on one man and drain the energy of all of us working while being no fun for the guests.

Looking around the room, you couldn't help but notice there were a couple of empty plastic mickey bottles of booze with the duffle bag wide open on the floor completely filled with mini bags of pretzels and peanuts that were also strewn across the room absolutely everywhere. As I slowly turned the dimmer switch up on the light in the room to brighten things up, some of his identification was on the side table indicating he was from Europe and worked for the airlines as a steward next to a couple of almost empty vials of liquid that I assumed was GHB.

In talking some more to him, he said he was ok and wasn't going to leave all the while still trying to feel me up. Gently pushing his hands away, I snagged his room key from the side table and gave it to the employee to hang on to, all the while his new admirers cruising the hallways were trying to get a peek into the room to catch another glimpse of this beauty and to see what was going on.

With him being all over the map and yet slowly getting louder and stronger with his intentions, I pretended I was his new best friend there to help him, and instead of talking in a normal tone, I was whispering to him because that seemed to calm him down and make him listen more intently. I urged him to leave the bathhouse, that I would help him pack up and get ready but told him things to make him move quicker as though a manager of some sort had called the cops on him so he should take off out of the bathhouse before they arrive and haul him off.

At first, he kept refusing to move but also thankfully became more alert to the situation and as I continued to whisper to him, he listened even more. It helped when he would see the other employee cause then he knew there was an urgency and that maybe he should leave before getting into trouble. What seemed to do it was when I told him having the police show up might affect his job, especially if he had to be handcuffed and taken out (not that this was going to happen) and that he didn't want to be embarrassed, so to this he agreed and started to move.

It did still take some convincing to get him to put his clothes on and leave, especially for him to get his pants on (over that big cock) and he was freaked out and focused about his bags of pretzels and peanuts, that not any of it was to be left behind and he wanted help putting his precious cargo back into his duffle bag.

Once that was done, it was a whole other plethora of issues for him once outside the rented room to get him moving towards the exit upstairs as his new fan club of admirers could see he was in bad shape yet some even asked to let him stay so they could possibly play with him to which both he and I ignored the request. Now dressed and making his way up the short flight of stairs, he was escalating like an angry drunk not getting his way yet not knowing what he wanted and was freaking out about his duffle bag of goodies, clinging to the bag for dear life.

When we started to approach the check-out counter, he became even more alarmed by what was happening so I told him this was the quickest way out as the managers have called the police so he should get out before they arrive. I gave the keys to the clerks while still whispering to him again more reassuring words but a crowd of patrons had started to gather because we had what many a gay man loves, drama and beauty on show.

As he was going through the first exit door and into the front lobby with his bag of goodies, that's when he became aggressive and literally wanted to fight.

Not about to deal with that, one big push out the front doors on the street solved that situation. Going outside with an employee a minute or two later, he was long gone.

The dichotomy in a bathhouse can be incredibly intriguing to watch, men come into a bathhouse of course for the sex so it can be their dick or headspace at the time that tends to lead to their ultimate motivations, what will actually happen though may not be as planned.

It's something you notice in a man's demeanor and overall self-confidence. There are men that come to a bathhouse feeling vulnerable and are seeking some kind of affection and validation, even if they don't end up meeting someone, they can be happy enough just to be surrounded by men who are hooking up or watching a movie on the big screen with others, they feel a sense of camaraderie and you just want to give them a big hug, and at times do just to let them know you are happy they are around.

Then you get the other kind who are also seeking some form of love and to them, that comes by way of letting themself become very open to anything by getting themselves on a sling in a public playroom and spreading their legs, open for whatever and whoever wants them. As odd as it sounds, this is also a way many men do end up forming some wonderful relationships by meeting their tribe so to speak.

In this kind of business, I was always taught to believe that with enough monitoring and communication between the staff and everyone else in the bathhouse in some aspect, the less you would hopefully have to deal with ambulance attendants or the police as it showed you were running a tight, safe ship.

When you're open 24 hours, 7 days a week though, naturally something is going to get missed and incidents will occur, that is why training is so important and even for the employees to have first aid knowledge and regular health and safety updates on some level.

When a patron rents a room, what they do inside of it really is their own business unless they start to disrupt the social activities of everyone, start destroying the room or other areas in the bathhouse, or if they are bringing harm to themselves or others.

Pride weekends and holiday long weekends, although lots of fun, can be the most stressful times so it's important to have everything ready to go at a moment's notice and for the employees to be more alert and aware of the surroundings. One way to do that is by regularly, casually walking around the venue just that little bit more but not to get into everyone's business. If some kind of monitoring is done at an appropriate level, then perhaps one can anticipate and rectify a situation before it gets full-blown.

Overall, it also lets people know employees are around in case they have any questions; it makes them feel more secure about the expansive business filled with men in a party atmosphere, especially if it's a first-time visit. And most often a customer will come to you if they have any concerns as customers do get protective of their safe space.

It's a given in this business that you are going to be dealing with people who might already be a bit high or drunk or both, just like in a nightclub situation whether it's against the rules or not.

Certainly not everyone but there is a percentage of men that sneak in some extra party substances and/or liquor and get carried away with it in their room or someone else's room and often in a bathroom stall. Some things you let slide because you know it's just part of the environment of a bathhouse and ultimately, it's up to what an owner or upper management dictates in terms of rules or might expect to happen. Although it's not unheard of for a few owners or managers to get in on it if they are around.

Depending on the situation, some things you give a light warning of to a customer to let them know that you and your staff are aware of what is going on. The ones that really go hard and don't seem to care are the ones that are on their last bit of rope anyway, meaning in their life in general so they give no fucks. We have routinely been watching these guys for a while and they might be on the verge of being barred for whatever reason and do get barred either for a week, a month, or for good.

When the shit goes down it's no fun at all. The absolute last thing you want to do is bar someone from the bathhouse or even more so, call for an ambulance and/or police as when they arrive that means the lights go up, the music stops and customers sometimes rush to check out in fear as it draws a lot of attention, then you have the rumor mill churning during and after it all.

How it might go down is, while doing a walk-around inspection of the bathhouse, especially during peak times on a weekend, you might come across someone throwing up or worse, passed out in a communal area. If an employee hasn't had the chance to notice this, most likely a customer will know something is not right with someone in the space and alert the staff.

Or a customer might even be late for check out so when you knock on the door of their room if there is no answer you politely knock again and then use the master key to open the door only to find booze and/or drugs paraphernalia next to someone passed out. That makes for a very scary situation for a manager and/or employee to have to deal with and even for those customers in the vicinity. It's been rare in my experiences to deal with but it has happened and is not delightful in the least.

Since the clubs I managed were always in the downtown core of a city, those in the medical and protection field have basically seen it all. It was fortunately not often when I worked in the baths to have to go to this degree, but we never hesitated about calling for an ambulance or the police as you wanted the right professional to come in and take care of the situation completely without us possibly missing or risking something a patron is going through.

No matter how much training we had, we are not medical professionals so when in doubt, it is always best to call for an ambulance or police as they can also refer to their knowledge, experience, and teams to take care of everything.

Ambulance attendants, police, and the fire department in my experience have always been extremely professional, calm, and very attentive. If it's the first time for them to be in a bath-house, they may or may not know what the place is about but will get right to the issue at hand and take your lead to where the customers are located in the venue.

After they may find the place a bit mind-blowing and inter-esting with a ton of intriguing questions but they were always non-judgmental and made not only the customer feel more confident and cared for in a situation but those around them.

One thing I always admired about my employees was how calm, thorough and responsive they were to an emergency situation while still managing to keep the patrons who are perhaps also witnessing a situation reassured as well, and we would follow through with a debriefing. For myself, I never panicked in an emergency and felt it was best to take care of the task at hand first effectively and efficiently for the client in distress and those around.

CHAPTER TWENTY
SEVEN

For those not familiar with the party and play scene in general or in a bathhouse. GHB, also known as: Lunch Money, Mind Eraser, Slippy, Horse Juice...among many other street names. Is used in all manners imaginable.

An individual can either take the liquid on their own as part of a euphoria they want to experience or it can be shared in groups and most tragically, it can easily be slipped into drinks which is what tends to transpire in unfortunately many date rape instances with women but it also happens between men quite frequently as well yet seemingly isn't spoken about that much.

According to Drugs.com. GHB or Gamma Hydroxybutyrate ($C_4H_8O_3$) is a central nervous system (CNS) depressant that is commonly referred to as a "club drug" or "date rape" drug. GHB is abused by people of all ages at bars, parties, nightclubs, bathhouses, and raves, and is often placed in alcoholic beverages.

Euphoria, increased sex drive, and tranquility is reported as positive effects of GHB abuse. Negative effects may include sweating, loss of consciousness, nausea, hallucinations, amnesia, and coma, among other side effects.

Normally carried in small vials, it is easy to travel with, sneak into a bathhouse, nightclub, or any other location to ingest or easily pour into someone's drink.

Then imagine people mixing that with other drugs such as cocaine, ecstasy, or booze.

It is all a matter of choice and I'm certainly not going to be the one to dictate anything, just offering up my own experiences in how this drug seems to flow like a wave within the community. It will be a large part of the scene or barely at all, as a trend, but it's always available and is widely known as one of the more popular party drugs.

And as you guessed it, some people take the drug while in a bathhouse. Nothing new there. Whether they are in a party mood on a late weekend night or just want the warm and fuzzy feelings while relaxing in their rented room or cruising the halls. GHB happens and when it does, no one knows until it's perhaps too late.

Although our bathhouse was now firmly established in the city and community, new patrons continued to discover the place for the first time, loved it, and kept coming back for more.

Even with house rules posted all over the bathhouse and noted on the website, men are going to do what they want which means they will also sneak in (or try to), whatever it is that will make the party happen for them.

Many items men also brought in which are allowed were full-on costumes of every kind, drag, fetish gear, and toys, food (slightly frowned upon because of the smell emulating from rooms) along with booze and drugs (a big no-no but it happens). With some patrons, we would wonder if they were trying to set up shop with everything they would bring with them to feel more at home.

Very late one evening, down one of the long mazes of hallways I spotted a muscular male, clean-cut and attractive, kind of leaning his back against the wall near a hallway light but not in a posing, cruising way. As I was approaching him to see if he was ok, he quickly went into a wall squat and since he was only wearing a towel around his waist, that easily fell to the floor and while that happened, he simultaneously shit all over the floor.

I'm not talking normal human feces, more like reams of diarrhea, as in a wet, flood of it that went everywhere.

He then abruptly dropped half on top of the diarrhea mess, immediately I was on the walkie talkie notifying an employee which hallway to come to for help and for the head cashier to call 911. By chance, in seeing his room key tag on the band around his wrist, his rental room door was across from where he was on the floor.

While attending to him we also closed off the area so that a crowd couldn't interrupt the scene or step in the mess and to also make way for the ambulance attendants while thankfully, surprisingly, there really was no overwhelming stench of shit as you might expect.

The employee and I tried to keep him alert as we got him into his room, which was an utter mess with weird things strewn around like Handi Wipes and at least three decks worth of playing cards, while we all kept in contact with the head cashier for updates on the paramedics through our walkies.

We got him onto the bed, he slowly seemed to be coming around, then while disoriented he started speaking to us, we calmly reassured him that the paramedics were on the way and that we were there for him. This kind of freaked him out yet he really couldn't move a lot as his body was too limp and exhausted.

Thankfully the paramedics came quickly. After spending some time with him he admitted he, "Might have overdone it on GHB". Do you think?! He somehow slowly managed to get himself together and the paramedics actually walked him out of the club and monitored him some more in the ambulance waiting out front then took him to the local hospital as a precaution.

Pulling this stunt would get a person barred from the club and this is what I initially did until I heard differently the next day. Again, since we were still considered the new boys in town (more than a year later), it was stated from those above that he would not be barred at this time and given a second chance.

This decision was made by Terry, as one of the head office managers who had recently come back to town with no real reason. Terry had seen this customer earlier in the night before he left to go to his hotel, thought he was a hot guy, and that he might be some fun to have around and shouldn't be a problem.

This same customer, two evenings later came into the bathhouse again. Since my office was near the entrance, by chance I happened to see him as he finished checking in and I was leaving the office. You could tell he was trying to go unnoticed, hoping no one would recognize him, and was meekly looking around.

When the GHB stud saw me, he tried to be even more inconspicuous and then acknowledged me as he might be in trouble. I just asked him if he was, ok? As I was more concerned about his health and was also amazed that he was back at the bathhouse again so soon.

He said he was feeling better and thanked me for the help. You could tell he was genuinely embarrassed. I just told him he should have fun in the bathhouse, but his mental and physical health comes first. To let him know too that his actions, although the employees don't freely talk about it to everyone, do affect them. Especially our new employees who have only started working at the bathhouse for their first time and also it can scare customers who are just wanting a safe place to play.

You could tell he didn't think about it that way, food for thought in a sense, he thanked me again and then went to his room. As nonchalant as possible, the staff and I kept an eye on him without being intrusive. When someone has acted like that in a place you work at, you feel the urge to want to do a pat-down and bag search them, but we had an honor system in place so we weren't allowed to. And if the decision was made by a higher-up, your hands are tied so you just try to watch and hope for the best.

This being a Friday night graveyard shift for me, although busy, was normal for the start of a weekend. We would all prepare as best we could for when men start rushing to the baths after the bars and nightclubs close. Being busy makes the night go by faster and it's fun to see everyone having a good time in a place where the party continues.

Check-in times and lengths of stay can vary depending on the bathhouse, city hall rules, establishment rules set up, and if you have a special, lower-priced time period on when a customer checks in.

In this case, the GHB stud who was practically overdosing a couple of evenings before, checked in just after 8 pm which meant he had paid for an 8-hour stay meaning his check-out time would be just after 4 am.

With that kind of time period, you tend to give more leeway with a patron's check-out time, in case they didn't think their time period through completely and you really don't want to kick someone out of the place in the middle of the night since all public transit will have stopped and you don't know how far they might have to go to get home, that's if they aren't driving.

Each situation is different, so you speak to the customer privately and just casually let them know their check-out time is up and ask what they would like to do. Our rule was they could stay with their same room or locker rental, just renew their time period at the front desk for another 8 hours or even 4 hours in some cases.

For some men, if they didn't have the funds, it's better to keep them in a safe space while downtown and let them hang out until the public transit system is in operation again for that day, for us that was at 5:30 am or 6 am. We were usually flexible about it. Some men abuse the privileges, some don't. We'd just roll with it all.

During this overnight, the GHB stud was seen at varying times throughout the bathhouse and everything seemed normal except for an instance when one of the housekeepers said they saw a guy come out of his rental room, still hard and with diarrhea shit all over his dick, across his hips and down the front of his thighs rushing to the showers followed by the GHB stud embarrassingly heading to the same direction. We used to jokingly refer to this as being an "Anal Chaos" situation as shit does happen.

Later, when the check-out time came up on the computer, one of the housekeeping staff went to his room, knocked on the door gently, and got no answer. It was just after 4 am, perhaps he was sleeping or hooking up with someone in the club. But because of the incident the other night, we thought it was best to actually find him to be sure he was ok.

After a very quick, yet calm-looking tour of the venue, we couldn't find him. My gut instincts were churning right away, so bringing an employee with me, I knocked a couple of times on his door and then used the master key to enter his rental room. As I did, the room was dark yet with my eye vision in sync with the dimly light atmosphere anyway, I could see a figure kind of splayed out on the bed.

I called to him quietly then a bit louder as I slowly turned up the dimmer on the light switch. No response at all. Having a staff member with me, we gently nudged him to try and wake him and noticed again, the room was strewn with his belongings, just not as bad or odd as the other night before besides the faint smell of shit.

His breathing was very shallow and he was still unresponsive, we radioed the head cashier to call for an ambulance again. This time they seemed to arrive even sooner which was a blessing. They were directed to the room where the customer was still unresponsive while this time the other customers were very curious as to what was happening.

The paramedics came with some of their equipment with two more heading back to the ambulance to get a gurney. We quickly gathered his belongings, threw it all into his backpack when one of the employees noticed some drug paraphernalia including small glass vials. It wasn't even a shock at this point. He was loaded onto the gurney while they tried to keep him revived, it was hard to tell what they were doing and how he was doing as he was hauled out in front of everyone with his belongings being carried out by one of the paramedics. With sirens blaring they headed off to the hospital.

Everyone in the bathhouse was buzzing about what just happened but then calmed down about it. All we could do is hope he was ok and reassure patrons that asked that things will be fine.

Terry, who never seemed to leave the bathhouse yet wasn't really doing anything work-related, saw what took place, let us handle it, and after asking us how we were doing. I told him, the GHB stud was going to be barred now, Kevin and I don't want the employees or customers to have to keep seeing or experiencing this kind of thing, but Terry acted like it was no big deal and dismissed it all.

The staff and I all had a quick, quiet debriefing with each other and made sure the whole environment was back to normal and calm for everyone in the place. I went back to my paperwork which included an incident report for Kevin to read when he came to work in the morning.

As 8 am rolled around, as I was getting ready to leave after my shift, a call came in with the head cashier telling me the person on the phone wanted to speak to the manager.

When I answered the phone, the voice on the other end sounded rough, sad, and tired. It was the patron who had been taken out on a gurney by the ambulance attendants. The GHB stud didn't sound right and given what he had been through I was just relieved that he was ok, just confused by what he would be calling about and why to the bathhouse?

The GHB stud told me he was still at the hospital and that he was told as they were approaching the hospital by ambulance, he had a mild heart attack but he wanted to let us know he was ok and would be in the hospital a couple of days.

It could be bullshit, it could be true, he could be looking for sympathy, who knew?

Yet it didn't even come as a surprise that this is how my overnight shift would end with this type of news from the patron.

After mentioning to me more of what had happened to him, the next words from his mouth were pleas for us not to bar him from the bathhouse. Like literally begging, weeping, and starting to freak out about it. I was barely getting a word in edgewise and didn't want him to have another heart attack over this so I tried to reassure him so that he would settle down.

My thoughts were, where are his priorities? Even in telling the other employees who were also on shift that night, we kept shaking our heads. You pull another GHB stunt, get hauled out by ambulance attendants again, have a mild heart attack, then call from a hospital begging not to be barred from our bath-house?!

This must-have happened before to him on some level and

maybe at some other place just in the way he was trying to make amends. Does it take possible death to learn a life lesson?

To me, he was barred. I wasn't putting the employees, customers, and myself through that again and Kevin backed me up.

We were the top bathhouse in town that everyone from everywhere was checking out but you have to set a precedent (more than once with a bathhouse) or else if word gets out with what you can get away with anything at that bathhouse, it becomes a free-for-all of trouble making it harder to succeed long term.

In the meanwhile, I put my foot down with Terry and he reluctantly let me have my way on this one after reading the incident report. It's funny how a gorgeous man to some can seemingly get away with so much through another man's eyes.

About a week later, the GHB stud called and we had a good discussion. He was still hoping to come back in as soon as that night. I told him not at this time. He had been barred, that we can't have the employees worried at work with their guards up in fear someone might overdose and possibly die while still trying to maintain a fun atmosphere for everyone else in a busy bathhouse.

Most importantly, he had to take care of himself first. The GHB stud mentioned he loved the atmosphere of the club and would do this kind of thing to ease his nerves and have some fun.

I told him he'd go a lot further faster by just being himself, there's nothing to be nervous about but at this time he needed to figure his life out more on his own and not inside the bathhouse. This was at least the tone of our conversation and he was being honest and appreciative of the decision not to let him back right now. Although disappointed, in the end, he actually seemed ok about it all. I was just glad he was still alive.

Period.

Months down the road, and with a couple more discussions, he was allowed back in with some minor restrictions at first pertaining to the length of stay and only being allowed to rent a locker. From there trust was built up and eventually he was good to go, probably still pissing around with GHB or something on occasion but he was never someone we had major concerns with again and he seemed to become closer to all of us.

As for Terry, he's a nice enough guy, a bit not all there from years of partying and very old school. When I first came on board, I was slightly warned about him and told he didn't really have a position; he had just been with the company for so long through who he knew and was a manager for a brief time at one of the baths but was now somehow considered a senior project manager at head office. I always felt whoever was in charge of that decision, kept him on so that he could make a living as they felt a bit sorry for him.

He could be funny and sweet, yet dated in his short-term business thinking and very nostalgic for the old times.

We were doing well on our own and of course, it would be expected that various people from head office and/or the owner would pay us visits from time to time which was something I looked forward to as then I/we could get answers to work and plans much sooner.

With Terry though, we were vaguely warned of his arrival just because you never knew what was going to happen and although he had a say, he also didn't in terms of business matters, yet was to be referred to for certain situations and liked to be thought of as a top boss.

Seeing him in action in the bathhouse, he certainly loved handing out his business card to customers he was attracted to, with the typical line of, "If there's anything you need..."

One way to put this was, if everyone was on board for a decision in the business, he would be the one man out that could hold movement up of any kind, just to be recognized for his "abilities."

For us, we just wanted to keep building the business and move forward long-term, there was always a lot to do and instead of having an encouraging member beside you, you felt there was someone in the house who could disrupt things, simply because he's bored as he certainly didn't even try to look busy.

Terry is a tall man who crouched a lot, late 50's at the time, and seemingly clinging to a form of youth. He could be hilarious and also completely condescending. It depended on his mood.

With no real reason for his visit, we suspected he was coming to us for an undisclosed amount of time mainly because of the city's very lenient marijuana laws. As minute one of us getting the bathhouse space, I'm not sure how but we were out of the blue delivered a box of his personal goodies to hide in the property before we had even started renovations for whenever he was in town.

I did not know what was in this sizable, black, locked container and did not care to know, just assumed it was something illegal where he lived or where we also lived. I wasn't going to find out more as it already told me a lot about him.

When he first arrived in town he stayed in an expensive hotel room a few blocks away. With the costs of that adding up, another manager at the head office saw those numbers and made him book a long-term Airbnb place if he felt he needed to stay longer.

After the first couple of weeks, once Terry got to know the city better, he mentioned in passing he didn't care for the place that much, although it was beautiful. Terry did however, seem to love being able to buy pot and whatever other drug of choice he enjoyed very easily.

We think that access to the party drugs is what kept him around as anything he did in the bathhouse, wasn't what one would consider work. He never did any kind of paperwork, would confuse the employees by changing the things they were officially trained to do or the rules to suit his agenda frequently.

Terry tended to only be at the bathhouse at night and sometimes into the morning.

Since I also worked mainly at night, more than once I'd come to work and see that he had already been preparing for his night ahead, and by that, I mean, he went around and twisted half of the lightbulbs out in the corridors in an already dimly lit bathhouse as he intended to cruise and hopefully hook up with customers on the night ahead with his thinking that the lower the lights, the harder it is for someone to judge if he is good-looking or not.

He'd also block out a few rental rooms at a time in various parts of the bathhouse so that he had a choice. The thing is though when you block off a room, you can't rent it out to a customer which means lower sales. He liked playing with elements of the whole club to suit his needs and in turn upset customers and messed with employees shifts and our sales and this was becoming a daily thing to try and manage, nicely.

Once when he was in a very high state, I happened to be walking from the laundry room back to the office and he stopped me in a hallway to tell me I wasn't what he expected from what he knew of how others work or were as a person in a bathhouse.

He thought I should be fucking the customers, literally, and hadn't come across me doing that yet. In a tone that, he wanted to watch me fuck or get fucked yet he also better not catch me fucking a customer as an underlying threat to being fired. Another one of those damned if you do, damned if you don't situations.

There were, of course, men I'd fool around with but work came first and it was also none of his business as my understanding from especially all the other managers was that it was a perk of the position to sleep around if you wanted and they certainly had their fun.

I just fake laughed though and told him, not to worry, I get some action. Just to play with his mind a little. He always creeped out everyone as it is with his sexual innuendos and almost forced intentions, the last thing I'd let him do is to watch me have sex.

This was just a colorful part of the job that everyone accepted and his sexual tone never offended me, if anything it let me know more of what that individual was about.

With that, it was on with the show.

CHAPTER TWENTY EIGHT

Our city during my time in the bathhouse industry wasn't considered a hub in terms of having any well-known porn stars or porn productions taking place, although plenty seem to keep trying.

Any activity in terms of money-making porn or even escorting then seemed to be for those in the transexual realm (to use an umbrella term), so if you were into that line of work, that is where the real money could be made in town if you met the right people and were smart about it.

At the first bathhouse, I worked at, just as the dawn of when the world wide web was coming to light. Porn was played in the bathhouse on VHS tapes. Gritty but still appealing to many even now and only at the end of the run of the venue were we able to introduce DVDs.

In this first bathhouse, there were a few dark rooms that played porn on small TVs, on a shelf high up near the ceiling. We'd have to bolt all that equipment into place and put duct tape over all the buttons on the TV so that no one could try and steal the TV, change the sound or station, or just for fun, break the equipment. Believe me, men would try it all. The TV would be wired in such a way throughout the club to the head cashier station where the clerk on shift would be able to notice when the VHS tape was done and then choose another 2-to-6-hour porn tape to pop into the player from his location.

We'd try to keep the porn as updated as possible and if it wasn't sent in by head office, a staff member obsessed with porn would make up several tapes to play at work. That would be fine but you'd have to also watch the tapes he made so that it wasn't all only one genre that appealed to that particular employee such as something geared only to the bear crowd.

It all seemed to work out though and was just how things were done at the time so no one complained and customers would ask who was what porn star that just appeared in the tape and one of the employees would know off-hand as though they were talking about a relevant pop star.

In those days, if men from the porn industry were passing through town, they'd show up at some point to the bathhouse either for some of their fun or also for "business" with a "friend". I'd somehow be alerted to it by someone's excitement of it all so that I could get a chance to see the individual too but there was never an issue with having them around, it was expected some caliber of a porn star would show up now and then.

As technology advanced, slowly the demand for more porn and TV screens came into play. At the time you would have to convince an owner that the money for a better TV or player system to be put into establishment was like an investment of sorts. For them spending small amounts of money was ok but spending a big chunk of cash on something like a large screen TV could be oddly painful for them or vice versa depending on who you were dealing with and what they wanted to achieve in the venue.

For added fun in the first bathhouse once in a while, we had a couple of staff members that liked to play pranks by getting on the club microphone and making sex noises with lots of moaning and groaning on the sound system while making it seem like it was coming from one specific part of the venue.

Just to see customers race in that particular direction thinking there was a big group sex session going on that they might be able to participate in was hilarious and once they found out, they couldn't stop laughing about it either.

In the second bathhouse, I helped construct and attempted to manage, the world of the internet was well into full swing by then but still not as solid when it was wireless like we have today, the massive size of the space didn't help either.

We did manage to place small flat-screen TVs into every rental room and other areas of the venue with custom made wood cabinets surrounding the TV with a smoked plexiglass screen (for a feeling of warmth to the eyes with no glare) so that customers wouldn't mess with the TV physically and could only manage it with the remote control given to them at the check-in counter.

The remote control would have a fresh piece of thin plastic shrink-wrapped over the buttons and enveloping the control device for every use so that it wouldn't get lubed up and was then slightly more protected, but as the place went downhill, that like everything else was thrown aside.

At this same bathhouse, we had all the screens individually wired to a technical room in the venue that was ventilated and with numerous DVD players playing all kinds of porn either purchased or burned onto DVDs. This was another thing Neil became obsessed with, the only problem is he would stupidly lend them out to random customers who asked and they would never get returned, or would he would do a bad job of trying to burn porn onto a DVD that he also never labeled then it would inevitability skip or stop the playing altogether.

Or worse, he would take them to wherever he was living at the moment and never bring them back to the bathhouse. Just having to deal with how he handled the whole DVD situation could be a job in itself as he never listened to any suggestions or set a rule about how they should be handled and yet it was something the customers expected to be a part of the atmosphere.

At this current bathhouse, porn was handled without issue and with ease. We could get whatever kind of porn we wanted at any time and were updated on new productions continuously while threading it all through a keen computer system to all the screens in the venue, set up by Kevin who developed and built everything.

We had one of the most up-to-date and technologically advanced bathhouses in the country, if not North America. Every bell and whistle one would expect and even be surprised to find out about was set into place along with any other updates frequently taken care of to help ensure that everything ran seamlessly as possible and was easy to maintain.

Like it or hate it, porn is a very valuable element to have in the bathhouse business as it helps feed the imagination of the patrons and keeps them wanting more. We had a large operation set in place for it all to the point that customers may not have even been aware of the extent of how much it was all so interwoven into every inch of the bathhouse.

To maximize the porn viewing potential, we had the biggest and best flat screens available on the market at the time installed in the lounge area (for normal day and nighttime programs), porn lounges, and other play areas. And fortunately, we were still able to utilize the flat-screen TVs that were set up from the previous bathhouse.

Every TV in those rental rooms now had access to over 30 different channels of porn in every genre available. Including live feeds at specific times directly from the San Francisco Armory when KINK owned that building.

This plethora of porn alone made clients very happy. Who could complain about porn when you have more than you can literally handle at your fingertips? Yet, some still thought it wasn't enough or not specific to what they exactly wanted. It could be hard to please a porn aficionado, so as a smart-ass remark we'd tell them things like, "Eyes off the screen, it's time to play with those roaming around half-naked in front of you".

With all of this was the introduction of porn stars into the establishment for special events or if someone in the porn industry wanted to film a whole movie or a specific kind of scene in the place.

Whoever else worked in the porn industry, as before, were also frequent visitors to the bathhouse. The difference this time to when I managed my first bathhouse was the internet was in full gear which meant more men were getting into the porn industry now as a side hustle or as an attempt at a career while setting up their own small social media networks.

If someone who did porn (or otherwise) was coming in as a customer, they could film basically whatever they wanted as long as it was in the privacy of their rented room with other consenting adults or if we arranged to set aside a certain part of the bathhouse for them.

Those filming in a predetermined public area of the venue at a set time we would discuss beforehand with them as in, do they want the patrons in the club to watch, or should we help set things up so it's a more private shoot? And even then, in both cases, we would put notices up that a porn scene or movie was being filmed in the space, where, and what time frame. This would bring in more clients if they wanted to see porn being produced, get off watching it being filmed, or even partake if allowed with everyone in agreement and paperwork all signed.

Each request and production were different so everyone worked with the idea at the moment and we moved on the plan from there.

Once in a while head office would fly in a big-name porn celebrity or two that maybe had a new film to promote on tour so that they could either put on a sex show together or solo and/or as a pre-arranged DVD signing meet-and-greet event. This too would attract a large crowd, even if a customer wasn't into the bathhouse scene, they would pay to come in just to watch the show, maybe get an autograph or photo with the star and leave.

The shows put on would either be a live sex event where one or two guys from the movie would strip down in an area, start with blowjobs and end with fucking to climax for the crowd.

For those into kink, that was covered too with the porn stars being in their fetish gear and perhaps getting their ass pounded by a fuck machine, with the dildo at first teasing their ass slowly and then aggressively as the mechanical device used was to simulate human sexual intercourse or other sexual activity. These devices can be penetrative or extractive and even if it wasn't your thing, most would watch out of curiosity.

Depending on the situation, Kevin and I usually shared the duties of booking their hotel room for their stay, per diem, and payment after the event. I only recall one porn star being strung out who was very striking but had a hard time getting and maintaining an erection but whatever he did seemed to be enough to satisfy the audience.

As I got to meet these porn stars, I found them to be extremely sweet, soft-spoken, and even shy in a one-on-one situation. The smart ones knew enough to realize it's a business, not a lifestyle and they kept a good track of their schedule, including when and how they should be paid, etc.

Some of the porn stars went all out when it came to planning large promotions to market what they do to make money. They'd show up early, be ready well ahead of time, and sign copies of their movies on DVD or a glossy photo and were great about having their photos captured with patrons. Depending on their mood they'd even let clients grab a couple of good feels and listened intently to their comments and questions.

Watching porn being filmed was a different experience. Obviously, it's not like you would expect and not always in a predictable sequence like watching a movie. A lot of pre-production was done with care and attention taking in all aspects of the set. The lighting had to be right, the sound managed with most of the sex scenes intentionally choreographed to help tell the story.

Some of the guys would be experts at this whole deal and took it seriously as a job and stayed within the time frames arranged and what kind of direction things should take, especially if they played multiple roles as both producer and director.

At the other end of the spectrum were the guys who were maybe new at running their own show and taking on the world while trying to micromanage everything as they were just starting their network for their fan base and couldn't yet afford extra people on set to help take care of it all.

You could tell these independent porn stars felt the pressure to have everything done just right and then to perform on top of it all. And although customers loved seeing a production in full swing, we couldn't hold up a section of a club, especially if it was one of the wet areas for 8-12 hours at a time, even on what could be considered a slow day. Time was money and we were letting them shoot for free since we promoted them being around as part of the deal to attract patrons.

It could be concerning seeing these porn stars very stressed out while trying to film with how they would treat their possibly, very new co-star who maybe hasn't done porn before. The co-star would look great, appeared confident on the outside but you could tell was a bit nervous and they might even say as much to whoever would listen.

To heighten the stress level even more, if they were filming in front of the customers who gathered around, say for a shower scene yet with everyone far enough away to not interrupt. Both the porn star and his even newer co-star would somehow have to shake off the nerves, be erect and go for it with the porn star getting right into the scene for a take and somehow the newbie just went with whatever was required or would flounder and even seize up in more ways than one.

There was a time this did happen, and the scene had to keep being reshot over and over, the pressure would increase and you'd witness the porn star even yell at his co-star right before the scene was being filmed.

"Spread that ass this time! Let's get this done! Do you want to get paid?!" Amongst many other demands. This was rare but did happen so then we'd step in and offer them bottled waters, anything to try and add relief to the moment. This is also when you would see men that were watching the film shoot slowly leave and go back to cruising in the bathhouse while others thought it was thrilling to watch those dynamics taking place.

The co-star you could tell was new to town, naïve, maybe stuck for cash, and just needed to pay their rent or whatever one does. Months later we'd find out the "star" that managed their porn film production this way ended up not doing too well down the road and giving it up while getting deep into the drug scene and letting other men, especially if they thought it would be a novelty, hire the guy to either perform privately for them or be a part of a weekend PNP gangbang.

We'd hear about this more often than we liked like he was just chewed up and spit out. Routinely by way of said porn star coming around to us at the bathhouse looking for freebies or getting into trouble, so then we would be fully aware of their circumstances.

You see all aspects of sex and men in a bathhouse and there are things you at times wish you never saw and it was these kinds of situations that would not be very appealing to me, but it was what it was. Knowing how hard it can be to try and make a living as a young person that moves to a big city, you only want the best for everyone to obtain their goals. You hope they have the strength to build something more tangible and learn lessons, like us all along the way.

With porn and everything else associated with bathhouses and through various social media groups and many online articles, the subject of sex addiction always comes up and whether it is a real issue or not.

As employees at the bathhouse back then we all used to get asked this both inside the establishment and from those outside as well that knew where we worked, even to this day I still get asked about sex addiction. From what I've witnessed over the years in a bathhouse, I personally believe sex can be an addiction, but like anything, if you try and have a well-balanced life it shouldn't overtake how you live.

Working in a bathhouse you see everything and the business are purposely designed around the whole idea of sex and all that it encompasses.

As noted previously, regular clients that come to the venue can almost be timed at the minute of their arrival and departure. If sex is the goal on every visit for a regular customer, as they will at times tell you whether it is or not as you get to know them, it can slowly become like an insatiable challenge for them, to the point that anyone will do and it becomes not very healthy.

Half the time things will be fine with a regular patron, they are just going about their business, have paid to play, can take rejection or two, and even have a visit to the baths of getting no sex at all, accepting that this is how life goes and love the fact that the bathhouse is part of their social life.

There are those though that possibly think because they have captured the ideal time at a bathhouse for sex, like an algorithm they have set for themselves as to when to strike it lucky so their visits are frequent and even daily based on a few prior sexual encounters.

If they haven't managed their external life well or found the habit, they have developed is starting to interfere with their normal life routine, that is when there can be some issues coming to the surface. And it doesn't have to be drug or booze-related.

You start to see it in their faces as they approach the check-in window. Even if it is their usual time, they will act rushed to get inside, and slowly start dropping some of the routines that they used to do, like change inside their rental room, go take a shower and start cruising the hallways. They might then skip the shower, or even skip cruising the maze of hallways and just instead sit in their room on the bed with the door open (which is a normal inviting gesture) and watch intently at every person walking by.

If their set time is almost up, they almost start to get frantic and possibly pace around the place if they haven't hooked up with someone yet, as anyone will do, in an attempt to achieve whatever kind of quota they might have set for themselves.

You can see the panic building up within themselves, just how they are more abrupt and hardest on themselves in the following visits. Good employees, especially the ones with a lot of life experience in general will be able to pick up on this and simply start having conversations with the customers. It may not ultimately end up solving the situation at the moment but will let that person know you are thinking about them, are a bit concerned, and discuss how things can be worked out better.

You want a regular customer to keep coming to the business but you also want to make sure their mental health is maintained as well; this isn't the feeling though across the board in the bathhouse industry.

Stepping into a bathhouse, especially if it is your first time discovering this world can be enlightening and offers a realm of possibilities you never knew before, but you also want to make sure your head is screwed on right because some people come to a bathhouse to get away from the outside world, which is great, but some people also come to a bathhouse thinking it will also solve their life problems only to discover when they leave, those problems are directly in front of them once again.

A solution for when you start to see someone is falling into a sex addiction pattern that is taking over how they live, at least in a bathhouse, is to encourage them to come back but in at least a week or two, don't tell them they are barred or even bar them, even give them a free pass for another visit on a specific future date. Just be honest with them that you have some concerns for their well-being and only want the best for them as long-term customers.

You won't get this level of service at every bathhouse, especially if it's all about making the money with owners and management but it does happen at really good establishments with a strong history.

Sex addiction can start to form for anyone that comes to the venue, perhaps once a week at the same time or twice a week and you'll see it building in frequency from there. It can depend on their motivations once inside or for even just showing up.

It's about the patterns and how high they set the bar. Keep in mind men don't typically come to the bathhouse to meet and have sex with one person. They can and do but since they feel they have paid for their time allotted which can be anywhere from 4 to 8 to even 16 hours, they tend to want to taste almost everything on offer. If they can get lucky once, why not twice or three times or more?

If it is their first visit and it's gone extremely well. You see it in their eyes, their mind has been blown that this kind of place even exists and they just want more. Some play it out by coming to the club as much as they can until that honeymoon is over and then calm down and realize what it's all about.

Especially if they recognize that the frequent visits are starting to hit their wallet, that is when you'll see these same men use the bathhouse more as a personal treat or reward as part of their entertainment instead of an everyday habit.

What can be scary to witness are the ones that within a short amount of time that take things to the highest level possible and quickly, while adding booze and/or drugs to the mix while they are at it. That just builds and feeds a possible addiction.

The establishment is set up like a party atmosphere, so with some men that are pushing the limits, trouble can and will happen at some point.

It's not unusual to see these types of men arrive at the bathhouse like anyone else off the street but once inside they've snuck in some booze or drugs and have just gone to town on the substances and end up spread eagle in a room, even yelling to those passing by to come and fuck them hard, and men do take them up on the offer. For some, there is no level of decorum, and that can be expected and fine too in this world.

Even without booze and drugs, there are men that just love sex and can't get enough of it. It's debatable if there is anything bad or good about it, again it depends on your lifestyle and what you want in terms of a sex life.

Men will sometimes be lined up outside of a patron's room to fuck him, and that will be exactly what the patron hopes will happen to feed his need, maybe he wants to (or thinks he wants to at the moment) have as many men as possible in one session treat him like a cum dump taking random loads after loads.

And there are those that come to a bathhouse with hopes of at some point finding the right bond with someone they have met and formed a lifelong commitment to each other, that happens too.

Your sex life is ultimately up to you and even in a bathhouse, those choices are yours to make.

CHAPTER
TWENTY NINE

Life at the bathhouse was as busy as can be with a never-ending list of things to do to entice and entertain the patrons of the bathhouse.

The employees had a great rapport with each other and with the customers, with many of the staff already considered long-term who put in a lot of effort and pride in their work.

Terry, who had been practically living at the bathhouse had mysteriously left to go back home for a while so everything went back to normal without daily, consistent minor disruptions.

The summer season was approaching, which means in the bathhouse business things will level off to an extent in terms of sales with everyone spending more time outdoors doing a string of activities such as going to the beaches, camping, or heading off on vacation somewhere.

About six months prior, when Terry was still hanging around, one day out of the blue he approached Kevin and me in a very matter-of-fact manner and told us we needed to hire his friend Taz. We didn't need to take on more employees at the time, kind of questioned it but since we were told otherwise for some unknown reason, we could hire him as a casual worker if we got stuck and someone called in sick last minute but if anything, we might have some part-time hours available.

In asking for more information since we didn't know who this Taz person was, we were just told that he was new to the country and we were to make it happen.

I set up the interview with Taz and when he arrived, he seemed a bit quiet but friendly and opened up slightly more during the interview process. Turns out he was from Europe so we connected on that; he had been traveling all over the world for a couple of years before now settling in the city with his new husband.

In mentioning that we didn't have a whole lot of hours available at first, we could probably give him more than the minimum at least by working part-time on evenings or overnights, which he seemed happy with as he also worked part-time at a local gay bar as a waiter/bartender.

Finding someone willing to work overnight shifts, even when half of the employees rotate on the schedule for work is a bonus. Along with the fact that he had a good, solid build for those shifts in case we had to bounce someone out of the bathhouse and having the bartending background helped as well. I was fine with hiring him and Kevin seemed to like him too.

Not that we had a real choice either way being told to hire Terry's new friend so that's what we did, even with the unanswered questions as to why it was so important.

In training, Taz did a good job, he could be a little lazy and not as thorough when it came to cleaning and appeared to take the role of cashier far better. This wasn't such a problem as at least he got trained on both sets of duties and some of the employees tend to prefer one role over another.

Taz seemed to get along well with the other employees and yet could be a bit guarded in his demeanor. With customers, he was fine, at times abrupt with them especially if it was super busy or if they somehow irritated him but we'd calmly talk things through if there was an issue.

He kept his private life to himself which can be a good idea in a bathhouse and you could tell he seemed to have a lot on his plate and under some sort of pressure. Giving off a combination of both urgency and stress in his mannerisms once in a while, though he put on a front like things were ok. No matter how much any of us tried to get him to relax and open up a bit more if something was bothering him that we could help with, he stayed silent and reserved, it was very rare that you'd see him happy.

His husband as it turns out, we already recognized as a much older, kind of messy semi-regular, and whenever he was around, if it was while Taz was working, you could almost cut the tension with a knife.

About a month and a half into the job, we had noticed some irregularities in his work, and even when one of us wasn't around, we would find out from other employees or customers that Taz seemed to do the bare minimum and would only leave the cashier area during his shift for frequent bathroom breaks. Even helping to take care of the laundry had become a chore for him and it would be consistently piled up for his co-worker or for the next shift coming on which was starting to also cause tension.

We also discovered when he was working an overnight shift, he'd spend most of that time on his phone either texting or we were told, calling friends and family overseas while feeling interrupted if a customer wanted to check-in or just needed something and he stopped monitoring the bathhouse altogether.

We also noticed his husband was hanging around the bathhouse more and was starting to disrupt customers with his antics. We then found out the husband was smoking crack in the toilet stalls and in his rental room along with doing meth, to the extent that we had to bar him for all of that because of the way he was escalating in his actions and for his health as the man looked practically dead and white as a ghost the last time I had seen him.

Taz was embarrassed and apologized profusely on behalf of his husband's behaviors, and understood why we had to bar him, at least temporarily. Time would shortly tell us though that Taz was possibly also partaking in some goodies too at work.

A signal of something possibly wrong down the road to a manager in a bathhouse is when you hear from an employee that they want or are very willing to work overnight shifts and this is all Taz wanted consistently during any kind of schedule rotation.

Granted, it does work better for their lifestyle because of another job or school, and in this case, he did have another evening job at a bar so for him, it made sense, even with his urgency about it. For anyone though, overnight shifts are hard and take a toll long-term if you are trying to have a normal sleep pattern and a life.

The first thing that can come to mind when you hear an urgency specifically for overnight shifts is why? Do they plan on playing an accounting game and skim the takings? Are they planning on dealing drugs? Do they plan on letting friends or customers come in and pay under the table directly to them? Any matter of concern can, but not always, come from wanting those particular shifts.

For myself and Kevin, too many minor infractions were adding up and being added to his file as our radars were setting off. We suspected more than a few things had been going on with Taz for quite some time and were on the verge of firing him.

When Terry happened to hear of this, we were told to give

him some more chances, hesitantly we did and like magic, Taz was all of a sudden being more of a team player, overall friendlier with the customers and his fellow employees, and things were falling back into place better. We were still suspect but feeling slightly more confident with how things were going yet he still stood out from the rest of the employees as something wasn't right.

What helped give us more faith in him, whether it was some kind of underlying wake-up call or an enlightened moment was Taz started chatting with one of our main DJs for the bathhouse during his sessions. They seemed to really get along, to the point they would be so enveloped in each other that we'd have to half-jokingly remind them they are both working as the DJ was also starting to let his playlists do the job and he wasn't even bothering to change the setlist anymore.

Taz and his new DJ friend both loved the world of fitness and since we had an amazing gym in the bathhouse, on their off time, they both started to use those facilities more and eventually became a couple although they didn't shout it from the rooftops at first. They did make a cute couple and seemed very happy and at the same time we never really heard about the husband much after that and none of us felt the need to bring it up in the gay world we were living in.

Seeing that things were going smoothly, I put in a request for a vacation with Kevin. I hadn't the chance to get back to Europe for a year or two and needed that cultural boost and a chance to unwind as we were constantly on call and overworked even with our rare days off from the bathhouse.

Kevin at first teased me as to why I needed to go on vacation, yet he was slightly serious about it too, probably because he knew what was going to be coming once head office found out. Yet by the government employment standards board, everyone at work is entitled to vacation time. I was giving a couple of months' notice of my plans and was only going to be gone for a couple of weeks and promised I would have things set up on my end to try and make work easier while I was away.

It didn't end there, once I had let members of the head office know too, what Kevin had assumed was going to happen turned out to be correct and I basically had to plead my case as to why I wanted to take time off. Especially with Terry when he found out as he questioned me intensely about it which I thought was over the top, weird, and a little unfair that I should have to justify having a vacation as Kevin and I basically gave up any kind of a personal life for the bathhouse when we came on board years prior.

Confused but not dismayed, I had to practically speak to Terry to a level (yet not in a condescending manner) he could understand since he didn't seem to know the process in a business was that people who work, and in this country, are allowed to take a short vacation, it's actually against labor board standards to deny this to someone.

In his eyes though, it's all about dedication. Bring in the men and the money, no personal life allowed, which explains why he was living from bathhouse to bathhouse, yet I never saw him attempt to bring men or money in, just creeped out the ones in the venue.

Summer months in the city were notoriously quieter as part of the history with any bathhouse where we lived so since I apparently had to make a deal in order to go (and still have my job when I came back). I told them where I would be in Europe and that I could make it part of a research trip and visit the local bathhouses and cruising bars wherever I went to get some ideas on what else we could add to our space.

This seemed to do the trick, yet I still felt uncertain about it, to the point that I was made guilty for wanting to go and yet disposable and easily replaced no matter how much experience I had and how devoted I was to the business, it just never seemed to be enough, more specifically for Terry. In talking to the others at head office further, they ended up being cool about it and I think we're just testing me more apparently.

With that, I was finally given word that I could go, so I booked my flights and left at the end of August until the middle of September.

Once back from vacation and feeling refreshed and inspired, I did in fact as part of my trip go to bathhouses and cruising bars, many of which I already knew the owners and brought back photos and descriptions of things we could possibly implement into the place but it was all dismissed because I was told by Terry, "How would North Americans understand what Europeans in bathhouses do?" That told me everything right there.

Moving on, as predicted, our summer sales had reached a plateau. Since Kevin and I were needed in the bathhouse most of the time, it made it hard to break away from work to go out to the bars and nightclubs like we had been doing to also promote the venue, but thinking of the sales, we still wanted to entice more men.

In discussions with the head office, we noted that the owner's other bathhouses all had one or two employees dedicated to promoting their own establishments so we thought we'd set up someone more specifically to be our promotions person. We were backed up by head office in this decision and they let us know to come to them if we needed anything.

We then decided, even with Taz's questionable work ethics and antics in the bathhouse previously, we felt he was now coming full circle. And since he was still working for us, plus he looked the part for what apparently gay culture strives for...beefy muscle men, that the idea of him in person out and about would help represent what one might encounter at a bathhouse. In various discussions with Taz about it all and he seemed very happy and excited to begin.

What also helped was Taz had some background experience in promoting nightclubs in London and he still had his other part-time job as a bartender at a gay bar in town, so the mixing and mingling of business could also be done there with the permission of that owner. It also didn't hurt that it was now public knowledge that he was dating one of the top DJs in the city at the time and they were both still connected with us.

It seemed like a winning plan and a new opportunity for Taz which made him happier in an already good place in his life.

To also get things rolling, we had Colin from head office, the main graphics and promotions guy, help us get the word out with stronger, more frequent advertising once we had promotional photoshoots done inside the bathhouse.

We arranged it so that Taz, his boyfriend, and a couple of other hot men we knew as friends with great bodies to be our models in provocative, semi-nude poses in various parts of the bathhouse both in and around the jacuzzi, the gym, lockers, rental rooms, steam room, sauna and lounge areas. Anything and anywhere to give a potential client an idea of the bathhouse and with the varying types of models to tempt customers to come for a visit.

Once those were done and ready to go, to coincide with it all, when the photos were released in our new advertising campaigns. Arrangements were made at all the LGBTQ bars and nightclubs for our promo men to show up as a group, just wearing towels with the logo of the bathhouse painted on parts of their bodies.

At these establishments, the promo models would then socialize with those patrons while handing out promotional packs that included free and half-price passes and other goodies like new cum rags, t-shirts, and keychains, etc., all with the logo printed on the items.

This seemed to get everyone talking within the community with people at the nightclubs having their photos taken with the models and from customers who would tell us they loved the new photos and the fact that they were shot in the bath-house, along with the new cheaper rates for specific times and events in the establishment.

All the while Kevin, Colin, and I helped train Taz more on anything to do with the promotional world of which he seemed to enjoy. He could still work at the bathhouse but also devote time to promotion in the city by being his own boss to a degree, it also added to his paychecks every two weeks, and he got to know more people.

When head office could see the more positive results from the sales, we were pushed on for even more (which is always the case and name of the game), so we continuously worked on new promotional schemes.

We already practically lived at the bathhouse working day and night and now we somehow were squeezing more work in on any hours left, sacrificing even more out of any personal life we might have had at the time but we loved the job and we didn't question it. Plus, although exhausted, we were happy with the results and thought that Taz earned his new position.

Then during a head office conference call one day shortly after Halloween, Terry, who hadn't been around our bath-house for a while mentioned he saw the new photo campaign with Taz and the other models and showed them in a prior, private meeting to Roy, the owner of the bathhouses.

Roy was a brutish-looking man, but laid back for the most part and yet could be a peculiar character at times of which I was also warned about before meeting him years before.

I liked him and his life partner, if you had the chance to be on your own with them both together, they were kind and down to earth.

Both of them also had a great sense of humor and you couldn't help but tell Roy was a party boy back in the day, and it showed in how he appeared now. Roy was also obsessed with the fitness world, which also explained why we had the most top-of-the-line (and very expensive) equipment available in the bathhouse. His partner was lovely one on one too and could seem like he was Roy's personal assistant and protector as he kept a very close eye on absolutely everything.

Apparently, upon seeing the new promotional photos, it was remarked by Terry that both he and Roy, were very impressed with Taz's new physique leading Terry to then mention out of nowhere that he should be our bathhouse's new night manager.

Kevin stated we didn't need a night manager (while we wondered where this was all coming from) and that since it was over a month since Taz took on this role being our promo manager, it was already not fair to keep Taz hanging on as we weren't able to give him explicit permission to be our promotions man yet.

Then the meeting took a twist and again from left field.

Another bathhouse the owner had in a different city was currently under renovations but it had been a slow, ongoing process, not helped by the fact that they decided all of a sudden to fire the manager there.

We were then told that Terry and Roy wanted Kevin to at some point soon go to the other bathhouse to work as manager there and help speed up the renovation process.

That Taz would be the new night manager and I would be the new day manager. We could understand changing things up but we also knew how Taz valued his personal time and he wouldn't then have any as manager, that he loved his other part-time job and this kind of position would also take time away from seeing his boyfriend.

The hours Taz was already working suited his lifestyle and besides, Kevin found it rude that our staffing had already started being dictated to by Terry and now this big shuffle.

Along with the fact that other employees who had been with us since day one might also be interested in stepping up the ladder to a different position that they could at least apply for, especially if they had more experience than Taz but that was never considered or the animosity it might create with our crew.

During the conversation, even with questions and concerns raised. It was decided to let it go for the moment until things could be thought out more.

Then, without hesitation, Terry called Taz directly who then told us that Terry officially offered him the position as our promotion manager but under one obligation. He had to fly to one of the other bathhouse locations immediately to do the training there for two weeks.

With this, all kinds of emotions and panic set in but we tried to handle it graciously and with some faith in whatever plan might be in place along with trying to support Taz who now had to immediately give up his shifts for two weeks at the bar and at our bathhouse which also meant our employees had to swap shifts right away with some having to go into overtime.

Taz begrudgingly told Terry that he would go but he told us he was extremely concerned about it and frankly did not want

to do it. We knew it was uprooting for him but couldn't understand why he was so upset until it all started to come to light
with the truth and then everything made far more sense.

We ended up finding out that Terry and Roy first met Taz
about a year ago prior to one of their visits to the city. This was
well before Taz and his DJ boyfriend were together but while
he was still married to his new husband (and still was at this
time). They had all met online where then a party and play
session was set up between them all at the competitor's bathhouse in town. {insert eye roll here}

From there, Terry clung to Taz, and given his position in the
company, probably used the famous line from the John Waters,
Female Trouble movie, "I can get you a job at the baths, Mary."
And that he did, with us.

It was not surprising and brought everything full circle. We
just couldn't understand why someone like Taz would allow
Terry to have such a stronghold on him but then realized, because of his immigration papers currently being processed to
become a citizen, having a job was important. Although Taz
did have another job elsewhere to help back him up, but then
again, choices.

Still, the wheels were in motion, and even with talking to
numerous head office personnel one on one, the big boss Roy
and Terry had made their decision.

It was strange that since Taz already had training through
Kevin, Colin, and myself with basically everything he would
need to know in terms of promotions, plus he was still grasping how our city worked on a social level, that he would also
now have to fly to one of the other bathhouses in a completely
different city for more training there.

With everything going on, while plenty was still being figured out, we kept having to reassure Taz who was absolutely

dreading flying across the country to do this training and leave his boyfriend.

We told him that it will give him a change of scene to a city he has never been to before, that more training for work can't hurt and that when he comes back, we would all take care of things. Kevin also reminded Taz that he's a grown man, that if he doesn't want to do that job, he doesn't have to accept the position if he doesn't want it, that he'd still have work with us as a cashier.

While Taz was away, work and life at the bathhouse carried on as normal as possible. Since his boyfriend who we were also friends with was still doing his DJ gig at our venue, we would get regular updates on how Taz was doing that wasn't somehow possibly altered coming through fellow colleagues we worked with, to be told that apparently Taz was taking to the training just fine but it wasn't what he expected and he was feeling set up.

At one point while there, Taz apparently confided to one of the managers at that bathhouse during lunch at a restaurant one day that he felt he was being trained to do my job. It didn't help that Terry had out of nowhere appeared in town at that bathhouse too while Taz was trying to work.

Taz was told by management while on location there that he was just learning more of the procedures that come with management because Kevin would be heading to the other bathhouse that was undertaking renovations so he would be needed as both a promotions manager and night manager, as I would be moving to the day time management position.

Yet those managers were just as confused about what was going on when they talked to us as well because Taz had adamantly told them he didn't want a management position yet they had been directed to keep training him as such in everything else besides just promotions.

With that added confusion, there was a pre-planned date for when Taz was coming back to town in which he would have two days off and then start his usual shifts with us from there and we were hoping we could now finalize everything by making him our promotions manager.

Without us knowing though, Terry had arrived in our city the day before Taz and only showed up at the bathhouse the day I was to come into work after having a day off.

Since I always worked the night shift, in the late afternoon I was to come into work. I got a frantic call from Kevin in the morning who sounded out of breath and upset. I asked him what was wrong as he sounded like he was outside, slightly hesitant and yet confused and angry.

He said he just stormed out of the bathhouse, that Terry was in town, and told him when I came to work later that afternoon to fire me. I was in shock and could instantly feel my heart sink. Kevin was extremely upset and just kept repeating how Terry told him to fire me today and for me to be gone. Kevin told Terry he had no reason to fire me, no warnings about anything at all, that he wasn't going to do it.

I think because of how close Kevin and I were as longtime friends, having been through everything, we started talking about our friendship while I pleaded with him to go back to the bathhouse as I didn't want him to get into trouble.

He told me he'd be ok, he just needed fresh air and to calm down. I assumed he was walking out in some sort of protest as employees had started texting me worried having witnessed Kevin leave.

Confused about it all, we spoke some more, then Kevin told me to go to work as normal but to expect that I might be fired. To act normal though, since I actually hadn't done anything wrong anyway.

We just kept talking about how upsetting this is, what did we do wrong? What did I do wrong? Why is this shit going on behind our backs? How they intertwined Taz and played games with him. It was all just shocking and I kept telling Kevin to go back to work as I was worried about him.

He said he would be fine and would call me later, to again, just come to work as normal but expect to be fired.

I spent my time at home pacing, worried, upset, and uncertain but thought Kevin will have more news before anyone and not to add to any more confusion, just wait for him to contact me again and he did at about 2 pm that afternoon. He was still not back at the bathhouse and he had spoken to a key head office manager and friend who was apparently not made aware of any of this news, was upset, and seemingly had no recourse.

Kevin again told me to go to work as normal but that Terry will likely fire me.

I showed up at my regular time at 5 pm, walked in, said hello to the staff that had just come on duty an hour before who all looked a little stunned and confused simply because Kevin wasn't around all day and they were very guarded with Terry hovering over them.

I casually waved to Terry as he was on his phone, went to the office, took off my jacket, and proceeded with work as normal yet knowing what was coming with all kinds of emotions inside.

Out of the office, as I was making my way to the cashiers, Terry was off the phone and told me that the employees were desperate for change, could I get them some from the safe as he didn't know the combination. I told him I would and did while sharing glances with the employees like what the fuck is going on?

After that, Terry asked to see me in the office in a few minutes, I agreed and went about my routine of doing a walk-through of the bathhouse to make sure everything was ok, clean, and topped up for the shift ahead.

Once back at the front of the bathhouse, Terry was still in the lounge area so I went into the office and he followed behind me. I sat at my office chair and he hesitantly sat in Kevin's chair and very nervously told me I was being fired today.

I asked him why? He just shrugged his shoulders. I asked, "What brought this up?" There was no answer. I told him that I've never had a warning, verbally or written, so what's the reason?! Terry then started to speak more but kept changing basically everything he had previously said without giving an actual reason.

Figuring I had nothing to lose, I asked him, even though I could guess, "Who was going to do my job?" He told me, "Taz." I asked him, "Does Taz know this?" Of which I got no reply while he kept his head down. Then I asked, "Did Taz even accept the position?"

I was to find out a couple of days later that Taz did get asked but turned down the position while still across the country if it meant I would lose my position and job.

Terry continued to avoid most of the questions or change answers. Even stated that Taz would be doing my job, but then retracting those words and saying he wouldn't be doing my job.

After asking him, still remarkably calmly, a number of times exactly why I was being fired, he gave no answer.

I mentioned that I know from past conversations with Taz that he doesn't even want a management position and if he feels forced into it, how long will that last? And how will the bathhouse manage?

To no answer, still, with his head down, not able to look at me.

Seeing this wasn't going anywhere, I asked him one last time if this was it? He just nodded yes and put his head back down. I grabbed my jacket, took my few personal things off of my desk, gave him back all my keys, and left while saying a very brief goodbye to the employees that were near the cashier desk with a look directed at them to take care of themselves.

That same afternoon, since Kevin wouldn't fire me, he was then fired too. This resulted in unbelievable mayhem of all sorts but there was nothing we could do, even with the endless calls, emails, and texts pleading otherwise from Taz and the other employees for help and from anyone else connected with the place.

Any predictions of what would happen after we left, without a doubt came true, sometimes three-fold and from evening one. Simply conjure up the worst things that could happen in a bathhouse and you'll probably be right.

Myself and Kevin were done. It was our final day in the bathhouse industry.

ABOUT THE AUTHOR

Jameson Farn

Originally from Canada with a mutual love of France for most of his life. Jameson has now resided for an extensive number of years in the Cote d'Azur region close to the Principality of Monaco.

For just over the past decade, Jameson has contributed articles for several European and North American online magazines along with his blog, Gay French Riviera, aimed at those in the LGBTQ community that either lives in or are seeking to travel to this beautiful region in France.

Always up for a challenge and with an ambitious drive, Jameson also manages three luxury real estate and rental agencies in not only France but for the global market.

Any media inquiries for this book should be directed to: bathhousebabylon@gmail.com

Made in the USA
Columbia, SC
20 November 2022

71799829R00215